LIQUID RACISM

Brexit, Education and Road Culture

Nathan Kerrigan, Damian Breen
and Yusef Bakkali

First published in Great Britain in 2025 by

Bristol University Press
University of Bristol
1–9 Old Park Hill
Bristol
BS2 8BB
UK
t: +44 (0)117 374 6645
e: bup-info@bristol.ac.uk

Details of international sales and distribution partners are available at bristoluniversitypress.co.uk

British Library Cataloguing in Publication Data
A catalogue record for this book is available from the British Library

ISBN 978-1-5292-1847-3 hardcover
ISBN 978-1-5292-1848-0 paperback
ISBN 978-1-5292-1849-7 ePub
ISBN 978-1-5292-1850-3 ePdf

Cover design: Lyn Davies Design
Front cover image: Unsplash/Omid Armin

Dedicated to our children:

Dylan, Archie, Nyle, Ella and Willow

Contents

1

Introduction: Zygmunt Bauman, Liquidity and Racism

This book is focused on addressing the relative overlooking of race in theories on late modernity, and utilizes three case studies – Brexit, education and road culture – to demonstrate the ways in which Zygmund Bauman's concept of liquidity can be applied to understand race relations in contemporary social theory. The case studies themselves are, of course, very different in nature, with Brexit being a historical moment, education an institutional site, and road culture a social phenomenon. However, as we will demonstrate, the liquidity of racism in contemporary society is such that it is able to permeate across these forms at the macro (Brexit), meso (education) and micro (road culture) levels. The experience of each of these cases is relational and can be felt at every level. It is important to note that the book's application of macro-/meso-/micro-scalar analyses is mostly used as a narrative framing device. For example, we look at Brexit as a macro-national and international phenomenon informed by relations between the UK and Europe, and the national public-political sphere. Similarly, we focus on education as an institution in the UK context and explore how race and racism function at the meso-level. Finally, road culture is discussed with an emphasis on the micro-level through its embodiment in the context of wider issues around social locatedness.

While the case study chapters are the key sites where the application of liquidity to race in late modernity is discussed, it is important first for us to provide an oversight of Bauman's work most relevant to this purpose. It is also necessary to provide an overview of concepts and terms which Bauman uses in his work on liquid modernity so that they can then be applied to the analysis in the case study chapters.

Zygmunt Bauman is one of the most prominent social thinkers of contemporary society and is often cited as one of the most influential sociologists in the world (Davies, 2013). Bauman's contribution to sociology spans six decades, addressing themes such as genocide (1989), consumerism

(2007), fear (2006a), morality (with Donskis, 2013), identity (2005), community (2001b), uncertainty (1991) and love (2003a). Bauman (2000) is most famous for his use of the metaphor 'liquidity' to capture the dramatic social changes taking place in everyday lives. In *Liquid Modernity*, he advocates that contemporary society is undergoing a melting of the 'solid' structures of modernity that once provided ontological security, and that have now been replaced with liquefied or liquefying structures and an overall sense of insecurity and malaise.

It is not the intention of this chapter to provide a formal introduction to the various contributions and theories covered in Bauman's work. The reader can find numerous collections on his various insights on the themes denoted earlier (see, for example, Beilharz, 2000; Tester, 2004; Blackshaw, 2005; Davies, 2013; Elliott, 2013; Jacobsen, 2016; Jacobsen and Poder, 2016). However, the authors are aware that an account of the relevance of Zygmunt Bauman's (2000) concept of liquidity needs to be unpacked in order to understand 'race' and racism under the conditions of late modernity. While Bauman's work has been influential on social theory, policy and the anti-globalization movement (see Garrett, 2012; Davies, 2013; Jacobsen and Poder, 2016), he has also received staunch criticism for staying within the white, Eurocentric tradition and not acknowledging concepts such as 'race' and gender (Rattansi, 2016). For instance, Raewyn Connell (2007: 379) critiques Bauman's central thesis on modernity for eliding theories of globalization taken from 'non-metropolitan social thought'. Connell argues that Bauman prioritizes an understanding of contemporary modernity in which state power is in decline and 'no one seems now to be in control' (Bauman, 1998: 58) to effectively regulate an international economy, tackle concerns of migration and mobility, provide security amid the growing difficulty in establishing stable social norms and reassurances, and tame the proliferation of negative capitalist and technological advancements and progress. All this presents Bauman's thesis of modernity as having a homogenized, we are ' "all in the same boat" trope' (Connell, 2007: 380) in which the social experiences of living in the 'Global North' are taken as the implicit norm and are rarely the specific concerns of individuals and nation states in the 'Global South' considered into Bauman's arguments surrounding modernity. This is despite the racialized and colonial violence which underpins northern theories of globalization and modernity (Connell, 2007).

However, recent scholarship (see, for example, Palmer, 2023) based on an excavation of the archives of Zygmunt Bauman at the University of Leeds has maintained that the positionality of Bauman himself is far more complicated than seeing his theorizing as yet another Eurocentric perspective. Jack Palmer (2023: 84) asserts that Zygmunt Bauman's philosophical project was a product of his own social location as a stranger *ante portas*, as someone who was born within a space of ' "inter- imperiality" between the Russian,

Habsburg, and German empires' and grew up in a Poland 'whose very existence [could] be put in question any moment' (Milan Kundera, cited in Palmer, 2023: 84). Because of this, Bauman's conception of liquid modernity needs to be thought of as inextricably connected to his social location: a Jewish man who experienced the extremes of 20th-century modernity in East-Central Europe prior to his exile to England and interpreted such extremes of 20th-century modernity from his exilic position in England. His concept of liquidity, therefore, is born out of a social and experiential knowledge of a fragmentary life. For Bauman, then, the very condition of liquid modernity is not a homogenized and generalized Eurocentric (Western) framework which ignores the specific and nuanced experiences of those individuals and communities residing outside of the Eurocentric explanatory framework of modernity, but rather a condition (and device) in which the manifold possible stories of modernity can be told (Bauman, 2003b: 1; see also Palmer, 2023: 81) based on an individual's own fragmentary and fluid lived experience.

It is the central aim of the authors in this chapter to make a theoretical case for the usefulness in applying Bauman's liquid metaphor to notions of 'race' and racism. There has been a small slurry of works (see, for instance, Weaver, 2010, 2011; Xifra and Mckie, 2011; Tsakona et al, 2020) that have attempted to connect Bauman's theorizations around liquidity to 'race' and racism; however, none have them has ever done so with the degree of depth covered in this book. The chapter begins by conceptually defining what Zygmunt Bauman meant by 'liquid modernity'. We then theoretically sketch out some of Bauman's previous works that have focused on notions of 'race' and racism, before highlighting the links and connections between Bauman's liquid metaphor and racism in the development of the concept of what we have called 'liquid racism'. Key terms are defined which will be applied throughout the book and used as a toolbox of concepts when thinking through how racism is enacted in late modernity before, finally, chapter overviews are provided.

Liquid modernity

The concept of *liquid modernity* was first coined by Zygmunt Bauman (2000). *Liquid Modernity* was the first of multiple books, including, *Liquid Love* (2003a), *Liquid Life* (2005), *Liquid Fear* (2006a), *Liquid Times* (2006b), *Liquid Surveillance* (with Lyon, 2013), *Management in a Liquid Modern World* (with Irena Bauman, Kociatkiewicz and Kostera, 2016) and *Liquid Evil* (with Donskis, 2016) that shifted Bauman's focus for many years away from ideas of postmodernity and postmodernism, and instead towards developing a more comprehensive theoretical framework of contemporary societies based on the notion of liquidity (see Chapter 2 for a more detailed discussion on the postmodernity/liquid modernity distinction in Bauman's thinking). According to Bauman (2000), liquidity can be seen as a metaphor for a society in which the social structures, systems and institutions of the past that previously held things together are now becoming rapidly disintegrated, dislocated, and dismantled as they can no longer keep their stable or solidified form for any substantial period of time (see also Bryant, 2013). All things – from intimate relationships to power structures, social identities, communities, moralities, ideologies and so on – begin to leak, seep, spill and fill from and out of their previously solidified states to become free-flowing without any apparent ability to or interest in being put back together into their previously solid and stable containers.

Bauman (2000) developed the metaphorical basis for liquid modernity from the assertion by Engels and Marx (1848: 9) in *The Communist Manifesto* that 'all that is solid melts into air'. This phrase is appropriate for Bauman's liquid modernity metaphor because it evokes the process of disintegration, with what was previously thought of as solid and stable now being characterized as fragile and motile. Bauman's metaphor to critically unpack the conditions of late modern society – 'liquid modernity' – only makes analytical sense if contrasted with another of his metaphors presented in *Liquid Modernity* (2000): 'solid modernity'. Liquid modernity is in diametrical opposition to the characteristics of solid modernity – societies built around and that involve control over nature, hierarchy, rules, regulation and categorization to organize the messiness and uncertainty of the human experience. While Bauman never dates the duration of the characterizing conditions of 'solid modernity', he does see it as an epoch spanning the centuries from the European Enlightenment to the latter part of the 20th century, a period which facilitated the conditions of the stable, heavy, lasting, condensed, systemic and orderly notions of 'solid modernity' to shift towards characteristics associated with 'liquid modernity': fluidity, lightness, capillary networks, and short term and fragmentary social relations (Bauman, 2000: 123).

There are five central features of 'liquid modernity' that differentiate the liquid-modern world from the solid-modern one (Bauman, 2000, 2006b). The first is the dissolution of 'society' – or an absence of *the social* – in which previous social bonds and relationships (for example, the family, friendships, intimate partners and a generalized sense of caring for the 'other') have been replaced by contradictory processes of heightened privatized individualization, technological connectivity and an 'absence of society' (Bauman, 2000) as society has become increasingly globalized. The second is the separation and pending divorce of power from politics, leaving the former without substance, purpose or direction and the latter totally impotent, emasculated and unable to have any real impact, rendering addressing and seeing the relationality of global problems such as racial (in)equalities unimaginable because the available political solutions and decision-making processes remain locally and nationally embedded. The third is the diminution or erosion of state-guaranteed insurance against individual misfortune that was previously available under the solid-modern welfare state model (Bauman, 1998). Processes of economic restructuring have replaced Keynesian economics with neoliberalism. Individuals are now expected to manage the concerns of social and economic status, of (un)employment, wellbeing/illness, the educational attainment of children, social inequalities and so on alone and with little state support. The fourth is the breakdown of any long-term planning, thinking and acting, and the subsequent lack of investment in the future. Instead of developing, building, learning and maturing, the most valuable skills – in the lives of individuals as well as in society at large – are those of forgetting, avoiding binding obligations and responsibilities, and constantly staying on the move. The final characteristic of liquid modernity is the responsibility for one's own life – its successes and failures, its victories and defeats, its triumphs and misfortunes – which now falls to the individual who has no one else to blame than himself or herself. Society no longer takes any responsibility – it is now all up to individuals and their own social networks. As Bauman (2006b: 1) states, 'living in liquid-modern society is like being on board a flight where all the passengers are painfully aware that the pilot – as a metaphor for those in control – has long since evacuated the cockpit and that the plane is set on a crash course'.

What is interesting about these central characteristics of liquid modernity is the overtly negative or disruptive aspects of social developments that have led to an irreversible state of being of always being on the move, under threat and experiencing feelings of ontological insecurity. Under this pretext, Bauman's (2000) sociological description and diagnosis of liquid modernity is almost one-sidedly sombre, pessimistic and dystopian, with Bauman (2000: 15) even going as far as to state that liquid-modern life is 'one fit to replace the fears recorded in Orwellian and Huxleyan-style nightmares' of solid modernity. But is society in a process of disappearing? Has everything 'solid' melted into air? Is everybody increasingly left to their own individual destinies and devices? Do we no longer care for the wellbeing of others? It is important to ask these questions as Bauman would not necessarily agree that as society shifts from solid to liquid modernity, specific social phenomena become wholly liquefied. Liquid modernity is 'open' to structural amnesia and reinvention. As social and cultural relations change, older historical patterned ways of social life present under the conditions of 'solid modernity' may be forgotten, leading to new social and cultural structures governing everyday life. However, the liquefaction of 'solid' social structure also means that the historical forms of social life may be forgotten, not that they inherently will, indicating a durability and tenacity of certain structures to persist under the liquefying processes of late-modern society.

Consequently, there is a need to see liquid modernity as an evocation of a wider conception that encompasses processes of fluidity, flux and turbulence (Bryant, 2007). Liquid modernity draws attention to the changing structures of solid modernity that are likely (not inevitably) to change under liquefying conditions of contemporary society, while simultaneously critiquing both the static nature of 'solid' social structures that have eroded, disintegrated and become dislocated as society has moved into a more liquefied form, as well as the pure relativist and absolute dissolution of structure within discussions and accounts of postmodernity.

The concepts of flux and turbulence are crucial to and enmeshed within Bauman's (2000) notion of liquid modernity. These concepts situate liquid modernity within the broader poststructuralist tradition of always seeing society under change in which it acts upon itself so that 'the ground is in motion' (Emery and Trist, 1973). In other words, under the conditions of liquid modernity, the only constant is change itself. The consequences of actions and events are increasingly unpredictable. Some social changes may lead to widespread and far-reaching effects, while others may only have a local impact. Such conditions lead to manufactured uncertainty (Giddens, 1994) and risk (Beck, 1992) within liquid modern societies (Bauman, 2000), conditions which are constantly shaping and are shaped by the plans and activities that actants make and perform while under the condition of constant uncertainty. The above theorizations around Zygmunt Bauman's concept of liquid modernity help to conceptualize the theoretical framework to be used throughout the book when thinking through notions of 'race' and racism in late modernity. The next section now turns to contextualizing racism within Bauman's wider body of work.

'Race', racism and Bauman

'Race' and racism are concepts that are rarely discussed – at least explicitly – within the corpus of Bauman's work, with a few notable exceptions (see Bauman, 1989a, 1993b, 1995, 2017, 2020). Within these works, Bauman draws upon the Derridean (1997, 1998) category of *the stranger*: a person who is present but unfamiliar. The stranger is someone who cannot be controlled or categorized into the (relative) established order of the dominant society. Thus, the stranger becomes the object of the fears of the majoritized; the potential criminal, one who is outside the limits of dominant society, but inside the same geographical borders, and hence a constant threat. According to Bauman (1995b), all societies produce strangers, but each kind of society produces its own kind of strangers and produces them in its own inimitable way. Strangers are the people who do not fit into the social, cultural, cognitive, moral and ideological cartography of the dominant society. They pollute the joy of majority societies with anxiety. They diffuse the boundary lines between the Cartesian categories of 'us' and 'them' which ought to be clearly drawn, and they manifest uncertainty, breeding discomfort and feelings of ontological and possibly existential insecurity. Each dominant society produces such strangers through delineating processes that simultaneously construct the social, cultural, moral, cognitive and ideological maps that define the dominant society. The alterity of strangers is not a new phenomenon, and nor can it be said to be any more or less evident than it was in the past. In his book *Modernity and the Holocaust*, Bauman (1989a) himself elucidates that the construction of the 'other' and the various prejudicial (and even genocidal) practices used to remove and to solidify such ambivalence were rooted in the processes of what he later would call 'solid modernity' (for example, the development of the nation state, bureaucracies and technologies of modernity).

Modernity and the Holocaust (Bauman, 1989a) is one of Bauman's most seminal texts where some sense of a racialized analysis is provided, although this is not always made explicit, with Bauman emphasizing an exploration of the structures of 'solid modernity' which made genocide possible and appear rational. Bauman's central argument, here, is that the construction of the nation state, and its underpinning rational bureaucratic structure(s), led to the mechanical killing of *the stranger* and that these were, in themselves, not anti-modernity but an outcome of modernizing processes. This is because the instruments of rationality – the bureaucratic organization that created a centralized power system – worked most efficiently and was based on notions of oppression, domination and alienation.

According to Bauman (1989), the Holocaust was deeply entrenched into the nature of modernity; into the rapid social change that modernity produced – processes of industrialization and urbanization, changes in political philosophy, dislocation, mobility, and the growth of nationalism. Such changes led to the development of 'race' and scientifically legitimated racism. Nazi ideology did not need to be imposed 'from above' onto scientists, doctors, 'expert' bureaucrats and the wider population. 'Race' was already there, seen to be part of a scientific and moral philosophy. The scale of extermination would not have been possible if it were not for the scientific and technological advancements of 'solid modernity'. Therefore, the administrative procedures and practices of the nation state, as exemplified by the bureaucratic organization, provided a vehicle for both the logistical intricacies of extermination, and of the moral absolution of responsibility. As Bauman (1989a: 17) notes:

> The most shattering of lessons deriving from the analysis of the 'twisted road to Auschwitz' is that – in the last resort – the choice of physical extermination as the right means to the task of Entfernung was a product of routine bureaucratic procedures: means–end calculus,

> budget balancing, universal rule application … At no point of its long and tortuous execution did the Holocaust come into conflict with the principles of rationality. The 'Final Solution' did not clash at any stage with the rational pursuit of efficient, optimal goal implementation. On the contrary, it arose out of a genuinely rational concern, and it was generated by bureaucracy true to its form and purpose.

Bauman uses the metaphor of the 'gardening state' to describe the ways in which the (solid) modernist project of the Enlightenment to the 20th century – through a combination of designed and planned order, social engineering and legislative reason – marked the transformation of society into an orderly and predictable one:

> The modern state was a gardening state. Its stance was a gardening stance. It delegitimised the present (wild, uncultivated) condition of the population and dismantled the extant mechanisms of reproduction and self-balancing. It put in their place purposely built mechanisms meant to point the change in the direction of a rational design. The design, presumed to be dictated by the supreme and unquestionable authority of reason, supplied the criteria to evaluate present day reality. These criteria split the population into useful plants to be encouraged and tenderly propagated, and weeds – to be removed or rooted out. (Bauman, 1991: 20)

Bauman (1991) thus argues that in Nazi Germany, the ambitions of the state were firmly set on eradicating all the dangerous and uncontrollable elements of society. Guided by the notion of a 'good' society, one in which the problematic and chaotic elements of nature are tamed using a systematic, rational scientific plan, Bauman argues that *the Jew* – as a literal and figural 'problematic' category – was constructed as the weed in the carefully designed garden of the future. There were, of course, other weeds; individuals with mental health issues, the disabled, nomadic groups (Bauman, 1991b: 29), all of which were seen and understood as weeds because state reason dictated that the space they occupied should be within someone else's garden, removed from the sites of purification of Nazi Germany.

For Bauman (1989a), genocide under the conditions of 'solid' modernity was purposeful. Something that Max Weber (1978 [1922]) would describe as formal, purposeful rationality. Genocide – in the context of the Holocaust – becomes a means to an end; calculative and therefore an element of the 'gardening state' which sought to bring 'a social order conforming to the design of a perfect society' (Bauman, 1989a: 91). The visioning processes of the gardener is to create a society based on 'ideal-type' (Weber, 2017 [1922]: 93); that is, an objectively better vision of society – through scientific modes of objectivity – better than the one that exists currently or previously. For Bauman, this is the product of the civilizing process (Elias, 1939) gone wrong. Instead of outlawing violence and celebrating difference, 'solid modernity' is characterized by a gardening culture: it defines itself as the design for an ideal life and a perfect arrangement of human conditions. It constructs its own identity out of a fear of strangerhood, chaos, uncertainty and insecurity through the removal of such 'threats', and the construction of a necessarily artificial order (Bauman, 1989a: 92).

The central tenet that could be extrapolated from Bauman's (1989a) argument(s) in *Modernity and the Holocaust* is that racism is one of the consequences of the (solid) modern project. In this, he does not mean that hate, tension and ethnic group conflicts did not exist premodernity, but rather that science defined 'race', and modern technology and state power made racism possible. Thus, (solid) modernity not only made racism possible – at least in its thickly, overtly hostile and politicized formation – but also created a demand for it. This meant that (solid) modernity was a necessary condition for the Holocaust. However, this conclusion was not deterministic, with a distinction being drawn between *necessary* and *sufficient*. This means that the conditions of (solid) modernity did need to be present for the Holocaust to take place, but the conditions of modernity were not the *only* conditions required. While (solid) modernity does hold a primacy in explaining the emergence of the Holocaust, for Bauman, (solid) modernity in and of itself is not *sufficient*. Rattansi (2017) evaluates these arguments by showing various moments which are comparable with the Holocaust (for example, the Viet Cong) as a criticism of Bauman's emphasis on the specificity of the Holocaust. However, in this process Rattansi only makes passing references to the African slave trade to demonstrate that racism has existed within the 'solid' modern project through ways which are not about extermination, and then argues that Jews were exterminated even when it did not make economic sense to do so.

Rattansi's (2017) point here is that Bauman (1989) gives 'solid modernity' a personality – an implicit agency – and fails to show the other driving forces of racism that a very specific history which eventually made dissenting dangerous was what underpinned the Holocaust. The inference was that the Holocaust did not happen everywhere where conditions of 'solid modernity' played out. Rattansi's critiques of Bauman are focused on raising potentially a more fundamental problem for his explanation of the Holocaust. For Rattansi, the idea that the bureaucratization of the Holocaust distanced actors and perpetrators paints a uniform picture which was fragmented according to actors' positions in the wider power structures of the Nazi administration. Consequently, those on the front line were not distanced, shielded or insulated from the horrors of the Holocaust because of the bureaucratization of society brought through with (solid) modernity;

rather, Rattansi argues that their compliance would be informed by either ideological radicalization or fear and coercion. This argument does raise some interesting questions about how far the Holocaust was ideologically rather than bureaucratically facilitated or driven, and the primacy of each of these relative to each other. But if we accept the inference that moments such as the Holocaust represent extreme moments of racialized violence which are primarily driven by ideological factors rather than representing a wider more problematic feature of 'solid modernity', then the African slave trade presents something of a fundamental problem. Rattansi does draw attention to the African slave trade as a way of demonstrating a distinction with the Holocaust. The Holocaust was primarily about extermination, whereas the African slave trade was about exploitation. But this distinction does not underplay the significance of the African slave trade in terms of its longer duration, the greater cumulative loss of life, its erasure of histories for enslaved peoples, and the violence used to sustain it as history's recorded most extreme episode of racialized oppression (see Sullivan and Hickel, 2023). Nevertheless, Rattansi (2017: 90) was correct to identify that:

> Bauman has a particularly acute understanding of the way in which the Jews who tried to assimilate were in fact only ever provisionally accepted … That this is indeed the fate of all ethnic minorities in liberal democratic states is something that Bauman briefly alludes to, but he fails to translate this insight into any broader discussion from the Jews in early 20th Century Western Europe to black and Asian ethnic minorities in the second half of the 20th Century. This omission is particularly puzzling given that Bauman cites the excellent analysis of this question by Dench but draws from it only lessons for the Jewish population of the early 20th Century.

Rattansi's (2017) point extends beyond failing to acknowledge the wider relevance of the efforts of Jewish communities to assimilate in 'Western' settings. The event of the Holocaust does make the narratives around Jewish assimilation distinctive, but arguably no more so than those around African Americans in the US, or Black British groups in the UK, each of which have a point of relationality to their countries of residence directly derived from abominations of Western European colonial activity which equal the horrors of the Holocaust and lasted over 400 years. Furthermore, the abolitionist movement was not comprised of allied outsiders, attacking the US for its uncivilized activities, but rather came from the oppressors themselves. Returning to Bauman's (1989) analysis of bureaucracy, his argument was that this was emergent because of the transitions of change brought through with (solid) modernity. This had primacy in facilitating the kind of dissociation required for individuals to carry out the horrors of the Holocaust. Parallels can be drawn with the African slave trade – also driven by racialized premises – with the rise of industrial capitalism dictating ever-increasingly dehumanizing methods of extracting capital from markets to great and tragic human expense. Such parallels make the omission of any meaningful discussion around 'race' in Bauman's (see 1989, 1995, 2017, 2020) work even more baffling than the apparent oversight of neglecting to apply the experience of Jewish assimilation to other ethnic minorities in Rattansi's initial critique.

In contrast to the Holocaust, the African slave trade represents an example which was the result of a much longer history, across networked modern European economies, and with a sedimentary legacy that is still present today in states with a European colonial history. The African slave trade and its aftermath for those colonized peoples has been a far more central feature of modernity than any of the examples given by Rattansi (2017). Its difference is that the African slave trade seems to be ever-present and therefore a more integral feature of modernity. The African slave trade was moderated bureaucratically in the process of the dissection of the globe by European colonial powers. Therefore, while specific histories may cast some doubt on the primacy of modernity in events such as the Holocaust, the longstanding history of the African slave trade indicates that racism has been endemic in modernity and across time and space. We cannot erase that history when considering moments like the Holocaust, which might more meaningfully represent extreme waves of racialized violence rather than specific historical moments which emerge as an endemic feature of modernity.

This is not to downplay in any way the atrocities of the Holocaust or the anti-semitism that led to it and still pervades society today. Indeed, racialized flows are a key feature in our application of Bauman's liquidity, and the nuances of racialized experience will include Jewish experiences of anti-semitism within these flows. What we intend is to extend Bauman's work to 'race' and racism in ways which go beyond his analysis of the Holocaust, and this requires close analysis of the European colonial project to make sense of racism in late modernity. However, we must also acknowledge, by way of reflexivity, that two of the authors identify as white and therefore do not have the same lived experiences as either Jewish or Black groups. We can foresee how this may bring into question our legitimacy in seemingly prioritizing one set of racialized experiences over the other in terms of understanding how racism emerges in the context of late modernity. Equally, these authors do not want to forgo the importance of the novelty in establishing a conceptual framework of racism in the context of late modernity on account of their whiteness. This would assume the need for a protected space within the scholarship on 'race' and racism resulting from our own white fragility around such topics and themes, topics and themes which themselves are predicated on the social construction of whiteness itself and the demarcation of racialized minorities as 'other'.

We need to see the African slave trade as a phenomenon for understanding racism within and as society shifts from 'solid' to 'liquid' formations of modernity through processes of solidification-liquefaction-resolidification. Under 'liquid modernity', the conditions that led to the exploitation and dehumanization of colonialized peoples within 'solid modernity' (for example, the extractive logics of capitalism that were facilitated by the rise of the nation state and systems of bureaucratization) do not disappear. They leave sedimentary legacies that – under the liquefying processes of late modern society – become resolidified as new, temporal structures around institutions, identity formations and places that are just as quick to melt away and resolidify again as new racialized structures. It is this notion of *liquid racism* to which we now turn our attention.

Liquid racism

Under liquid modernity, where accelerated social change has facilitated a solidification-liquefaction-resolidification process of social identities, communities, moralities, ideologies, power structures and institutions that govern everyday life, racism has become increasingly complex, ever more present but equally invisiblized, surfacing as solidified moments of extreme political tension and upheaval (for example, Brexit, the murder of George Floyd and so on), all to be melted down and become imbricated within processes of consumerism and embedded in key social institutions (for example, education and the criminal justice system). The term *liquid racism* acknowledges a racism that is premised on the conditions of late modernity. It is a racism that is fluid and difficult to identify because it may escape or dissolve into confluences of public-political, institutional and sociocultural spheres, and as a result of neoliberal policy making before it can be resolidified, manifesting in overt acts of hostility, racialized violence and oppression. In other words, liquid racisms are racisms whose structure has changed and are less solid than they were in the past. However, the historical manifestations of racism have not gone away and been fully melted down; they are constantly reproduced as new racialized flows and/or brought into being through meeting points with other flows of power and relations (for example, consumer capitalism) of late modern society.

This existence of an ambivalence and contradiction in the ways in which racism manifests itself has been documented in the social sciences (for example, Billig et al, 1988; Hall, 1988; Gallagher, 2003; Rattansi, 2007; Bonilla-Silva, 2013). Such research suggests that because notions of racism are based on contradictory processes – some constructed as racist and others constructed as nonracist – a singular, homogeneous racism or racist subjectivity is difficult to locate, leading Rattansi (2007: 118) to argue that there can be no essentialized racist subjects or processes in contemporary society (see also Weaver, 2010, 2011). The conditions of racism are contingent upon sets of actions, routines, discourses, policies and power structures that may give way to heating or cooling effects, solidifying racism into more overtly, hostile and thickly politicized formations or liquifying racism to spill and fill into other public-political, institutional and sociocultural arenas. The application of Bauman's (2000) liquid metaphor to explain the conditions of contemporary modernity as a society without solid patterns or routines, undergoing processes of constant change that have accelerated, is also fitting when we are wishing to grasp the nature of contemporary racisms within late modernity.

Bauman (2000) reminds us in the foreword to *Liquid Modernity* that liquid – unlike the composition of solids – cannot hold its shape very easily. Whereas solids have clear spatiotemporal dimensions that can resist any sort of fluidity – for example, the flows of time – that could compromise the structural properties of the solid (that is, its space), liquid does not have any spatiotemporal dimension to it, holding no shape and being prone to constant flux and change. Because of this, it is the flow of time that comes to count more than the space liquid occupies (Bauman, 2000: 2). Space is filled, but only momentarily. In a sense, then, 'solid racisms' are those highly politicized moments of racialized violence, oppression and domination that occur under a specific set of circumstances and within a temporal period of history (for example, the Holocaust). 'Liquid racisms', on the contrary, are those actions, routines, policies, institutions and power structures that transcend time (for example, the African slave trade) that 'flow', 'spill', 'splash', 'pour over', 'leak', 'flood', 'spray', 'drip', 'seep' and 'ooze' (Bauman, 2000: 2) into the different public-political, institutional and sociocultural spheres of contemporary society, resulting in a racism that is ubiquitously present but not clearly delineated, sometimes overtly politically hostile and at other times in a mundane manner and woven into the quotidian routines and discourses of everyday life.

Such 'liquid racisms' – unlike 'solid racisms' – are not easily noticeable. They meander around some historical racialized structures and dissolve and/or seep their way through others. But what constitutes liquid in the context of 'liquid racism'? In *Liquid Modernity*, Bauman (2000) is never fully clear on what sort of liquid he was referring to. He assumes that liquids are simply the antithesis of solids, underpinned by their characteristic of fluidity as opposed to the solids' fixedness. This has led to a series of critiques in Bauman's application of the 'liquid' metaphor, with Davies (2013: 6) asserting that Bauman's use of liquidity was more of an 'artistic, literacy discussion rather than a scientific one', and Rattansi (2017: 205) maintaining the use of the term as 'disappointingly unimaginative' in explaining late modern social relations and change. Despite these critiques, the 'liquid' metaphor is still useful in helping us to get to grips with racism in late modernity. But to do this, the 'liquid' metaphor needs developing. The flows present within 'liquid racism' are – and should be, as Bauman (2000) at least implied – water like flows of 'race' and racialized structures and of flows of power relations by dominant society that influence the production and reproduction of racialized outcomes and consequences within different public-political, institutional and sociocultural spheres. Much like water whose individual flows are not unidirectional, predictable and that are instead constantly leak and spill into each other, the flows of racialized structures and power dynamics of dominant society are constantly colliding and pouring over the other, facilitating 'new' confluences of racialized systems of domination, exclusion and marginalization. Bonilla-Silva (2013: 40) alludes to such processes of water-like flows of 'liquid racism' in his book *Racism without Racists*. His conceptual framing device of abstract liberalism involved seeing how existing historical racial structures seeped into discourses around political (for example, 'equal opportunity') and economic liberalism (for example, individualism) in an abstract manner to explain racialized outcomes. Bonilla-Silva's argument is that by framing race-related issues in the language of liberalism, majoritized white groups can appear *reasonable* and *moral*, while opposing most (if not all) practical solutions to deal with embedded institutional racial inequalities. For instance, the principle of equal opportunity – central to reducing the structural inequalities that minority groups experience within the labour market and education – is drawn upon by white majority groups to oppose equality, diversity and inclusion policies because they supposedly represent the 'preferential treatment' of racially minoritized groups, often ignoring the fact that racialized minority groups are severely underrepresented in most jobs, schools and universities. Through the confluence of these two flows – one of existing racialized structural disadvantage and another of political discourse that promotes shallow notions of equality – we see the emergence of an abstract utilization of the idea of 'equal opportunity' used to legitimate not supporting the diminution of racial inequalities in favour of a postracial state discourse where all groups are on an equal footing (see Chapter 3 for a detailed discussion of the problematics around 'race' and 'postrace').

Bauman (2006b) indicates such ambivalent processes through his discussion of mixophilia and mixophobia in *Liquid Times*. He notes that '*mixophobia and mixophilia coexist in every city, but they coexist as well inside every one of the city's residents*' (Bauman, 2006b: 90, emphasis in original text). Because liquid modernity has necessitated individuals to make company with the stranger without any prior relationship or future expectations of having to form social bonds, people have adopted strategies of encountering and consuming difference – for example, the cosmopolitanism of shopping centres and food courts (see Gallagher, 2003; Anderson, 2004) – that allow white majoritized groups to buy into racialized sign systems, thus benefiting from mixophilia through liquid racist flows. Nonetheless, despite such encounters of difference, the fears and concerns geared towards the stranger have not gone away. They are still constructed as a floating signifier (Hall, 1997) that brings problems in from a variety of 'elsewheres', reproducing mixophobic attitudes that the stranger is the deviant 'other' in need of damming to restrict a flooding of issues likely to create further fears and ontological insecurities in the minds of white majoritized groups.

Our aim in developing the concept of 'liquid racism' is to build upon discussions that have been had elsewhere (see Weaver, 2010, 2011; Xifra and McKie, 2011; Tsakona et al, 2020) to probe and problematize conversations and discourses around locating racism in the context of late modernity. While the authors recognize that there has been theoretical developments in recent years in relation to understanding racism as liquid flows, especially within the postcolonial literature (see, for example, Cruz and Sodeke, 2021), the intention of this book is to situate the ways in which racisms manifest within the late modern period through a direct conversation with and about Bauman's (2000) work on liquidity, addressing current criticisms (see Rattansi, 2016, 2017) and therefore identifying a novel way of locating the dimensions of 'race' and racism within Zygmunt Bauman's wider theorizations regarding liquid modernity. Now that we have provided a conceptualization of what liquid racism is in the context of this book, we want to briefly sketch out and provide definitions for some of the key concepts and terms to be used in unpacking the various ways racism can be understood using the liquid metaphor.

Key concepts and terms

Liquid racism is a term for a complex range of contradictory and conflicting sets of processes that facilitate a liquifying of the solids or a solidifying of the liquids of racism (Bauman, 2000), requiring a specific level of reflexivity when questioning its meaning, influences or implications for understanding the condition(s) of racism within late modernity (Weaver, 2010, 2011). Therefore, in the following section, the authors outline and define the key concepts and terms used throughout this book when examining how processes of liquid racism work when mapped onto certain macro (Brexit), meso (education) and micro (road culture) public-political, institutional, and sociocultural spheres. These concepts and terms are by no means exhaustive, nor do they all have to be applied when exploring racism as liquid. Rather, they are deployed as a toolbox of concepts to be used and applied when considering the ways in which racism works in late modernity. This is not to suggest that such dimensions of liquid racism are exclusive to the period of late modernity. We acknowledge that they have been historically part and parcel of racialization and racism. The concepts ascribed to liquid racism have been utilized to analytically examine the ways in which racism is experienced under late modernity.

Ambivalence of Uncertainty: An ambivalence of uncertainty in the context of liquid racism is rooted in society's position towards strangerhood. In late modernity strangerhood and ontological ambivalence are enmeshed. It does not offer any routes to inclusion for the stranger, nor does it fully exclude them from public-political life. The stranger in modernity – where movement was fixed and less mobile – is different from the stranger in late modernity where the world is always on the move. Because social norms and values were clearly defined, there was an uncontested authority around the position of strangers in relation to 'host' groups in modernity. The 'hosts' were seen as the socially included and universally dominant group, rendering the stranger's position to the 'host' group parochial and shameful (Bauman, 1991b). Therefore, for 'modern' strangers, the effort of assimilation to the dominant groups' values and norms with the promise of inclusion was more about the dominant group's structuring capabilities to remove encroaching strangerhood and solidify cultural sameness and the homogeneity of the dominant group. However, for 'late modern strangers', strangers remain strangers. In the absence of the social – where individualization is one of the new rules of the game of late modernity – strangerhood is a permanent state of being. Encountering of difference is part of daily routines and yet it is also a hazardous condition (Beck, 1992) of late modern life – leading to feelings of ontological insecurity – so people adopt routines and strategic performances as coping mechanisms against the fear of the unknown, against strangerhood (Giddens, 1991). Underpinning the experiences of strangerhood in late modern society is ambivalence. Difference (or strangerness) is embraced and even enjoyed fleetingly – leading to mixophilia – through the propinquities of strangers while moving through city streets and consumed in the purchasing of goods and services under capitalism. However, on the other hand, the stranger is still the stranger and constructed as 'threatening'. This is even more present in a late modern world of increasing globalized hazards (for example, refugee crises and terrorism) where the stranger is posed as coming from a variety of 'somewheres' and bring with them a number of 'new' risks, leading to feelings of mixophobia for those individuals whose daily life is (perceived to be) perilously threatened by strangers showing up at their doors (Bauman, 2017; Goodhart, 2017).

Confluence(s): Confluences are an important part of water networks. They represent a flowing together of two bodies of water at one point – either from a tributary stream feeding into a larger stream or river or where two smaller streams merge to become the source river – forming 'new' or repatterned flows of liquid. In the context of liquid racism, confluences occur where racial flows connect or merge with other structural flows, producing new racialized assemblages that re-embed historical manifestations of racism in more fluid and mobile ways. An example of this is the confluence of consumer capitalism and 'race' signs (see Gallagher, 2003). Under capitalism, 'race' signs become commodified to signify diversity, but are intended for consumption across the racial divide. Individuals from any racial background can listen to drill music, eat their favourite ethnic cuisine and cheer for their favourite, majority racially diverse, professional sports team. However, this confluent flow between consumer capitalism and 'race' signs does not ignore 'race'. It acknowledges 'race' while disregarding any sort of racialized privileges for white majority groups by taking racially coded styles and products, and reducing these symbols to commodities or experiences that white majority groups and Black and ethnic minority groups can purchase and share. This reproduces systems of structural whiteness by ignoring the reflection of power and privilege for white majority groups (Frankenberg, 1993) as they have a greater range of racially coded styles and products to buy into due to whiteness being the implicit norm and therefore cannot be consumed.

Damming: Dams are structures designed to capture water and modify the magnitude and timing of its movement. The central purpose of damming streams and rivers is to serve as an instrument of water management and provides a specific level of security for the functional existence of urban and rural places, reducing hazards and allowing individuals to settle and reside in certain areas without risk. Damming is used as a metaphor in chapters throughout this book to explain the ways in which racial flows are restricted or prevented by hegemonic power structures. Take, for example, Brexit (see Chapter 4 for a detailed discussion of this). Part of the narrative around Brexit was about the reassertion of control over British borders to maintain ontological security against the (perceived) increased levels of uncertainties of uncontrollable migrations and terrorist activity. Both Leave campaigns – *Vote Leave* and *Leave.EU* – employed discourses of damming to restrict the racialized flows of migrants who were constructed as hazards (Beck, 1992) that needed to be prevented from flooding into Britain. In the context of Leave.EU, politicians such as Nigel Farage constructed migrants as an economic and security threat to the British public. Thus, the withdrawal of the EU was worked up as a system of damming by drawing on Powellite narratives of retreat from a globalizing world that was no longer recognizably 'British'. This was made most evident in the lead-up to the 23 June vote through Leave. EU's infamous 'Breaking Point' poster, which pictured Middle Eastern refugees queuing at Europe's borders, with the subheading reading: 'We must break free of the EU and take back control'. Vote Leave, on the other hand, used the rhetoric of a 'Global Britain' to invoke collective memories and remind the British public of the 'glory' days of the economic, political and cultural superiority of Britain, where everything from ships to spoons were marked with a 'Made in Britain' stamp while failing to talk about the corrosive legacies of colonialism and racism, both past and present (see Virdee and McGeever, 2017; Kerrigan, 2018). While both Leave campaigns mobilized different narrative accounts towards migration, they both attempted to dam the racialized flows from seeping and leaking into Britain. This was either by re-establishing Britain's global position through an erasure of its colonial history (Vote Leave) or using explicit racialized discourses of purification (see Sibley, 2002) and bordering practices (Leave. EU). However, damming does not occur only from majoritized groups to prevent racialized flows from seeping in; it also occurs from anti-racist groups and social movements (for example, Black Lives Matter) to restrict the damaging effects of racist flows that may spill into populist discourses among the wider public. Therefore, processes of damming can restrict both the mobilization of racist and anti-racist flows contingent on context.

Sediments: Sediments are the remains of solid material that has been moved and deposited from one location to another location. They can be transported by flows of water which move them between different geomorphic zones in and across different landscapes. As they move, they settle, slow down and cluster together with other sediments through processes of sedimentation giving rise to new geomorphic forms and structures. Drawing on the concept of sediments as a metaphor allows the authors to unpack how older historical manifestations of racism break down as they move from 'solid modernity' to 'liquid modernity', carrying with them remnants of racialized violence, marginalization, exploitation and exclusion which, when compounded together under and through processes of late modernity, lead to new sedimentary structures and compositions that can explain contemporary issues around institutionalized racism and exclusion. For example, the rates of school exclusion for Black British groups are the result of sedimentary legacies of colonial histories, with Black African and Caribbean British groups experiencing the highest level of vulnerability because of the slavery element of that history being the most violent, disempowering and marginalizing for these groups. This can then explain why Black African and Caribbean British groups experience the most extreme accounts of marginalization among other Black British groups (for example, Black African British groups). However, this is not to say that other Black British groups do not experience the same sedimentary legacies of colonialism in the same way. Rather, their sedimentation of colonialism under liquid modernity has compounded in such a way where their experiences of marginalization – at least within the institutional sphere of education – is lower than Black African and Caribbean British groups (see Chapter 5 for a more detailed discussion of this).

Meandering: Meandering is the self-induced deformation of a stream (or other bodies of water, such as rivers) that is anti-symmetrical with the axes of such water flow, which may or may not be exactly straight. In a similar way to the meandering of streams or rivers, racialized flows also meander. Racialized meandering occurs when there is an interest convergence between politicians and social policy and/or organizations and institutional policies and minoritized groups which allow minoritized groups superficial and conditional routes to inclusion based on the interests of the dominant group. The rhetoric surrounding New Labour's postracial state ideal is an example of this. State-driven policies around multiculturalism and social equalities provided minority groups with room for manoeuvre in terms of belonging and securing of rights. This was only conditional based on the state wanting to be seen as promoting racial equality by moving beyond racialized discriminatory practices. However, the sets of policy discourses that attempted to promote the postracial state ideal were less about equality and more attributive to deracializing race relations. This process individualized structural disadvantage and any experience of racial inequality was the result of the neoliberalized subject and not wider structural conditions (see Bonilla-Silva [2013] for discussions on cultural racism). Such process meanders the direction of structural racism around the overt hostilities rooted in the colonial project towards the strategic performance of an equality policy discourse that, while contributory to the postracial state ideal, is still very much about sustaining domination, marginalization and hegemony over minoritized groups.

Filtering: Filtering is where solids are removed from liquid. This occurs through the process of separation, where solids go one way and the remaining liquid moves in the opposite direction. This is achieved through a mechanical filtration mechanism. As liquid flows through the filtration mechanism, it gets diverted around the centre of the machine, leaving any solidified materials – as they tend to move in a unidirectional flow – to hit the mechanism and be removed. Under liquid modernity, the compounding of sediments of 'race', socioeconomic position, gender, sexuality and other identity markers, lead to a similar filtration of racial flows. Those powerful and dominant groups – 'all those infamous straight white middle class privileged and abled-bodied men' (Bhattacharya, 1999: 81) – are guarded from such filtering processes of racism. This is because when white groups come into contact with racialized flows, they do not experience the same levels of marginalization and disadvantage that Black groups do. Instead, the compounding of identity sediments over time leads to a filtering process which, when connected with whiteness, invisibilizes (for white majority groups) the ways in which racial flows are experienced by racially minoritized groups, leading to the notion of racial progressivism and the idea of a postracial state (see Chapter 3 for a more detailed discussion around filtering and postraciality).

Soaking: Soaking means to become drench or completely saturated by liquid (for example, water). The processes of soaking in the context of liquid racism refers to the ways in which racialized flows are perceived differently by white majoritized and Black British minority groups contingent on the level of penetration by the racialized flow experienced. An example of this is how white majoritized and Black British minority groups experienced the murder of George Floyd and its subsequent Black Lives Matter protests. For Black British minority groups, the racialized flow of seeing George Floyd's murder was able to soak more so than when observed and witnessed by white majoritized groups. This is because of the sedimentary accumulation of racialized flows over time due to the African slave trade was able to penetrate into the experiences of Black British groups as they observed his murder. Because white majoritized groups do not share such colonial histories, when they observed the same moment of racial violence, they were not soaked as deeply. This process of soaking relates to Frantz Fanon's (2008 [1952]) account in *Black Skin, White Masks.* Fanon demonstrates that Blackness (but also, by the same criterion, whiteness) are phenomenological forms of lived experience; both white majoritized and Black British minoritized groups will experience the same racial moment, but only through the racialized registers of their lived realities.

Viscosity/viscosities: Viscosity/viscosities is a measure of a fluid's resistance to flow or fluidity. Viscosity is defined as the internal friction of a moving fluid. A fluid with large viscosity resists motion because its molecular make-up gives it internal friction due to the fluid's density or stickiness. Much like some liquids, not all 'liquid racism' has the same consistency – that is, constantly fluid, and permanently on the move, spilling and pouring over and into one another. As Rattansi (2017: 204) points out, liquids come in a variety of viscosities. Some liquids (for example, honey) have a specific level of stickiness and are difficult to move through and navigate. They tar individuals, leaving residual residue and create an environment where detaching from others is increasingly challenging. A 'liquid racism' that is also composed of such viscosities not only allows us to see the conditions and possibilities for the fragmentation and disembedding of historical manifestations of racism into 'new' confluent flows, but also the conditions for the re-embedding of historical manifestations of racism that may result in more solidified moments of racial tension, conflict and violence. Drawing on Rattansi's (2017: 204) examples of honey and treacle, certain liquids have different degrees of viscosity and fluidity contingent on temperature. Racism under the conditions of liquid modernity experiences a similar process. Liquid racisms are not wholly fluid all the time; they encounter moments of stickiness. These moments of stickiness are brought into being either through the racialized viscosities of dominant political power structures or events (for example, Brexit and education policy; see Chapters 4 and 5) – facilitating the production and reproduction of more solidified racist flows – or mobilized through anti-racist activism (for example, Black Lives Matter protests) which attempts to push back and resist the hegemonic racialized flows of dominant majoritized groups. Each of these flows – racist or anti-racist – creates a damming effect (see the preceding definition) which seeks to prevent or restrict racialized flows from soaking minoritized groups even further or producing further ontological insecurities for the majoritized.

Glaciation: The process of glaciation refers to the way in which liquids (for example, water) can freeze and, as such, has the possibility to expand and solidify, all to be melted down again as soon as temperatures rise and increase (Rattansi, 2017: 204). This liquefaction-solidification-liquefaction process is important when considering the way in which 'liquid racisms' become glaciated into 'solid racisms'. Under liquid modernity, racism is never wholly mobile. It goes through periods of cooling and heating, moments of time which make racism more or less visible contingent upon a range of public-political, institutional and sociocultural factors. For instance, education policies under New Labour were aimed at competing in a global marketplace where Britain could afford the risk of offsetting local labour – facilitating a brain drain in human capital terms – through the recruitment of migrant and foreign labour that would result in achieving an overall gain in terms of skills. This supported the EU's agenda of creating a flexible, motile labour force. Not only did such policy reinscribe – through processes of liquefaction – the logics of extraction imbricated in the African slave trade, but it also facilitated the conditions for waterfalls of resentment for those groups left behind by the flows of globalization, specifically the retrenchment of the 'solid' welfare state, in supporting and thereby solidifying the concerns of 'host' white majority groups leading to a glaciated, cooling period for 'solid racisms' manifested through anti-immigration and 'island retreat' (Winter, 2016; Virdee and McGeever, 2017) narratives around Brexit and the growth of alt-right politics nationally – to occur (see Chapters 4 and 5 for more details). These processes – both 'liquid' and 'solid' – have facilitated an ambivalence of uncertainty (Bauman, 2000; see the earlier definition) produced through the meeting of strangers under the conditions of liquid modernity. Liquid racism signifies an ambivalent experience of both a tolerance of strangerhood – through labour migration and the consumption and propinquities of otherness within liquid modern life – as well as a fear of strangerhood due to the diminution of trust because of individualizing processes and (perceived) erosion of community and local, regional, and national identities as strangers continually show up at our doors (Bauman, 2017).

Overview of the chapters

This book is structured into six central chapters. In Chapter 2, we contextualize how racism can be understood within the social thought of Zygmunt Bauman around postmodernity/liquid modernity. The chapter begins with a critical discussion of the delineations between modernity and postmodernity in social theory. This discussion is strategically deployed to allow us to map out the ways in which racism has been approached and theorized under the conditions of modernity and postmodernity. Contextualizing the ways in which racism has been mapped onto the conditions of modernity and postmodernity provides the authors with a milieu in locating Zygmunt Bauman's position within the modernity/postmodernity debate in social theory. Here, we argue that the shift in Bauman's thinking around modernity, from the vocabulary of postmodernity to a vocabulary of liquid modernity, was not an epistemological break in his wider social thought. We maintain that Bauman's thinking has always been based on notions of liquidity, seeing the conditions of the social world has always on the move fluctuating between solidification and liquefaction (known to Bauman as the period of liquid modernity). This contextualization of Bauman's theorizations of (liquid) modernity affords us the opportunity to locate racism within the very conditions of it as to make a conceptual intervention into ways of understanding racism in late modernity.

Developing themes drawn out of the previous chapter, Chapter 3 will focus on some of the problematics around notions of postrace. This critique lays the foundations for exposing the dangers of 'colorblind' reasoning around 'race', while setting a rationale for a critical enquiry to address the void in addressing 'race' in existing theorizing around late modernity. In 2010, almost immediately after assuming office as Prime Minister, David Cameron declared that 'state multiculturalism had failed' (Helm et al, 2011). This marked a significant moment in the state actively distancing itself from any interest or responsibility to pursue the promise of New Labour's multicultural project – a series of promises and premises which were superficially manifested in state strategies for achieving 'cultural pluralism' dating back to the Swann Report (1985) – and the notion of becoming a postracial state. The US has seen a more marked U-turn in relation to public political attitudes on notions of 'post-race'. Prior to Donald Trump's 2016 election, the US as 'a post-racial society enjoyed significant popularity' (Speed, 2020: 77). Against the illusory representation of America's postracial moment manifested in the election of Barack Obama, public debate has suggested that Trump represented a 'backlash against the assumed progress of a multicultural and potentially even post-racial society' (Speed, 2020: 76). Therefore, within the context of late modernity, postracial society, as the designated goal, failed in its efforts to construct notions of postracial social dynamics in the wider public consciousness. This argument is developed in Chapter 4, where we argue the conditions around Brexit provided a perfect storm for a resurgence in both explicit ethnocentric English nationalism amid more thinly veiled and nuanced articulations of white resistance to the postracial project manifested in deracialized concerns around the implications of immigration for employment. Thus, the state politics surrounding the postracial 'ideal' has not moved society towards a 'postracial' future, but inevitably, and unwittingly, has produced a resurgence in ethnocentric nationalist ideologies.

Chapter 4 provides an analysis of the ambivalence of racism within and through which Brexit occurred. It starts with a contextualization of how liquid modern processes – globalization, or more specifically, the intensification of mobilities of people from a variety of 'somewheres' that have ended up at the shores of Britain – have produced feelings of fear and ontological insecurity for 'host' citizens (Goodhart, 2017). The authors maintain that these liquid modern processes – of which migration and mobility is of legitimate concern – have manifested in what Bauman (2006a) identifies as 'liquid fears'. Liquid fear is the name Bauman gives to the scale of uncertainty and risk individuals experience in the face of the dangers that characterize the liquid modern age. We demonstrate how the conceptual category of the migrant 'other' has become the source of uncertainty and fear in the lives of much of the British public in which Brexit becomes the management of such fear through a discourse of retrotopia (Bauman, 2016). The chapter then proceeds to establish the ways in which a racism that is liquid is maintained through the discourses of migration that underpinned much of the Brexit debate. Both 'Leave' and 'Remain' campaigns are presented as articulating a position where the rhetoric of 'race' and racism became liquefied. For Vote Leave, liquid racism emerged via discourses of empire 2.0 that meandered around the historical legacies and structures of the original empire project by maintaining the narrative of a globally connected Britain with an emphasis on increased trade with Commonwealth nations that sought to dam public concerns of migration. Leave.EU, on the other hand, attempted to circumvent their intrinsic, Powellite racist sentiment towards migration through processes of deracialization (for example, the social and political retreat from Europe was used as a damming response towards the late modern risks and fears of continuous migrations and not about the exclusion of migrants themselves). The Remain argument, concurrently, used the same strategies of meandering and damming to present itself as inclusive and outwardly facing and globally aligned in support of migration. We argue that such Remainer discourses of the importance of labour migration (specifically from Eastern Europe) were built upon the sedimentary logic of extraction which saw individuals and resources from different areas and regions throughout much of the 'Global South' redirected towards the British metropole as part of empire building. The final section of the chapter highlights that the liquid racist narratives underpinning the Brexit debate facilitated a resolidification process, demonstrated by the increased racialized violence seen directly after the Brexit vote. Racialized minorities represented the personified threat of late modernity in which the Brexit decision to leave the EU reinforced a sense of white superiority and where racialized violence was understood as a celebratory victory over the 'threat' from racialized minorities (Taylor, 2017).

Chapter 5 examines education. Nowhere more substantively have we seen the embedding of the multicultural project than within education policy in the UK. This chapter develops themes introduced earlier around 'race' and liquid modernity to provide a critical account of the extent that racist outcomes persist in education. The project is focused on demonstrating how relationships between structure and agency, which characterize late modernity, manifest through persistent racialized inequities across public-political, institutional and sociocultural spheres. Education has been selected as a site for demonstrating how these processes persist (and have persisted) in the institutional sphere throughout late modernity. In the context of late modernity, 'race' and racism have come to be characterized by ambivalence, shifts towards more 'colourblind' notions of 'race', and unfounded claims around the realization of the postracial project. In this context, this chapter outlines how various active and passive processes collude to ensure the sustaining of highly racialized inequities in educational outcomes and experiences. These processes exist at the macro-structural, meso-discursive and micro-agential levels – through policy, institutional discourse and educational practice. The primacy of education in the continuation of racial domination and inequity is significant, due to the continued implementation of strategies which have a proven record of disadvantaging racialized minority groups. To draw on part of the apparatus of critical race theory, this represents a form of tacit intentionality on the part of policy makers (Gillborn, 2005). In the context of ambivalence around racism in late modernity, tacit intentionality can be read in two ways. The first reading is that intentionality is actively embedded in policy and practice in ways which evade obvious detection, hence functioning in tacit or unseen ways. A second reading might assume that policy makers are not actively conspiring against the interests of racialized minority groups. This passivity perhaps represents a position within which 'good intentions' are seen as enough to avoid accusations of racism in policy and practice, while ensuring that racist outcomes persist. This chapter develops these themes to incorporate an understanding of institutional discourse to bridge the gap between the macro-sphere within which policy making is constructed within late modernity, and the micro-sphere within which the agential action of educational practitioners is framed.

Chapter 6, the final case study chapter, focuses on youth road culture. The deep ambivalence of late modernity is lived out in the everyday lives of socially excluded young people, as the commonalities in their experiences of marginalization fail to 'congeal' into collective social issues, experiences of marginality become subsumed into the sphere of private troubles. Focusing on 'road culture', a contemporary Black-influenced street/youth culture emanating from the UK's urban centres, this chapter explores how the historical tensions of racism still weigh heavy. Building on the previous chapter, it focuses on the ways in which persisting inequalities and social exclusion, perpetuated by racist structures (such as education, as demonstrated in Chapter 5) are increasingly internalized as personal deficits. These processes contribute to a sense of social malaise, termed the 'munpain' (Bakkali, 2019), which places the subject as the central site of a struggle to alleviate their suffering. Reflective of the conditions which produce it, this struggle is also deeply ambivalent as the liquefied currents of historical racist structures flow through contemporary youth cultural practices, especially at their confluence with popular culture, which sought to connect young people with a sense of value and autonomy. This analysis focuses on the ways in which an urban youth culture, in which Black youth often take centre stage, is celebrated and commodified while simultaneously and paradoxically being maligned and feared. Young people arising from these communities themselves have a stake as they seek to ease their suffering and develop strategies to overcome their private troubles. The chapter seeks to understand the complex and ambivalent ways in which this process sees young people seemingly resisting their excluded status, while in some ways reproducing the tropes underpinning the fears and desires, and power and fantasies (Hall, 1997) connected to historical processes of racism. This is not a straightforward process of individual agents reproducing the conditions of racism, but demonstrates the ways in which resisting racism and social exclusion is increasingly ambivalent, as the traction required to overcome private troubles often requires the commodification of problematic tropes in popular culture.

In the concluding chapter (Chapter 7), key theoretical themes are further extrapolated. A detailed summary is given of how liquid racism contributes to ongoing discourses of 'race' and racism as well as the novel way in which it situates understandings of racism in the context of late modernity. Themes covered across each of the chapters are drawn together, highlighting wider research implications and trajectories in relation to illuminating further the importance of Zygmunt Bauman's liquid metaphor when thinking through notions of 'race' and racism in contemporary society.

2

Revisiting the Postmodernity/Liquid Modernity Debate

Introduction

The analysis and critique of modernity is a central theme in social theory. In the writings of major contemporary theorists (see the works of Habermas, 1985; Giddens, 1990, 1991; Touraine, 1995), the claim that we are living in unprecedented times, or that we are undergoing processes of major transformational social change, has been powerfully explored in some detail. These major social transformations associated with modernity have been generated by a range of processes – namely, the global expansion of capitalism, new technoscientific discoveries (for example, digitalization and the internet revolution) and the advent of globalization (for example, ongoing mobilities of goods, people and services) to most areas and regions of the world. Such processes are referred to in the sociological literature – though suggestive of the sociological fiction and subsequent collapse of the Western stadial model of development – as 'post-industrialism', 'postmodernism' or 'post-capitalism' (Elliott, 2013: 46). Recent social theorists (see, for instance, Beck, 1998, 1999, 2009; and Lash, 1992 (with Friedman), 1995 (with Featherstone and Robertson), 1996 (with Szerszynski and Wynne) and 1999) have instead chosen to refer to these contemporary social processes as constituting a new type of social system: that of late modernity (Giddens, 1991), second modernity (Beck, 1992) or *reflexive modernization* (Lash et al, 1994). In this latter intellectual tradition – what could be called late modernism – there is another important sociologist who has had wide reaching social, cultural and political significance: Zygmunt Bauman. Despite having an expansive career – writing on topics of class, socialism and Marxian social theory (see, for instance, Bauman, 1957, 1964, 1972, 1976) – Bauman did not receive sociological recognition until the publication of his now-renowned book *Modernity and the Holocaust* (1989a). In *Modernity and the Holocaust*, Bauman maintained the Nazi's Final Solution did not contradict the rationalization of modernity; it was predicated upon its very condition. Simply put, modernity's claim of order building and certainty making was also simultaneously about the removal of cultural and social ambivalences which – for the Nazi Party and the Holocaust – was the extermination of specific racialized 'others' as part of a wider visioning process of the 'good society' (see Chapter 1 for a more detailed discussion of Bauman's modernity and the Holocaust). Only a few years later, Bauman began analysing what he called the novelty of contemporary social processes and their ever-shifting guise and mutation, from the economy to entertainment. He identified these contemporary social changes as producing the new social system of postmodernity (see Bauman, 1992, 1993a, 1995 and 1997). He later rejected the discourse(s) of postmodernity and postmodernism for his formulation of modernity as liquid (see Bauman, 2000). This led to him writing a series of books on various topics such as love (2003a), everyday life (2005, 2006b), fear (2006a), culture (2011b), surveillance (2012, with Lyon), evil (2016, with Donskis) and management (2016, with Irena Bauman, Kociatkiewicz and Kostera). Topics and themes Bauman saw as central to and being influenced by liquid modernity.

The central aim of this chapter is to theorize the concept of liquid racism further by situating it within the broader debates around modernity in social theory. The first section provides a critical discussion of modernity and postmodernity, before turning its attention to the ways in which racism can be read within the contours of 'modern' and 'postmodern' thinking in the second section. Situating how racism is understood under the conditions of modernity and postmodernity allows us to perform a 180° turn back towards the work of Zygmunt Bauman to explain his manoeuvre in theoretical orientation away from the vocabulary of postmodernity to a vocabulary of liquid modernity. It is within this discussion that we maintain that Bauman's thinking has always been one of liquidity. It is just that the wider field of social theory gave him a language in which to finally actualize and describe his conceptual worldview. This discussion of Bauman's position on modernity is crucial. It affords us the opportunity to contextualize his theorizations of (liquid) modernity as to then locate racism within the contours of it. We now turn to the first section of the chapter.

The modernity/postmodernity debate in social theory

To situate our theorizations of racism within Bauman's theory of liquidity, or liquid modernity, we must firstly contextualize some of the key themes from the modernity/postmodernity debate in social theory. Modernity is largely understood as the institutionalization (or what could be called in Baumanian terms a solidification) of a specific (European) and universalizing sociohistorical and epistemic meaning through the emergence of scientific, political, bureaucratic and technological rationality that serves as an ordering framework for such ontology (Elliott, 2004). The development of modernity involved the rejection of 'traditional' modes of social organization in which tradition and custom were regarded as the way things were and held legitimizing authority. Modernity radically transformed the dynamism and complexities of social relations and processes by removing the certainties of tradition and custom, and replacing them with the social, economic and political upheavals of capitalist development, industrialism and urban expansion, the creation of parliamentary democracy, and mass social movements, resulting in technological transformations in the experience of space and time through the generation of information and knowledge.

Social and cultural theory has drawn attention to the problematic nature of the rise of large-scale bureaucratic institutions based on scientific, economic, political and technological rationality, and the influence it has on depoliticising the personal sphere. The rationalization of public life is seen to weaken the role of the personal sphere insofar as individual autonomy retreats against an all-encumbering public realm. In this regard, notions of 'self' and personal identity become increasingly precarious under the conditions of modernity in which the individual loses all sense of cultural anchorage as well as inner (psychic) reference points to 'self' and the wider social world. This has led the American historian Christopher Lasch (1979) to declare that at the centre of modernity – especially capitalist modernity – lies a 'culture of narcissism', a cultural form in which selfhood retracts to a state of defensiveness. Personal life becomes ever more parochial, and this parochialism of 'self' becomes a psychic coping mechanism against the social, cultural and political changes brought in by modernity. The German philosopher Jürgen Habermas (1981: 367) provides a more sophisticated analysis of this process, referring to the formation of modernity as an 'inner colonization of the lifeworld by technical systems'. What Habermas means by this is that 'modern' social life has become increasingly regulated by administrative and bureaucratic control, which has led to a stripping away of individual agency.

In his book *All That Is Solid Melts into Air*, Marshall Berman (1982) highlights the cultural possibilities and limits of modernity. He maintains that modernity produces a cultural ambivalence, facilitating a schizoid splitting of contemporary social life into either affirmation and idealization or condemnation and denigration. Such conceptual bifurcation is understood to be intrinsic to modernity itself (for example, 'modern' social life oscillating between the overly regulatory effects of the bureaucratic iron cage [Marcuse, 1941; Weber, 2013 (1922)]) and the zealousness attributed to 'modern' sensibilities (Simmel, 1903; Benjamin, 1929; McLuhan, 1962) producing a binary distinction between constraint and empowerment. This either/or logic can be seen as representing a hauntology (Derrida, 1993) of modernity, becoming a cornerstone of 'modern' thinking because of the proliferation of rationalizing systems. Berman explores the ambivalence of the 'modern' experience through the lens of the city. He argues – as a cultural field – the city represents a simultaneous fragmentation and liberated sense of contemporary urban living, of personal isolation and loneliness on the one hand and intense social proximity and cultural interconnectedness on the other. Drawing on modernist social theorists (in particular, Johann Wolfgang von Goethe, Charles Baudelaire and Karl Marx), Berman suggests the very dislocations of the social process which modernity brings into existence – of isolation and connection paradoxically – serve to create a social world of both cultural possibilities and perils. As Berman (1982: 13) observes:

> To be modern is to find ourselves in an environment that promises us adventure, power, joy, growth, transformation of ourselves and the world – and, at the same time, that threatens to destroy everything we have, everything we know, everything we are. Modern environments and experiences cut across all boundaries of geography and ethnicity, of class and nationality, of religion and ideology: in this sense, modernity can be said to unite all [*sic*] mankind. But it is a paradoxical unity, a unity of disunity: it pours us all into a maelstrom of perpetual disintegration and renewal, of struggle and contradiction, of ambiguity and anguish.

Modernity is thus a double-edged sword. Instead of being governed via a system of patrimonialism – where individuals are assigned preordained roles based on social status – as was the case in premodern (feudalist) societies, modernity succeeds in structuring individuals into a dynamic making of self-identity and the fashioning of lifestyles according to personal preference. Such a social transformation provides opportunities and possibilities through providing individual agency and autonomy. However, modernity has a darker side (Mignolo, 2011). The implementation of rationalizing systems as to legislate rational order – or, more accurately put, to imagine a utopian vision of the 'good society' – has regularly come at the cost of destroying individual human life. In the wake of Nazism and the Holocaust, for instance, rational 'modern' systems were used to remove the ambivalencing effects of otherness, and to therefore solidify a vision of a (perceived) utopian society based on the (genocidal) removal of the cause of such ambivalence (Bauman, 1989a; see also Chapter 1 for discussions of racism and the gardening state in Bauman's writings on the Holocaust).

This response to the ambivalence of modernity (even in its genocidal consequences) is the result of the certainties of tradition and custom under the conditions of premodernity becoming replaced by the anxieties of 'modern' life. Such anxiety is symptomatic of the rapid social change(s) characteristic of 'modern' societies. From the increased mobilities of people crossing borders in search of employment, security and escape from global conflicts to the existential risks of climate collapse and the implosion of global economic markets and political systems, the 'modern' world is not one envisioned through (European) modernity – a rationally controlled and predictably ordered world. Instead, it is beleaguered with multiple risks and dangers (Beck, 1992), many of which arise directly because of modernity's systems of rationalization – facilitated by what Theodor Adorno (1966) called 'negative dialectics' – creating an uncontrollable and unpredictable world (Giddens, 1999). These risks and dangers have only served to highlight the limitations of (European) modernist epistemology, necessitating a call for a new social and political way of thinking and imagining of the world: a way that seeks to reimagine the oppressive and destructive features of modernity. This new social and political way of imagining the world is postmodernity.

Postmodernity problematizes the relationship between theory, identity and politics through a blurring of their once concrete boundaries; it levels the hierarchies among them through favouring interpretative polyvalence and self-reflexive pluralism. In other words, postmodernity precipitates cultural heterogeneity. It refers to a range of cultural and critical theories that deconstruct the totalising narratives of modernity, the operationalization of power and epistemic legitimation. Postmodernity also produces new (re) articulations of personal and cultural experience, affording the concept of 'self' to no longer depend on the epistemological and ideological domination and oppression of modernity's search for universalism. While postmodern theorists (see, for instance, Lyotard, 1979; Baudrillard, 1981) acknowledge that we are still living in a time of transformational social and political change, individuals are no longer committing themselves to a Kierkegaardian (1846) *leap of faith* to grand narratives of scientific knowledge and technological advancement(s). A recognition of the limits of rationality has facilitated a cautionary manoeuvre away from the emancipatory claims of modernity such as rationality and liberty. This is echoed by Lyotard (1979: xiv) in *The Postmodern Condition*, in which he defines postmodernity as an 'incredulity toward metanarratives'. Therefore, the grand narratives of (Western) science and philosophy that attempted to ground truth and meaning in the presumption of a universal subject and the goal of emancipation no longer appear convincing or even plausible. Instead, postmodernity's rhetoric of anti-totalities attempts to understand knowledge as multiplicities; localized and perspectival. Knowledge is constructed, not discovered through positivist premises of validity and verification.

Social transformation(s) are understood to have played a crucial role in the diminution of the grand narratives of modernity. The scale and intensity of the globalization of social institutions and transnational communication systems because of digitalization, ongoing mobilities of individuals, goods and services, and cheap air travel have accelerated the distanciation of time-space to a greater degree than the social and political changes that reshaped the 'modern' world, resulting in the turmoil and flux of personal and cultural life. This has resulted in the blurring of the boundaries of social and cultural life, leading to what Baudrillard (1981) sees as an imposition of all boundaries, an erasure of the distinctions of high and low culture, of appearance and reality, of past and present. Postmodernity, under these conditions, is the abandonment of the modernist goal to find foundationalist knowledge systems underlined by scientific principles. Conversely, postmodernity maintains there to be no foundationalist presumptions of the world. Social and cultural life is decentred and dispersed: everything has an equal valid-truth claim, which means that nothing much counts in terms of meaning, distinction and hierarchy. In this context, postmodernist culture dislocates structures and materialist explanations for identity, politics and sociospatial inequalities in favour for constructions of the social world through signs, symbols and codes, constituting reality in Baudrillardian (1981: 17) terms as a 'simulation' where the world is only merely experienced: '"The real" becomes that of which it is possible to give an equivalent reproduction – the real is not only what can be reproduced, but that which is always already reproduced, the hyperreal.' Postmodernity is thus a society (or state of being) that is only experienced through an assemblage of transient signs, symbols and codes. 'Reality' – or more accurately put, the 'modern' conditions that attempted to solidify and tame the ambivalencing effects of modernity insofar as to control and make possible a more orderly future – are not achievable within the contours of postmodernity. Reality (and thus social and cultural life) is always contingent on the symbols, signs and codes that come to signify a particular experience (or sets of experiences), but which are as easily reproduced and given new designations of meaning: reality is only experienced, but never fully actualized.

However, postmodernity is never only purely cultural. The scale and intensity of globalization and informational communication technologies, which has further compressed time and space, have not only fragmented and dislocated personal and cultural experiences – which were once grounded in the rationalizing systems of modernity – offering new textures to, or reproductions of, such personal and cultural experience, but also enter the psychic structures of the individual too. In other words, the free-floating nature of sociocultural meanings in postmodernity has an impact on the psychic space of the individual as disorientation, discontinuity and fragmentation. As postmodernity erodes the scientific, bureaucratic, technological and political structures of modernity, the remit of an individual's life is increasingly one of what Anthony Giddens (1991: 209) calls 'life politics'. A person's identity, as well as their ability to meet the demands of the market and the health and wellbeing of their loved ones and communities, is dislocated from the social, economic and political contexts which once framed them under the conditions of modernity. The individual is now free (or, more accurately put, necessitated) to choose their identity and to deal with the associated risks of postmodernity (Beck, 1992). Fredric Jameson (1991) maintains that the social and economic world which facilitates this is late capitalism. The rhizomatic communicational and computational networks of late capitalism, with its ever-pluralizing of surplus-generating forms (for example, the personalized consumption of identity markers), disrupt the materialist framing of reality, facilitating a psychic dislocation, and therefore a deterritorialization of social space between 'self' and 'other'. As Jameson (1991: 27) comments:

> If, indeed, the subject has lost its capacity actively to extend its pro-tensions and re-tensions across the temporal manifold and to organize its past and future into coherent experience, it becomes difficult enough to see how the cultural productions of such a subject could result in anything but 'heaps of fragments' and in a practice of the randomly heterogeneous and fragmentary and the aleatory.

This fragmentation between the social world and the psychic subjectivity of the individual – or what Deleuze and Guattari (1977) would term schizo-fragmentation – is one of the central themes of postmodernity. The disintegration of the individual within postmodernity is related to the intensity and scale of consumer capitalism (Jameson, 1991). The extent of such scalability and intensification of mediated signs and technological codes in postmodernity are initiated by, and indeed are deeply imbricated in, the commodification of abstract categories within the late capitalist marketplace. This contemporary pluralism – with its manifold subjectivities, fractured and competing discourses, and the diversification of identities and cultural worldviews which are all of equal value – is for Jameson capitalist exchange-value, but in its radical, nascent state. It is a kind of perversion of the extremities of consumer capitalism itself, a cultural mutation of commodities as simply fetishism which accompanies postmodernity's ability to dehumanize the individual through replacing materialism with a process of signification. Put another way, postmodernity is the ability of capitalism to transmute the materialization of Foucault's (1988) *technologies of production, sign systems and power* into the human psychic sphere via processes of internalization (or, to use another Foucauldian term, *technologies of self*). For Jameson, therefore, because late capitalism is so saturated with goods, services, information, codes and signs, it is as if we all now live in some communicational network of random signifiers, a network which produces radical cultural possibilities and dominations in equal parts.

Under such fragmentation, individuals live moment by moment, adopting a 'until-further-notice' (Bauman, 2006b) attitude and, consequently, nothing lasts very long. As such, postmodernity – in the very act of fashioning itself as a period of rapid territorialization-deterritorialization-reterritorialization – subverts all features of previous historical development, in particular the universalizing effects of modernity, instead spawning a conception of the social world that is only accessible (but only ever in its hyperreal state; see Baudrillard [1981]) as discursive formations. This produces an endless proliferation of social forms and adaptations, an unstoppable breeding of the signifying chain which disrupted structuralism's attempt to produce ontological meaning through the relationship between signifier and the signified (see de Saussure, 1993). In postmodernity there is a breakdown in the relationship between the signifier and signified. Social and cultural experience(s) exist without the codifying effects that occur between the signifier and the signified, dislocating the individual from the concept of 'selfhood'. Selfhood is instead constructed in Lacanian (1977) terms through 'signifiers in isolation', as a breaking of the signifying chain, a 'schizophrenia in the form of a rubble of distinct and unrelated signifiers' (Jameson, 1991: 26). Despite this, the individual's engagement with 'signifiers in isolation' never produces pure fragmentation, but rather an intensification of fetishism with the signifiers of contemporary culture. According to Jameson (1991), such fetishism takes the form of a 'cognitive mapping', a kind of reimagination and respatialization of the relationality between subject and object. This 'cognitive mapping' occurs through the personal, social, cultural and political reflection upon the rhizomatic connections, as well as the deconstruction of, different conceptual bifurcated categories (for example, local/global, same/other and present/past). Ultimately, Jameson sees such theorization of postmodernity as a form of emancipation for individuals, between the subject and collective autonomy, a countertrend to the overly negative effects of postmodernity; that of fragmentation, dislocation and dispersal.

Jean Baudrillard (1981) provides a more sombre reading of postmodernity. Postmodernity, for Baudrillard, is seen as reframing the individual within the simulatory dimensions of hyperrealism, of taking perception prisoner and locking it away inside the prison of an aesthetic hallucination of culture, while also inscribing desire, where desire in this instance is understood in Lacanian (1977) terms as the surplus production of demand once need is taken away, within the seductiveness of consumer signifiers in contemporary society. In contrast to modernity, then, Baudrillard speaks of postmodernity as a world of excess symbols, signs and codes that are nondetermining, of seduction and domination, a stage of consumer capitalism that continually outstrips all assigned representations, boundaries and limits of the consumer object. As Baudrillard (1981: 26) notes:

> Things have found a way to elude the dialectic of meaning which bored them: it is to proliferate to infinity, to fully realize their potentialities,

> to surpass their essence in going to extremes, in an obscenity which henceforth takes the place for them of an immanent finality and of an insane rationality.

This is understood by Baudrillard (1981) as hyperreality: a simulational excess, devoid of logic or direction, produced by a proliferation and acceleration of the representational sign value of commodity objects (for example, the stylish shirt or dress is more stylish than the designation of stylish the shirt or dress gives to the model in the magazine). This produces a form of social logic in which the multiplicity of commodity objects dominates over individuals, rendering subjectivity defeated, outdated, old-fashioned and redundant. The psychic arena under the conditions of postmodernity is so immersed and seduced by a world of things that any attempt to ascribe any form of identity or identification to oneself or to that of 'others' will always be reabsorbed or already caught, within the aesthetic of the hyperreal. Put simply, there is nothing beyond the representational sign value of the hyperreal. Therefore, the message of pessimism outlined by Baudrillard is that postmodernity is the era in which the commodity object reigns supreme, and that every mode of thought is at once found and lost in the simulacrum.

The critical theories of the Frankfurt School (for example, Theodor Adorno, Max Horkheimer and Herbert Marcuse) conceptualized the result of these postmodern conditions 20–40 years prior to the works of both Baudrillard (1981) and Jameson (1991). *Dialectics of Enlightenment* (Adorno and Horkheimer, 1944), *Composing for the Films* (Adorno, 1947), *Night Music: Essays on Music 1928–1962* (Adorno, 1964), *Negative Dialectics* (Adorno, 1966), *Eros and Civilisation* (Marcuse, 1955) and *One-Dimensional Man* (Marcuse, 1964) all distilled the essence of Marxism into a reflexive critique of the cultural sphere. These texts claimed that it was the logic of capitalist economic exploitation that drained individuals of psychic significance by generating an exhilaration of forgetting, an addiction to mindlessness because of the Lacanian (1977) desire for 'signifiers in isolation' (or, more simply put, commodity objects), all resulting in the embodied pleasures of the immediate – that is, the ongoing search for the next big thing in which once the state of instantaneous satisfaction is achieved, the individual is in search for the next big thing; another exhilarated high, the next 'signifier in isolation'. The consequence of this, according to the ideas and works of the Frankfurt School, is that the postmodern period comes to be understood as a culture permeated by fragmentation and dislocation where individuals are continuously and more deeply alienated from themselves (in the psychic sense), other people and the wider (materialist) social world around them. Instead, individuals operate in a social world constructed out of signs, symbols and codes which are created by capitalist institutions as *false needs* that attempt to integrate individuals into the dominant system of production and consumption through mass media, advertising, industrial management and contemporary modes of thought, leading individuals to become what Herbert Marcuse (1964) calls 'one-dimensional'.

Within postmodernity, identities (or, more precisely, the identification) of the individual is no longer based on economic, racialized and gendered reductionism – as a way of solidifying and removing the ambivalence of difference and diversification – but rather the relationality of symbols, signs and codes which come to signify a person's identification with a 'sameness' or 'othering' presence and designation. By distinguishing the periods of modernity and postmodernity in this way, theorists such as Judith Butler (1997, 2004) and Stuart Hall and Paul du Gay (1996) have maintained that the identification of individuals is produced through an assemblage of signs, spectacles, and simulacra (see also Debord, 1967) that do not emanate from a purely materialist 'external outside' (even when such signs, symbols and codes are produced on the contemporary capitalist marketplace in the vein of the social analyses provided by the Frankfurt School), but rather through intersubjectivity and the relationship between subject and object. Baudrillard (1981: 19) maintained this to produce a 'death of the social' and articulated there to be nothing but a pure base of existence and of identity in which no one could ever ascertain among the depthless, fragmentary possibilities of postmodernity, anchored with the seductive charm(s) of being one move away from choosing or having the next-best identity in town to fit in with or become included or assimilated into the majoritized population or become structured into a designation of otherness based on how you are identified (or a mix of both). Within a postmodern period, where every sign simply refers itself to another, and that to another, in an infinite regression (Baudrillard, 1981), leaving the psychic sphere disconnected from the wider social world, immersed instead in the perception of (commodity) objects, notions of difference and diversification are addressed through an embrace (or better yet, consumption) of the 'other', approaching the negation between sameness and otherness as one of mixophilia as opposed to mixophobia under modernity (Bauman, 2006b). In the next section, we continue our theorizing around the modernity/postmodernity debate in social theory to unpack how racism has been situated in the broader contours of the modern/postmodern distinction.

Racism and the modernity/postmodernity debate

Racism – under the conditions of modernity – emerged out of (European) Enlightenment rationalizing practices. The legitimation of science – as the guiding principle of modernity – opened society up to 'objective' enquiry; that is, everything (from personal identity to economic and political systems) should be put under the microscope to determine its reliability and valid truth claim(s). Every social, cultural and political institution – those which are current and those which ought to be – had become a legitimate object of systematic, precise observation. It was only through such precise observation that social, cultural and political institutions could legitimize themselves. Zygmunt Bauman (1993b: 218) in his chapter 'Modernity, racism, extermination' cites the work of American historian George Mosse to document the relationship between modernity and racism: 'it is impossible to separate the inquiries of the Enlightenment philosophies into nature from their examination of morality and human character … [From] the outset … natural science and the moral and aesthetic ideals of the ancient, joined hands'. In other words, racism in its 'modern' form was shaped by scientific activity that was marked by an 'attempt to determine man's [*sic*] exact place in nature through observation, measurements, and comparisons between groups of men [*sic*] and animals' (Bauman, 1993b: 218). This led to the development of pseudo-scientific fields of research such as phrenology (the study of character from the measurements of the skull) and physiognomy (the study of character from facial features) which best captured the confidence and ambition of scientific modernity. Human character, intelligence and aesthetics were seen as determined by natural predispositions, which could be captured, understood and categorized through observation. Such human characteristics were merely 'raw facts' to discover the mysticism of nature; signs and codes to be read, interpreted and analysed by science.

Therefore, 'modern' racism emerged as an attempt to postulate a systematic understanding and distribution of the characteristics and features of human populations. This is seen in the scientifically legitimated racism of Robert Knox (1850) in his book *The Races of Men*, in which he inferred from physical qualities of human populations a series of speculations of the differences of temperaments, intelligences and abilities between what he understood to be different racial categories. Knox's racialization of anatomy led him to conclude that there were various racial groups throughout history which were distinctive and that they could be positioned on a scale according to their civilizational abilities. According to him, no racial grouping was incapable of some sort of civilizing process, yet there existed distinctions between limited civility of Black groups on the one hand, and the much greater past achievements and future potential of white groups on the other: 'The Black differed from the White in everything else as much as in colour: He is no more a white man than an ass is a horse or a zebra' (Knox, 1850: 245). However, Knox's scientific legitimation of racialized distinction had more to do with the political and religious ideological domination of European societies than it did with any scientific basis for racial difference. Knox was concerned about Europe's ability to expand its colonial and imperial project. Colonialized peoples had already expelled the French from Haiti. Knox feared they might soon expel other European settlers from the West Indies and Brazil, and prevent European occupation of Africa itself (Biddiss, 1976). Proclamations of a scientifically justified racial superiority of Europeans were thus needed to vindicate their incursion into other areas and regions of the world as a matter of empire building. Similarly, Knox's scientific legitimation of racial difference was able to fuse with elements of Christian doctrine. Christians – clergy and the most devout among the laity – could take a teleological position and justify specific religious teachings (for example, the 'sons of Ham') and uphold the belief that Christianity was crucial to Europe's civilizing process, while simultaneously seeing non-Europeans as culturally inferior.

From such Enlightenment scientific rationalization came what Bauman (1993b) calls 'engineering attitudes' towards nature itself. Science was not to be conducted for its own sake; it was seen as an instrument of eliminating and solidifying the social and cultural ambivalences of modernity – of which one was the coming to terms with the confronting of *the stranger* or *strangerhood* – through the visioning of the 'good society' via planning and bureaucratic administration. Bauman (1989a, 1993b) used the metaphor of the *gardening state* to explain this process: 'like garden vegetation or a living organism they could not be left to their own devices, lest should they be infested by weeds or overwhelmed by cancerous tissues' (Bauman, 1993b: 219; see also Chapter 1 for a more detailed discussion on Bauman's gardening state metaphor in his writings on *Modernity and the Holocaust*). Therefore, under modernity – where there is the capacity to improve human conditions through the reorganization of societies based on rationality – racism was maintained because of scientific, technological and cultural manipulation. Racism is the outcome of the removal of certain categories of people that are (perceived) to be at odds with the visioning process of the 'good society'.

Nazi Germany is an example of such 'modern' racism(s) on a large scale (see Bauman, 1989a). For Nazi Germany, the notion of a 'good society' was only attainable through the splitting of human life into categories of 'worthy' (Aryans) and 'unworthy' (Jewish communities). Drawing on Bauman's (1989a) 'gardening' metaphor, the 'worthy' needed cultivating, while the 'unworthy' needed to be removed. To the Nazi administration, Jewish communities were not a 'race' like other groups; they were a group constructed as contaminating the ambition or goal of achieving the vision of a perfect society, a society that was based on a particular racial order. Thus, the removal of Jewish communities, by keeping Jewish individuals outside the borders of the German nation state (for example, the Nazi Party's Madagascan refoulement plan) or through internal racial social policies (for example, the creation of Jewish ghettos, or – in the case of the Holocaust – extermination), served to solidify very racialized ambivalences and render a racially organized humankind (see Bauman [1989a] for a more in-depth discussion of this).

If the condition (or conditions) of racism in modernity was framed through a solidification effort to remove cultural and social ambivalences, how does racism manifest in postmodernity? Postmodernity preoccupies itself with fantasy and the imaginary as the process of self-construction and otherness. As Stephen Mitchell (1993: 21) observes, 'the bridge supporting connection with others is not built out of a rationality superseding fantasy and the imagination, but out of feelings experienced as real, authentic, generated from the inside, rather than imposed externally, in relationship with fantasy and the imagination'. What such imaginaries and fantasy does is facilitate a permanent transitional space of rolling identifications, where someone's personal identification or the identification given to someone from others is built on a range of assemblages and framed through reverie, containments of selfhood placed onto oneself or by others, and semiotic forces; in other words, within postmodernity, imagination and fantasy constitutes human subjectivity. Imagination and fantasy are thus generative forces. They are forces in and through which individuals create meaning in the moment of differentiation between 'self' and 'other'. Through these premises of self-construction and otherness, racism emerges within postmodernity via multiple meanings and codes, the schizoid dissolution of personal identification and signification. The disconnection of cultural and ethnic representation is a precondition for the emergence of 'postmodern' racism. The suspension of hostile socially reproduced thoughts of otherness, coupled with an immersion in the unfolding of cultural and ethnic ambiguity, is the central means from which racism gets brought into being. More precisely, racism is embodied through personal subjectivity, of the multiplicity and fluidity, and narrative reconstructions of identity and identification without beginning or end; a conception of racism that emerges out of the imagination and fantasy which are enacted via the 'subject-in-process' (Kristeva, 1982). Simply put, racism becomes enacted through intersubjective identification(s) because of cultural fragmentation, political and social dislocation, and the economic interchangeability of commodities and objects on the late capitalist marketplace (Jameson, 1991). 'Postmodern' racism is thus the creative and reflexive psychic organization underpinning the construction of subject positions and identity; an alternative to the mixophobic removal of cultural ambivalences under modernity (Bauman, 2006b). Otherness is handled through a mixophilia of the 'other' (Bauman, 2006b), the removal of otherness through an assimilation into majority subjective positionalities (or what bell hooks [1992] identifies as a process of eating the 'other').

Gallagher (2003) observes this emergence of 'postmodern' racism through the commodification process. Under late capitalism, the commodification and mass marketing of products that signify 'race' are intended for consumption across the 'colour line' (DuBois, 1903). Individuals from any racial or ethnic background can listen to drill music or cheer on their favourite, majority

Black, professional sports team. Racial symbols are bought and sold in the late capitalist marketplace, denoting a 'colourblind' logic where 'race' no longer plays a role in the consumption of specific commodity objects to the (re)construction of personal identity or the identification(s) of 'others'. However, such colourblind logic does not ignore 'race'; it acknowledges 'race' while sidestepping racial disadvantage and discrimination by reducing racially coded symbols and signs to commodities or experiences that both majoritized white groups and racialized minorities can purchase and share. It is through such acts of shared consumption that racism becomes an outcome of 'signifiers in isolation' (Lacan, 1977), commodity objects devoid of any sort of racializing identification(s). Seeing 'race' only as 'signifiers in isolation' that are for sale allows majoritized white groups to consume the identification(s) of racialized minorities to construct their own identity, or that what majoritized white groups are purchasing is a racially or ethnically authentic experience or cultural artefact. In other words, racism is no longer a solidifying effort to remove the cultural ambivalences of the 'other', as was the case under modernity. Instead, late capitalism has constructed a postracial society which is perceived to have homogenized culture (by creating the illusion that we are all the same) through the ubiquitous consumption of racially coded symbols and signs (see Chapter 3 for a more detailed discussion on 'race' and postrace). Such consumption of otherness refocuses relations between identity and difference, subjectivity, and politics. The pervasiveness of the racialized 'other' has left the 'white' self to feel the full force of its inner pain, of the intensities of the anxiety caused by diversification and of the loss of security produced through the diminution of what once was. Drawing on Baudrillard (1981: 81), then, we could describe 'postmodern' racism as 'playing with the pieces'; that is, the personal identification of majoritized white groups and the identification of 'others' is about an increasing awareness of the creativity of fantasy and imagination of consuming racialized signs, symbols and codes.

The production of identity/identification of majoritized white groups through the consumption of racialized sign systems forms the basis for 'postmodern' racism. Such identities/identifications are produced through reflexively organized narratives around commoditized culturally diverse 'signifiers in isolation' (Lacan, 1973) in the constitution of the 'white' self and racialized 'others'; representations fabricated out of fragmentary racialized (but also other identity) aesthetics. This connection between the aleatory (re)configurations and psychic reorganization of white selfhood based on racialized sign systems results in the decentredness of the subject. Decentring, in this context, is not understood as the separation of ego (whiteness) from the subject (the individual reproducing whiteness) in a Lacanian (1973) sense, but rather in terms of a representational contingency through which the filtering of self and other occurs because of the consumption of racialized sign systems that attempts to assimilate difference and solidify otherness through mixophilia. Whiteness, in this context, represents a complete mastery, self-sufficiency and the jouissance of otherness; a racialized totality in the overcoming of difference and an enjoyment of absolute wholeness (Seshadri-Crooks, 2002: 8) – in other words, a lack of recognition of one's raciality on account of whiteness itself (Andrews, 2016). 'Postmodern' racisms are thus about the questioning of fantasy and the imagination or, perhaps more accurately, seeking to turn fantasy and imagination back upon itself, to glimpse the creative workings of the unconscious desire, for the postcolonial longings of white supremacy.

This representational contingency of meaning and racialized signs is never purely unconscious, lost in the simulacrum (Baudrillard, 1981) of the late capitalist marketplace. Majoritized white groups are aware of them; they acknowledge that meaning (and by extension their own identities and the identifications of others through the consumption of racialized symbols and signs) is not fixed once and for all, but rather that the racial signification given to a person's identity/identification is creatively fabricated and negotiated through fantasy and imagination (or, in this context, the reproduction of domination and white supremacy). Such creativity of fantasy and imagination – on the part of majoritized white groups – is about the reordering of structural whiteness. This is done through the 'colourblind' discourses of late capitalism, which remove from personal thought and public discussion any taint or suggestion of white supremacy or guilt while legitimating the existing dominant social, political and economic arrangements which privilege majoritized white groups. After all, 'colourblind' consumption habits within the late capitalist marketplace allow majoritized white groups to see themselves as racially progressive and tolerant as they can proclaim belief into a system which does not see 'race'. Instead, all individuals can consume into the same racialized sign systems, commodities and products regardless of 'race' or ethnicity to (re)construct one's own personal identity or to demarcate the identification of the 'other'. This enactment of 'postmodern' racism filters out whiteness as a marker for structural (dis)advantage and racial dominance in society (Frankenberg, 2001: 76) by resisting reflexive awareness and thinking, leading to what Bonilla-Silva (2013) would term a *racism without racists*. It evades the power differential within 'postmodern' racism through an immersion in unconscious denials, disavowals and negations (of white supremacy). The personal confusion and dislocation of majoritized white groups – the feeling of ontological insecurity due to the postcolonial melancholia of whiteness (Gilroy, 2004) – becomes hidden behind the logic of late capitalism, consequently invisiblizing the assimilatory dynamics of otherness under the conditions of postmodernity that perpetuate and resolidify racial inequality. Such resolidification of racial inequality casts doubts on whether postmodern thinking in relation to racism is at all adequate or whether alternative premises are needed to conceptualize the enactment of racism in late modernity. This necessitates us to perform a 180° turn back towards discourses of modernity, specifically the postmodernity/liquid modernity distinction in Bauman's own thinking on modernity, in order to contextualize the enactment of racism(s) within a liquid modern world.

Zygmunt Bauman: from postmodernity to 'liquid' modernity

Zygmunt Bauman is seen as one of the most prominent social theorists of postmodernity (Best, 1998). Throughout the 1980s and 1990s, Bauman published a range of scholarly texts around the theme(s) of postmodernity and postmodernism. These texts include 'Is there a postmodern sociology?' (1988), 'Sociological responses to postmodernity' (1989b), 'Philosophical affinities of postmodern sociology' (1990a), 'A sociological theory of postmodernity' (1991), *Intimations of Postmodernity* (1992), 'Postmodern ethics' (1993), *Life in Fragments* (1995a) and *Postmodernity and Its Discontents* (1997). Zygmunt Bauman understood postmodernity as a new cultural and social experience, a milieu where individuals have a 'painful and sickening feeling of perpetual uncertainty in everything regarding the future' (Bauman, 1997: 192). This is because, for Bauman (1992: 35), contemporary cultural and social experiences are 'disorderly, to wit plural, rhizomically growing, devoid of direction'. Postmodernity is thus about the dissolution of *the social.* The structures that bound people together into groups and communities under the conditions of modernity (and thus reproduce feelings of security) are no longer stable, fixed and long term. Postmodernity has facilitated a pluralization of activities, identities and ways of being to the extent that the premises underpinning the 'modern' project can no longer help people make sense of the world and their place within it. This is because the postmodern condition is one of fleetingness; short-lived and aleatory – a condition that, according to Bauman (1992), arises from the subject's immersion in the social world without any illusion of modernity's structures to produce a secure, controlled and orderly world, as well as having a tolerance for the ambiguity and confusion facilitated by postmodernity.

As Bauman shifted his analysis of contemporary society to that of liquidity, those who read his works closely would be able to see little fundamental difference in theoretical orientation between his postmodern phase (for example, Bauman, 1991a, 1992, 1997) and his liquid modern phase (for example, Bauman, 2000, 2005, 2007). There is much overlap between Bauman's conceptualization of liquid modernity (see Chapter 1 for a more detailed account of this) and that of his examination of postmodernity. This has led Ray (2013: 66) to ask: 'Why did this transition in Bauman's thinking occur'? Bauman addresses this observation in an interview from 2002 where he maintains that the reason for the shift in his conceptual focus was because of the reservations he had about the theoretical adequacy of postmodernism as a framing device to understand the contemporary conditions of society:

> I've some time ago distanced myself from the 'postmodern' grid of the worldmap. A number of reasons contributed … the concept of 'postmodern' was but a stop-gap choice, a 'career report' of a search – still on-going and remote from completion. That concept signalled that the social world had ceased to be like the one mapped using the 'modernity' grid … but was singularly un-committal as to the features the world had acquired instead … About the qualities of the present-day world we can say now more than it is unlike the old familiar one. We have, so to speak, matured to afford (to risk?) a positive theory of the novelty. (Bauman and Yakimova, 2002)

What we can see from Bauman's comments given earlier is that, despite some observers (see, for instance, Rattansi, 2017) denoting him as a postmodernist, he was never a postmodern social theorist to begin with. Bauman's theoretical orientation has always been one based on liquidity – a condition whereby individualized reflexive awareness rebels against the unpredictable social changes of the modern world (Camus, 1951) by refusing to be constrained within the limits of 'what is' through attempting to solidify certainties of anything concerning the future, and thereby transcending the present insofar as the actions used to conceive of the possibility of the future are short term, aleatory and can easily be melted down again due to the scale and intensity of contemporary social changes requiring individuals to reflect on new alternative possibilities and futures to avoid the trap of the present – throughout his various analyses of contemporary society. The concept of postmodernism or postmodernity was merely used as an *epistemological* 'stop gap' to the absence of appropriate descriptors or explanatory power of his account of the contemporary social world. It was not until the wider field of social theory developed the theoretical parameters around understanding the social changes of the present (for example, neoliberal economic restructuring, intensification of the mobility of people, goods and services, and the emergence of new communicational networks due to digitalization) and their consequences that Bauman had a vocabulary with which to conceptualize the contemporary social world. Paralleling Ulrich Beck's (1992) dichotomy between *first* and *second modernity*, as well as Anthony Giddens' (1991) separation of the modernity of the 19th and 20th centuries to the *high modernity* characteristic of the 21st century, Bauman (2000: 28) also saw society in the 21st century as 'no less "modern" than the society which entered the twentieth'. Therefore, while previously describing postmodernity as 'an aspect of a fully-fledged, viable social system which has come to replace the "classical" modern, capitalist society and thus needs to be theorized according to its own logic' (Bauman, 1992: 52), he later rejected the term, proclaiming that '[p]ostmodern was … flawed from the beginning. Disclaimers notwithstanding, it did suggest that modernity was over' (Bauman and Yakimova, 2002). Bauman's (2000) employment of the conceptual category of liquidity afforded him the possibility to still theorize the themes of ambivalence and uncertainty – themes he identifies as characteristic of the novelty – but now with a clearer attempt to work through the 'logic' of the new social system of the present and without the need of straightforward periodization. This is probably why many scholars have tended to still view Bauman through a lens of the postmodern. Sceptics of modernity viewed the 'modern' project's ability to periodize time (or what Jacques Derrida [1981] calls chronophonism) as oppressive and rooted in colonial logics as to civilize Europe through decivilizing countries in Africa, Asia and South America. This resulted in many philosophers and sociologists to develop a genealogical account of European/Western knowledge construction, leading to such intellectual figures (for example, Jean Baudrillard [1981], Jean-Francois Lyotard [1979] and Michel Foucault [1969]) being seen by those sympathetic of the 'modern' project's promises of Enlightened scientific discovery, verification and validity of a universalizing homogeneity of the social world as postmodern (although the only scholar to identify as a postmodernist was Lyotard himself). In contrast to these (what are actually) poststructuralist interpretations of modernity, Bauman developed an original formulation of postmodernity as a generalized social system, in which the postmodern did not function as a point beyond modernity, but rather as a condition onto modernity itself. This led Bauman (1990b: 98) to see modernity through 'the non-feasibility of its original project'. In other words, postmodernity is modernity reconciled to its own impossibility, contained with itself and determined to forever live with it. This is what Bauman (2001a: 339) meant by the now influential claim 'postmodernity as modernity minus illusions'. It is this formulation that has made scholars declare Bauman to be postmodernist. However, Bauman is not suggesting postmodernity is an illusionary end point here, beyond modernity and the systems of rationalization underpinning it. He is detailing the ambivalent character of the present in terms of current and future prospects of self, social relations and everyday life. The language of postmodernity facilitated him to do this, given its domination within academia and popular culture. However, once Bauman had the appropriate vocabulary – largely taken from the works of Ulrich Beck (1992) – he felt the need for new terminological descriptions of contemporary culture. Thus, for Bauman (cited in Tester and Jacobsen, 2005: 149), postmodernity was always a '"fleeting affair", but in its time it was indispensable. Like many other good intentions, it went astray'.

Bauman's (2000) eventual employment of the concept of liquidity is him finally actualizing (in theoretical orientation) the contemporary experience of the social world which, in a sociological sense, is a far better conceptual category than that of postmodern or postmodernity.

Bauman's (2000) concept of liquidity or, better put, 'liquefaction', arose from his critique of the theoretical presuppositions and social and political consequences of the category of postmodernity. A category that reinforces a stadial model of society whereby postmodernity represents the 'end of history' (see the works of Fukuyama, 1989; Giddens, 1991; Jameson, 1991; Beck, 1999). Bauman saw social theory's conceptualization of the postmodern and postmodernity as too fatalistic. He maintained that social theory had more to say about the state of the contemporary world than simply modernity was over and had been replaced with a cultural and social relativism which indefinitely reproduced societal meaning and individualized personhood. Bauman saw that social theory had the potential to engage with what he called a positive account of the novelty of contemporary social processes. Therefore, the deployment of the concept of liquidity was purposefully chosen to capture the contemporaneity of modernity. Liquidity, or liquefaction, makes salient the fleetingness of society understood in the 21st century, a fleetingness premised on a culture of ambivalence – of societal opening and closure in equal measure premised on the human condition to open up new worlds and possibilities in order to safeguard, protect and maintain security against unanticipated future hazards and risks. These possibilities and new worlds can lead to the production of new risks and hazards, necessitating individuals to identify further new possibilities and worlds that go beyond the limits of the present. This means late modernity is characterized by a 'reflexive imperative' (Archer, 2012) which helps to break past human volitions that now have structuring effects over the present. Such structuring effects which are also contained within each new possibility via the process of sedimentation. Put another way, society is prone to structural amnesias over time and space, but is also always reinvented through a restructuring process – a process which itself does not last very long and so can quite easily become liquid again. Thus, for Bauman (2000: 2), this is the most compelling reason 'to consider "fluidity" or "liquidity" as fitting metaphors when we wish to grasp the nature of the present'. The notion that society goes through periods of liquefaction and resolidification – although he only ever makes passing comments concerning the latter and never actually names it as a resolidification process – affords him the possibility to analyse and make sense of the series of fragmentary sketches (or themes) that he sees as being constantly reshaped under the conditions of a liquid modern world, including (but not limited to) morality and ethics (Bauman and Donskis, 2013), individualization and everyday life (Bauman, 2005), love and sexuality (Bauman, 2003a), human rights and social exclusion

(2003b, 2011a), and risk, fear and terrorism (Bauman, 2006a). One theme that Bauman ignores as being reshaped and made under the conditions of liquid modernity is racism. This is something for which he has been criticized within the sociological literature (see, for instance, Rattansi, 2016, 2017), and quite rightly so. In the next section, we will discuss the application of the Baumanian lens of liquidity to racism.

Racism in a 'liquid' modern world

The category of *the stranger* has been a constant fixture within Zygmunt Bauman's writings, from *Modernity and the Holocaust* (1989a), where he denotes the construction of the 'other' as part of a wider modern process used to remove cultural and social ambivalence and maintain ontological security in the utopian visioning process of the 'good society' (mixophobic attitudes and responses), to *Liquid Modernity* (2000), where he describes the meeting of strangers as unstable and unsatisfying mis-meetings in which their encounter has no past referent point or any future set of expectations and obligations, thus requiring a strategy to make these mis-meetings or mis-viewings less risk-laden and more meaningful and satisfying for the dominant (majoritized white) group (mixophilic incorporation). Using both examples, it is not difficult to see how Bauman's theorizations of the stranger and on strangerness throughout his work can be used as a description of understanding racism and racialization within the contours of liquid modernity, which we have coined in this book as a process of *glaciation*. In other words, racism under the condition of liquid modern society oscillates between 'solid' and liquid forms which simultaneously also 'co-exist in every situation' (Mestrovic, 2010: 48), with each form of racism – solid or liquid – representing a hauntology of the other. For instance, there are spatiotemporal moments which solidify racism into racialized violence and exploitation (for example, colonialism and the imperial expansion of empire that led to the African slave trade), while in other spatiotemporalities, racism manages to meander, seep, spill and fill into the quotidian lives of racially minoritized groups and key social, cultural and political institutions insofar as it results in structural and instutionalized racism, domination, oppression and subjugation. All of this is underpinned by the racialized violence and exploitation of the former (for example, the murder of George Floyd and the routine over policing of Black subjects being the direct result of sedimentary racialized colonial flows).

Racism under the condition of liquid modernity is therefore based on the *ambivalence of uncertainty* of the 'other'. Bauman (2007) expresses this ambivalence of uncertainty of the 'other' through the concepts of mixophilia and mixophobia. His focus on the mixophilic and mixophobic tendencies towards the stranger and strangerhood is a direct application of French anthropologist and structuralist Lévi-Strauss' (1955) conceptualization of anthropoemic and anthropophagic strategies towards 'others' (see Bauman, 2000: 101). Bauman argues that all strategies used to deal with the 'other' resemble one or part of these distinctions in late modernity. Mixophobia is the fear of the 'other' which results in the expulsion of otherness, while mixophilia concerns the consumption of the 'other' that leads to the incorporation of otherness into the dominant culture. Each tendency always results in a form of objectification (Bauman, 2011a: 58) that attempts to stabilize the perceived ambivalence of the 'other' (Bauman, 1993a) in a late modern society where the propinquity of strangerness has resulted in a range of fears and insecurities, which are themselves fleeting and aleatory, and subject to the same process of glaciation (solidification-liquefaction-re-solidification) as racism itself.

Mixophobic responses to otherness in liquid modernity map onto the solidification of racism. The 'other' – constructed as a danger 'lurking just around the next corner, oozing and leaking' (Bauman, 2011a: 57) – is feared in what Bauman (2011a: 57) describes as a 'permanent state of alert' by the dominant (majoritized white) group because of the ubiquitous status of otherness itself under the conditions of liquid modernity. 'Others' are everywhere, but, due to the liquidity of the concept and category itself, are nowhere to be seen. When otherness is made visible and rendered threatening, 'others' are to be removed from society, both literally and figuratively. This occurs through techniques of *viscosity* and *damming* such as violent antagonism (for example, physical assault and verbal abuse), stereotyping, state strategies of refoulment and the biopolitical governance of rights. Mixophobic responses to otherness result from the diminution of community and subsequent growth of individualism in liquid modernity (see Chapter 1 for a more detailed account of the characteristics of liquid modernity). The (perceived) erosion of community becomes a source of ontological insecurity that leads to increased anxiety towards otherness. The fragility of human bonds lead to fear as there is no expectation or obligation to connect to 'others' but there is the certainty of the ubiquity of otherness itself. These fears are themselves liquid and subject to change and new flows as the dominant (majoritized white) group define and redefine the parameters of self-identification, or the identification(s) of 'others' (see Chapter 4 for a more detailed discussion of liquid fear). The dominant group – all those individuals who construct themselves and 'others' with a normative identity of whiteness (Bhattacharya, 1999) – demarcate the otherness of the 'other' through the process of deracializing themselves. For Bauman (2000: 107), these constructions and demarcations of (racialized) identification facilitate a 'withdraw from the frightening, polyphonic space where "no one knows how to talk to anyone else" into a "secure niche" where "Everyone is like anyone else"'. It is this demarcation of otherness that produces its visibility and renders it threatening. Manifesting feelings of collective fear and the subsequent creation of 'peg communities' (Bauman, 2001b: 15): 'an imagined community identity [among the dominant group] that offers collective insurance against individually confronted uncertainties'. And it is because of this that the 'strangers, the newcomers, and particularly the newcomers among the strangers [become blamed] for all aspects of social malaise' (Bauman, 2011a: 56) and thus need to be removed from society.

Alternatively, mixophilic approaches to otherness can be located within the liquefaction of racism as a conceptual category under the conditions of liquid modernity. These forms of racism are based on the jouissance of otherness. For instance, the *confluence* between 'race' and consumer capitalism provides a distanciated space for mixophilia to develop – an environment where otherness can be embraced, enjoyed and consumed as spectacle (Debord, 1967), but never actually directly experienced. Mixophilia as spectacle can be seen within the musical field where the consumption of music produced by racialized minorities (for example, drill) – which detail the lived experience(s) of Black subjectivity – by white (middle-class) individuals encourages a partial view of the 'other' in which some aspects of otherness are reified, while at the same time the complexity of the 'other' due to a *filtering* process is erased or removed. This shows how the ambivalence of uncertainty expressed towards the 'other' results in the reproduction of both mixophobic and mixophilic tendencies through the consumption of racially coded signs and symbols. While the consumption of racial codes and signs displays the incorporation of otherness as spectacle, it does so by removing difference through strategies of 'incorporation and expulsion' (Ahmed, 2000: 97), which are premised on and framed by the sedimentary flows of colonial extraction (see Chapter 6 for a more detailed account of this process). Therefore, it is glaciation (solidification-liquefaction-resolidification) that underpins the conceptual framework of a racism that is liquid, forever changing and always on the move within the contours of late modernity.

Conclusion

This chapter has situated our theorizing of liquid racism by contextualizing and conceptualizing how racism has been understood in the wider debates around modernity, postmodernity and liquid modernity in social theory. In the first section of the chapter, we outlined the contours of what constitutes modernity and postmodernity. Modernity was defined as the solidification of a particular European epistemology which, through systems of scientific, political, bureaucratic and technological rationality, served as an ordering framework. Postmodernity, on the other hand, was discussed as problematizing the relationship between the *political*, the *theoretical* and the *social* that were once seen as being able to provide a universalization of experience under the conditions of all that was 'modern'. Postmodernity was understood as being suspicious of the claim to grand narratives – of universalizability and homogeneity – of modernity. Postmodernity maintains an understanding of the social world based on the fragmentation, disorientation and discontinuity of selfhood. Selfhood is only ever experienced, but never actualized through the endless proliferation of social forms facilitated by the break in the signifying chain, between subject (self) and object (the seductive charm of consumer signifiers) within the late capitalist marketplace. The second section of the chapter then examined how racism has been located within the wider discourses of modernity and postmodernity. Drawing on Zygmunt Bauman's (1989a, 1993b) work itself, we highlighted how the racism(s) of modernity represented a solidification of otherness through 'engineering attitudes'. Scientific rationality became an instrument to remove 'modern' social and cultural ambivalences, and solidify cultural and social certainties via idealization of the 'good society'. Alternatively, postmodern racism(s) were explained using fantasy and imaginary as processes of constructing sameness and otherness. Postmodern racism(s) emerge in the consumption of racialized sign systems for majoritized white groups. It was this commodification process of culturally diverse 'signifiers in isolation' (Lacan, 1973) that constructs notions of 'white selfhood' and racialized otherness under the conditions of postmodernity. It solidifies otherness through a jouissance of otherness; the assimilation of racialized codes, signs and symbols into whiteness facilitates a racialized totality – an overcoming of otherness through an embrace of racialized wholeness.

The third section focused on how modernity is approached in Bauman's own theorizing. We maintained that social theorists and sociologists of Bauman have misconstrued his thinking around the theme(s) of modernity. This literature (see, for instance, Beilharz, 2001; Gane, 2001; Blackshaw, 2005; Elliott, 2013; Jacobsen and Poder, 2016) has presented Bauman's conceptuality of modernity as epochal, distinguishing between a postmodern phase (Bauman, 1991, 1992, 1997) and a liquid modern phase (for example, Bauman, 2000, 2005, 2007). We argue that this periodization of Bauman's thinking of modernity is superficial. The theme(s) of societal liquidization or, better yet, liquefaction – that is, his thesis of liquid modernity – is scattered throughout various points in the corpus of his writings. Liquidity was not simply a repackaging of other contemporary social theorists' thinking on late modernity (namely, the works of Ulrich Beck [1992, 1999] and Anthony Giddens [1990, 1991]). There were traces of liquidity throughout Bauman's writings on postmodernity. The growth of what could be termed late modernist accounts of the novelty afforded Bauman a vocabulary to actualize the theoretical project at the centre of much (if not all) of his work. The final section provided an analysis of racism in the context of liquid modernity. Under the condition of liquid modernity, we contended that racism undergoes a solidification-liquefaction-resolidification process (*glaciation*). In this process, racism can manifest as solidified mixophobic attitudes and responses (for example, violent antagonisms such as physical assault, verbal abuse and stereotyping), but can just as easily become liquid again before very long, resulting in the mixophilic incorporation of otherness (for example, consumption and jouissance of the 'other') – in other words, racism(s) that are liquid constantly flow between expulsion and incorporation. They are neither about the removal of 'modern' cultural and social ambivalence, nor are they wholly about the 'postmodern' assimilation of racialized assemblages to invisiblize the presence of otherness and difference. Liquid racism is a constant oscillation or flowing between the two. Such racism (or racisms) distinctively maps onto the ways in which liquid modern social life is experienced – one that is short-lived, aleatory and fleeting. Liquid modern social life is experienced through moments of structural amnesias (a range of forgettings, changes, fluctuations and flows) that simultaneously become reinvented – solidified once again – into new ways of doing and being, doings and beings that are anchored in the sedimentary flows of things that once were. Zygmunt Bauman has therefore afforded us an ability to imaginatively capture the racism(s) of the novelty through the application of the concept of liquidity. In the next chapter, we continue along the lines of such theorizing by providing a critical analysis of the debates around racialism/postracialism to further extrapolate the contours in which racism can be located within liquid modernity.

3

Race, Postrace and the False Promises of the Postracial State

Introduction

As explored in Chapter 2, postmodernity – as a conceptual category to explain the novelty of contemporary social processes – does not have the same explanatory power of liquid modernity. The liquefaction of older modern structures does not represent a unidirectional or irreversible process. As the solid structures of modernity remain part of the flows of liquid modernity, so too remains the opportunity for increased viscosities within such flows, facilitating transient or sustained periods of resolidification. There is a necessity to rely on some of the premises which underpinned notions of modernity as a way of advancing the incorporation of theorizing 'race' in the context of liquid modernity. For instance, the premise of be 'modernity' as a European project governed by rapid processes of change against Eurocentric indicators of 'progress' is useful in critical terms and is not accepted as a singular model of modernity to displace other parallel 'modernities'. However, the canonical theorizing of modernity in the social sciences *only* provides this Eurocentric account (see Chapter 2 for a full discussion of modernity and postmodernity). This chapter will focus on what this means for some of the problematics concerning notions 'postracialism', whether this is desirable and what we will call the 'multicultural project'. The ambivalence around engaging in any meaningful discussions about 'race' in the context of late modernity has been a prevalent feature of what could be called the *meta* end of the social science theorizing scale. While there have been collective bodies of work on theorizing multiculturalism, anti-racism, postcolonial theory and critical race theory (CRT), these areas of scholarship have consistently been compartmentalized as distinctive subject topic areas rather than being drawn upon to inform wider theorizing around the state of society in late, or *liquid*, modernity. The dismissiveness with which these critically important bodies of work become reframed as subject topics sees their intellectual contribution conveniently fragmented, where experts from liberal to radical discuss the intricate nuances of differing critical positions on 'race' in a level of detail apparently too intricate, complex and intimidating to incorporate into wider main*stream* theoretical projects. While these bodies of work have been positioned at the fringes of canonical social theory, this does not mean that the subsequent absence of theorizing around 'race' in theories of late modernity makes 'race' any less relevant for their enquiry. On the contrary, this chapter will explore how public-political aspirations towards a notional 'postracial state' effectively served as a mechanism to erase meaningful discussions on 'race' in the main*stream* public-political sphere, while simultaneously allowing disparate racialized inequities to continuously play out. The ways in which these processes have operated has varied from the explicit to the implicit, with intermittent and varying impacts on racialized inequities. It is the fluidity of these processes and the variances in the intensity of their flows which have allowed racialized marginalization to reconfigure itself in the context of liquid modernity.

This chapter will explore a range of examples which contest the notion of the postracial state, including debating the extent to which this would be a desirable feature of society. More significantly, this discussion lays the foundation for discussing the state of race relations in liquid modernity, and the extent to which the fluidity of progressiveness, race equality and race consciousness through new channels such as social media impact the extent to which any of these phenomena can be explored or realized. While these phenomena have been omitted in canonical theories of late modernity, their relevance has clearly remained significant. One of the key features of late modernity has been the notion of change under the premises of progress. Increasing flows of interests towards progressive politics around 'race' might be seen as a feature of liquid modernity. This chapter will interrogate the extent to which this has been facilitated or realized, and in doing so will establish how far aspirations towards (and perhaps even the realization of) a *postracial* society have been manifested in liquid modernity. More interestingly, the chapter demonstrates that it is the specific conditions of liquid modernity which allow particular nation states to present a highly convincing picture of progressiveness in relation to 'race', fuelled by a notional postracial project, while ensuring that highly racialized inequities continue to be manifested in agential, structural and discursive flows.

What is a postracial society?

In the context of liquid modernity, social identities begin to seep, leak and spill from their previously solidified states. This raises an important question for 'race' in the context of liquid modernity: does the liquefaction of the older structures of modernity mean the liquefaction of race, and therefore racism, itself? But before we can consider how far liquid modernity might (or, as we contend, does not) represent a postracial society, we need to consider what such a society might look like. Questions we might ask could include the following: is a postracial society a 'raceless' society? Or is a postracial state within which diversity is acknowledged, but which has zero discrimination across ethnic, cultural or racial lines? Both positions would incur further questions such as 'what does a raceless society look like?' and 'how would we know a postracial society was completely devoid of discrimination across ethnic, cultural or racial lines?' In order to entertain these practical questions, we need to engage with established work on 'postracial' society.

The work of W.E.B. Du Bois (1897) might help us to engage with the first of these questions. In his public address *The Conservation of Races*, Du Bois argued that the default strategy laid out for those of African descent attempting to achieve 'salvation' in the US had been to aspire to *losing* one's 'race identity' (Du Bois, 1897: 10). He posited that 'salvation' lies in the collective mobilization of that which is culturally Black – including colleges, business organizations, newspapers, schools of art and literature, and the 'institutionalization of intellect' – all cultural spaces demarcated across race lines (Du Bois, 1897: 13). These mobilizations would be not only necessary for positive *advancement* but also imperative for negative *defence* (Du Bois, 1897: 13). While the overtones of Du Bois' position leans into notions of separatism across racial lines, his work has to be read temporally. His critique of the pursuit of a state of 'racelessness' as the most effective strategy for Americans of African descent and advocating for the preservation of 'that which is culturally black' certainly indicate that his position on what the future of society *should* look like regarding race relations is not one which would see a postracial society as entirely 'raceless'. Rather, this premise is more complex than it initially seems. Du Bois argues that aspiring to a 'raceless society' for *Africans of American descent* is an ineffective strategy. This is not the same as suggesting that the notion of a raceless society *in and of itself* is an undesirable future to aspire to. While he is clear on emphasizing cultural preservation in the context of American society, he did anticipate that race relations would change over time. In his unpublished story entitled *A.D. 2150*, Du Bois provides a vision of exactly what a postracial society might look like (Du Bois, 1950, in Warren, 2016). The fictional scenario, set 200 years after Du Bois' death in 1950, sees him wake 200 years later to explore New York City over the course of a single day in the year 2150. He awakes to find a postracial society (Warren, 2016: 54), describing the vision as follows:

> I remembered that the matter of colored people [*sic*] getting meals was one of the great problems of my other life so that when I came opposite the really beautiful, small and quiet restaurant, I naturally

> hesitated, hanging on the outside until I saw a black man enter. He not only entered, but he went right to one of the front tables. At the table was one white girl, reading. The black man sat down. I stopped stock still and stared. Here was something that would tell me what 200 years had done in America quicker than anything else. I waited for the explosion. I did not expect the black man to be put out (that would have been 1850). I did not expect that he would be refused service (that would have been 1900). I did not expect that the woman would ask for another seat (that would have been 1950). I did expect her to move decisively, quickly, with an affronted look. But she did not. Quite evidently this was 2150! She did not move, she did not speak. She casually glanced up, bowed courteously, and went on with her breakfast and with her reading. The black man bowed just as courteously … and went on with his reading; save their reading and their eating, nothing happened. (Du Bois, 1950, in Warren, 2016: 54)

Du Bois' vision is interesting for two reasons. The first is that we might not be particularly struck by the way in which these kinds of events might unfold in 2025, so does this indicate that we are at least on our way to realizing Du Bois' vision for a postracial society? The answer to that question lies in the extent to which we might expect this scenario to be a *typical* experience. How likely is it that these events would be allowed to flow without resistance in the way described by Du Bois in contemporary society? In what scenarios and to what extent might we see viscosities in the form of the kinds of reactions Du Bois anticipates, resulting in varying degrees of resistance to the postracial ideal he presents? As Du Bois takes us through his vision, many other indicators are noted, including the absence of residential areas demarcated across racial lines and the ability for American citizens of all racial backgrounds to have the ability to live where they wish according to 'their desires and friends and income' (Du Bois, 1950, in Warren, 2016). As they day progresses, Du Bois discovers that that the Mayor of New York is African American, which he finds shocking, and questions a police officer about perceptions of racial difference in 2150:

Du Bois:	You have demolished the color line [*sic*] I see?
Police officer:	I don't know that I understand you sir
Du Bois:	I mean there is no distinction between people of different color [*sic*]
Police officer:	Oh yes there is. Some people are black and some are brown [*sic*], some are yellow [*sic*] and some are white, or a sort of pinkish color which we call white
Du Bois:	But I mean there is no difference between them?

Police officer:	On the contrary, there is as much difference as there always was. Of course, there is no difference in the treatment, there is no difference in the law, there is no difference in privilege. People do not choose their friends simply according to their skins [*sic*]; mostly, I should say, according to their abilities, characters and likes and dislikes.

Du Bois' account, while fictional, clearly serves as a vehicle for him to convey his ideas about what typical postracial experience might look like. His narrative only offers us single instances, but this is still intended to convey what is typical in his vision of a postracial society. But this is not a raceless society. In Du Bois' vision, while the 'color line' has been demolished (or, as we prefer, liquified), a postracial state has been achieved without the need for aspirations towards a race*less* society. While this does allow for a more nuanced understanding of what the postracial might look like beyond a homogenized aspiration towards 'racelessness', this does not mean that we are near to achieving such a state in the context of liquid modernity. While race – as a feature of social identity – may well be experiencing liquification, this is not to suggest that 'race', or racism, is any less present in liquid modernity. Nor does it suggest that racial identities in liquid modernity are transient or established solely on the bases of self-identification. The legacies of white majority societies with colonial histories are laden with sediments which ensure ongoing racialization and the persistence of racism in liquid modernity. Moreover, the variations in both flows of racialized power relations (as will be discussed later on in this chapter) and resistance to those flows (through mobilizations such as Black Lives Matter) would suggest that race remains very much on the agenda.

The continuing presence of public political debates around 'race' necessitates the question of where we are up to in terms of race relations, and what are the aspirations *for the future* of race relations in liquid modernity. Recent developments have seen a sustained emergence of 'woke culture' (see Roberts, 2021) alongside 'cancel culture' (see Duque et al, 2021) in social media spaces, and these phenomena are often discussed with regard to issues around contemporary attitudes towards issues relating to a range of factors including 'race'. With regard to race in the contemporary context, the notion that an individual can be 'cancelled' for not being 'woke enough' has come to be a signifier for online spaces becoming too sympathetic to perceived priorities of what might be called the liberal multicultural and/or postracial project (which will be discussed and outlined in detail later on in this chapter) to the detriment of the basic principles of free speech. Alongside issues of sexuality and gender fluidity, this tension has positioned discussion around 'race' in something of a fragile position within online spaces – a topic many wish to avoid engaging with, and with which some have engaged too freely with little to no lived experience or evidence-based expertise. This dynamic is interesting, not least considering the emphasis on individual accountability and responsibility for one's own life as one of the conditions of liquid modernity. While we might be inclined to think about what this means as a strategy for eroding away the legitimacy of claims to racist experiences in liquid modernity, it also has implications for those even engaging with discussions around 'race' in social media spaces. Where individuals who engage with public discussion around 'race' online, it is entirely of their own making in liquid modernity. Bauman's (2001) emphasis on individuals and the role that their social networks play is important here, especially when considering the implications of 'cancel culture' for individuals in social media spaces. This phenomenon demonstrates how the politics of online spaces has come to be characterized by an increasingly fluid negotiation and renegotiation of what constitutes an acceptable state of public relations around 'race'. At one end of this spectrum, there are voices committed to drawing attention to the ongoing relevance of issues around social justice and advocating for the utilization of 'cancel culture' as part of a strategy for negotiating a future postracial state. At the other end of the spectrum, there are voices exemplifying a conviction that a notional postracial 'state' has already been achieved or even exceeded, and that this renders ongoing discussions on racialized inequalities unnecessary or even problematic in themselves. The notion of 'state' here is also interesting in how 'postracial' refers to a 'state' in terms of a set of conditions or understood norms and values which define a given political space versus how far a given 'nation state' might exemplify such conditions.

The question of how far society has become postracial remains at the centre of much of the academic literature on race relations. Goldberg (2015) exemplifies a notion which maps onto some of the core assumptions and premises attributed to modernity when viewed through a Eurocentric prism – notions of change in the form of progress, represented by the specific progression of cultural, social, scientific, economic and political institutions in the Western world (Mouzakitis, 2017: 17). With regard to race relations, such change and *progress* implies an inevitable flow of race relations into a postracial 'state' of being as an unavoidable outcome over the life course of modernity; thus reproducing the sociological fiction of the 'modern' project itself (Bhambra and Holmwood, 2021). Indeed, it can be argued that any theory of racism is necessarily a theory of modernity, always reckoning with modernity's complexity in circulating racial frameworks (Valluvan, 2016: 2242). Arguably one of the most significant mechanisms, and indeed products, of late modernity by which these frameworks continue to be formed and reformed through the process of glaciation has been via the neoliberal political ideal. All neoliberalism is about writing out attentiveness to structural constraints (Valluvan, 2016: 2242), including those pertaining to 'race'. This process has been described elsewhere as the neoliberal erasure of the structural conditions of racial reproduction and racist articulation (Goldberg, 2015: 34). Subsequently, iterations of racism or race inequality in this context are considered an unfortunate echo of a residual and rapidly fading legacy, operating under neoliberalism's preferred modus operandi – instances of racism are reductively located at the individual level by constitutionally 'bad' individuals (Valluvan, 2016: 2241). There are two issues to contend with here. The first is to return to our point of caution given earlier regarding the implications of the Eurocentric lens for what we understand as being characteristic of modernity. We can also draw on Titley's (2016) excellent deconstruction of Goldberg's question 'Are we all postracial yet?' in the process of considering *what* or *who* the notion of the postracial is for. Titley draws attention to the phrasing of the question and its overtones. Principally, the question is posed in one voice, suggesting a uniformity of aspiration towards postracialism, a 'definitive claim about the contemporary achievement of a post-racial ideal' (Titley, 2016: 2269). The phrasing 'we all' suggests that the question is being asked from a postracial position, from a position itself devoid of racial identification (Titley, 2016: 2269). Finally, 'yet?' suggests the inevitability associated with modernity, and also a sense of impatience and implied frustration with ongoing conversations about 'race' which do little else but keep the concept alive (Titley, 2016: 2269). Can postracialism then only exist as an aspirational state in the context of the modernities of the Global North? What might the postracial look like in the Global South? Have postracial ideals similarly been seen as indicators of progress in the Global South? And how does liquid modernity figure in all of this?

Perhaps notions of the postracial have been most intuitively relevant as a signifier of progress in the Global North rather than the Global South. There might be some merit in this idea, as the notion of achieving a postracial 'state' has arguably been fetishized as an indicator to signify a rebalancing of the historical evils of the European colonial project. How far then does the postracial ideal apply outside of this context? Is the notion of the postracial a concept which only makes sense in the context of the Global North? Does the fact that the Global South is characterized more by populations of the 'Global majority' than the Global North mean that it is already postracial, or postracial by default? This final question requires that we clarify the terminology here – specifically with regard to what is meant by 'Global Majority' and why this is significant in considering how far, and in what ways, notions of the postracial might be relevant for the Global South. The term 'Global Majority' emerged through the work of Rosemary Campbell-Stevens (2020) as a critique of the widespread use of the term 'BAME' to refer to 'Black and Asian Minority Ethnic' groups in the UK. By way of contrast to BAME, which emphasizes 'Minority', 'Global Majority' emphasizes a sense of global critical mass for individuals who identify as Black, African, Asian, Brown, dual-heritage, indigenous to the Global South and/or have been racialized as 'ethnic minorities' (Campbell-Stephens, 2020) in white majority societies. Globally, these groups represent approximately 80 per cent of the world's population (Campbell-Stephens, 2020). In the context of the Global South, this raises questions as to what a postracial society might look like *for* the Global South, as well as how far postracialism might represent an inevitable outcome in the context of modernity as it plays out *in* the Global South. Indeed, this is a question which has been considered by Franco (2019), whose work on how place making and belonging remain governed by race in Brazil raise interesting questions around notions of the postracial in Global North and Global South contexts.

Franco (2019) argues that Brazil and South Africa represent examples of nation states which probably exemplify subscription to notions of the postracial, albeit from quite different perspectives. Even though the recent postracial rhetoric that has characterized debates around 'race' in the Global North has 'only barely echoed' in Brazil and South Africa, both countries forged comparable understandings before the 2000s (Franco, 2019: 962). For Brazil, the notion of 'racial democracy' is longstanding and has been characterized by the absence of any laws prohibiting racial conviviality, interracial marriage or interracial sexual intercourse and racial mixing (Franco, 2019: 964). For Franco, the legacy of this has been a 'lax approach to racial classification in which racial boundaries were much more permeable and fluid than in the USA and South Africa' (Franco, 2019: 964). South Africa represents a more straightforward example in principle, operating a system of apartheid before transitioning into a rainbow nation led by Nelson Mandela. This model maps onto the American model (which will be discussed later on in this chapter), with racial boundaries sustaining more of their previously solidified form, even in the context of apparent aspirations towards a postracial South African state. The Brazilian example is slightly more complex, not least because the very term 'racial democracy' suggests that racial disparities have been, to some degree, transcended through the apparent presence of equal rights within the legal-formal realm (Franco, 2019: 965). Yet racial disparities do exist, and such disparate racialized flows are manifested in the landscape of Brazil – perhaps solidifying most significantly in the history of the Favelas which characterize Rio de Janiero (Franco, 2019: 965). The favelas were part of the urban structure of Rio dating back to slavery, and Black groups had a formative role in their creation as well as making up the majority of their populations (Oliveira, 1996: 75). Brazil's history of slavery is striking, with an estimated 3.6 million African slaves entering the country over three centuries, compared with an estimated 404,000 slaves entering the US over a similar period (Oliveira, 1996: 73). Brazil was also the last American nation to abolish slavery in 1888. The history of public policies enacted in the period immediately following abolition were also responsible for the pooling of African Brazilians in Rio and other large cities in the country (Oliveira, 1996: 74). Against this history, the ideals of 'racial democracy' and the notion that these ideals have even been achieved through norms and institutions upholding 'more or less equal' citizenship rights (Franco, 2019: 965) represent, in principle, a rapid and successful melting of the racial structures of modernity into a postracial 'state', against the most unlikely circumstances. The sense of inevitability around postracialism implied in canonical social theories of modernity would make Brazil an ideal model for demonstrating a rapid erosion of racial inequality in liquid modernity *in the Global South*. Unfortunately, the extent to which such principles of racial democracy as a set of public political ideals map onto the realities of racial dynamics in Brazil is easily brought into question. Urban segregation along racial lines still characterizes many large cities in the country, and the poorer districts of Rio specifically (containing over 1,000 favelas) are mainly occupied by Global Majority groups, with residential areas catering to the upper classes almost exclusively being occupied by white groups (Franco, 2019: 971). While this disparity might seem problematic for the postracial ideal, it raises an interesting question as to what the function of the postracial *ideal* is and, in fact, just what the postracial *itself* is.

As such, this requires us to take a step towards considering that the postracial *ideal* might not necessitate the *realization* of postracial dynamics in postracial societies. One of Goldberg's (2015) most striking conclusions revolves around the implications of aspiring to postracial ideals as we might understand them in the Global North, but, considering the preceding points, arguably as we might also in the Global South. In synthesizing Goldberg's analysis, Valluvan (2016) posits that in this context, aspiration towards a societal transcendence of 'race' results in a situation where discursively time is called on racism, while structurally it continues unabated (Valluvan 2016: 2242), and it is this that facilitates what Goldberg identifies as 'racisms without racism' (Goldberg, 2015: 159). The implications here are twofold in that the postracial is not only a significant feature of contemporary racisms, but is its very constitutive *base* (Valluvan, 2016: 2242). This mechanism has constructed distributary channels that divert racisms away from mainstream flows, which subsequently become discursively characterized by decreasing interest in entertaining any meaningful engagement with issues around race inequalities. Rather, any increase in racist flows which poses a threat either through risk of contaminating the mainstream or spilling out of these distributaries is controlled either through their immediate dilution in mainstream flows or the reinforcement of the ever-increasing banks of the mainstream, through the resultant sedimentary deposits of postracial idealism.

This suggests that the postracial ideal is a far more dangerous notion than simply aspiring to a society devoid of racialized marginalization or inequalities. In the context of any society claiming to have achieved *progress* in working towards postracial ideals, accounts of racism are highly problematic to this agenda and, as such, rather than being considered as evidence to the contrary of postracial claims becoming realized in some sort of progressive process, they are increasing doubted, treated with suspicion and dismissed as paranoia. Charges of racism become diluted by claims that it is anti-racists themselves who fetishize race, a fetishism for the discredited logic of the past that any self-respecting progressive is implored to renounce (Valluvan, 2016: 2243). This manufactured postracialization acts as a form of what is known in CRT as *tacit intentionality*. Tacit intentionality refers to the notion that public policy is laden with a latent intentionality which disadvantages particular racialized minority groups and reproduces racialized educational inequities either actively or passively (for a full discussion of tacit intentionality, see Chapter 5). We apply this concept beyond policy here to argue that the very public political discourses around postracial idealism are themselves laden with a tacit intentionality, laying sediments which convey false notions of progress around race relations as they flow through the main*stream* public political sphere. However, what we have also seen from the preceding discussion is that while it makes sense that the source of postracial idealism may lie initially within the public political 'aspirations' of the Global North, in particular with nations keen to shake off their colonial histories, these aspirations have flowed within and between the Global North and the Global South in tidal patterns. The aspiration to 'racial democracy' in Brazil following substantive trading in the African slave trade by the Portuguese, along with the apartheid regime in South Africa following colonial rule by the Dutch, then the British and finally the internal colonial rule under the white minority of Afrikaners, suggest that historically these sediments flowed initially from North to South. However, these flows would subsequently follow tidal patterns, with increasing transference of postracial *ideals*, rather than any real measurable *realities* arising from the liquefaction of the racial. While we acknowledge the nuances in racial dynamics across the Global North and the Global South, as well as the presence of multiple and concurrent modernities, we also suggest that the tacit intentionality underpinning postracial idealism, and its dual-edged purpose as a tool to dilute and neutralize race consciousness, has saturated and soaked public-political arenas in the Global South as well as the Global North. We draw upon this to contend that a state can be postracial without having to evidence an absence of racial inequity; rather, the postracial state is one which ensures that highly racialized inequalities are allowed to flow unobstructed. These conditions are facilitated through the precipitation of wider postracial narratives designed to undermine the perceived legitimacy of any attempts to build up resistance to such flows of race inequities on the premise that if we're not 'postracial yet', it is because we are unnecessarily still talking about race.

The postracial state is the embodiment of the ambivalence of uncertainty concerning 'race' in liquid modernity. The postracial state facilitates ontological insecurity, a *state of being* which hides the realities of racial marginalization deep below the apparently calm and progressive waters at the surface. Postracial idealism manifests the promise of racial equity and freedom from racism, and the apparent realization of such moments, while sustaining a façade that not only ignores the ongoing relevance of 'race', but which actively works to ensure persistent racialized outcomes for racialized marginalized groups in liquid modernity. Perhaps it goes without saying that while Bauman (2000) was hesitant to identify liquid modernity as a necessarily dystopian reality, we do contend that the postracial state *is* a dystopian reality, and a *state of being* contingent with the liquefaction of the old racial structures of modernity – a racial dystopia indeed for those who become swept into liminality through the racialized flows which sustain the kind of liquid racisms facilitated through postracial idealism in liquid modernity. In the following sections we will consider what this has looked like in recent history in the contexts of the US and the UK.

The postracial state as postracial fallacy: the US and the UK

Since the election of Barack Obama to the presidency in 2008, the US has been an interesting case study which can be used to explore the enactment of postracialism. Obama's successful election victory represented a victory for race equality in the mainstream American public political sphere – the final realization of a postracial moment for US politics and society more widely. However, the initial contradictions in what this moment demonstrated were manifested in the events leading up to Obama's first successful presidential election victory. Questions were raised initially about the legitimacy of his identification as African American, ranging from his background as a biracial man to the observation that his Blackness comes from Kenyan rather than African-American heritage. This scrutiny, which was played out in the public political sphere, went as far as casting doubt around Obama's own right to citizenship in the US, with a media circus surrounding these debates leading to the actual publicization of his birth certificate (Pham, 2015). The apparent concern around Obama's racial identity demonstrates both the liquidity of Black racial identification and also how this was weaponized to imply ambiguity around eligibility for the US presidency. The presidential victory represents something of a significant moment, an intermittent flow of power resulting in the appointment of a person of colour to the presidential office. But in no way did this demonstrate that the US had become postracial in any solid or permanent sense. The political backlash against Obama's presidential election would ultimately culminate in shifting currents manifesting in the election of Donald Trump, a figurehead for extreme right-wing libertarian and populist public sentiment which appeared to have soaked through enough of the American public political sphere to secure his own presidential victory.

Crenshaw's (2017) critical discussion on Obama's election and what it meant and continues to mean with regard to postracialism in America affords some interesting insights into the dramatic variances on the flows of apparent political consensus in recent years in the US. For Crenshaw, at the surface level, the election of Obama was perceived as significant for marking a defining moment whereby America 'had put its race problem decisively in the past' (Crenshaw, 2017). In this context, Obama represented an impeccably credentialled presidential candidate, and even a product of American meritocracy (Crenshaw, 2017). In the wider American public consciousness, Obama's successful election in 2008 was evidence that: 'The painful, violent legacy of white supremacy had been repealed, in one miraculous fell swoop; the guilt-averse white majority and the grievance-prone Black minority could come together as one' (Crenshaw, 2017).

How then could this lead to the stark shift in political consciousness manifested in the election of Donald Trump to office in 2016? If Obama's election had facilitated a unified American republic characterized by notions postracial idealism in the name of progressive democratic politics, how did this 'progress' become undone? This process represents a clear example of the ways in which political collective consciousness and the resultant flows of public consensus can shift and meander on their journey towards informing outcomes of the democratic process. The stark shift from 2008 to 2016 saw collective public opinion in the US filling streams and tributaries which have a clear pathway to sustained progressive politics around 'race'. Yet somehow these flows became redirected quite dramatically into channels with a clear pathway towards a return to the kind of uber-neoliberal political climate of Ronald Reagan's 1980s, under the direction of another big screen personality: libertarian business mogul Donald Trump. For Crenshaw, in just eight years the symbolic breakthrough of Obama's election had given way to 'a terrifying new political order that is anything but post-racial' (Crenshaw, 2017). Furthermore, if the election of Trump immediately following Obama's presidential administration did not expose the fallacy of the notion of the US as a postracial state, then the death of George Floyd in March 2020 surely did. While the election of Obama to the presidential office for many will continue to represent the archetypal postracial moment, the resurgence of the Black Lives Matter movement in the wake of the murder of Floyd demonstrated the extent to which racialized tensions have remained for African Americans in the post-Obama era.

What happened? Was Obama's presidency a legitimate postracial moment which, like any other political moment in the context of liquid modernity, was transient – a tidal current rushing inland, peaking in a wave of interests around progressive politics which would inevitably crash and eventually be drawn back by opposing tidal forces? There is an alternative scenario. The political transition from the Obama to the Trump administration represents a postracial state in action. Crenshaw outlines how the paradox of postracial idealism actually facilitated this process:

> The rhetoric of post-racialism that greeted Obama's ascension to power has proved instrumental in the dumbfounding political rise of Donald Trump, the man who is in every way the photographic negative of Barack Obama. The feel-good presuppositions of post-racialism played directly into the evasive habits of the white supremacist heart, permitting Americans to congratulate themselves for achieving a historic breakthrough that had very little to do with our actual racial history. (Crenshaw, 2017)

This represents a clear example of what is known in CRT as *interest convergence* (Bell, 1980: 94). Interest convergence is a process whereby the marginalization of racialized minority groups is addressed only where gains are also facilitated for white groups (Breen, 2018: 17). In much work on CRT, interest convergence is discussed in relation to policies and strategies that on the surface level appear to be focused on benefiting or advancing the interests of racialized minority groups. In practice, however, these policies and strategies bear convergent interests across racialized minority groups *and* the wider white majority society implementing them. In short, there has to be *at least an equivalent gain* for white groups when compared with any possible gains for racialized minority groups in order for interests to converge enough for a policy or strategy to considered viable for implementation in white majority societies (see Bell, 1980; Ladson-Billings, 1998; Gillborn, 2005). Thus, 'racial remedies' are based on an unspoken understanding that they will 'secure, advance, or at least not harm societal interests deemed important by middle- and upper-class whites' (Bell, 1980: 523). From this position, such policies and strategies are therefore illusory and merely serve to enfranchise white groups, while sustaining the relative marginalization and disadvantage experienced by racialized minority groups in white majority societies. The seminal example used by Derrick Bell to demonstrate this point is that of the desegregation of schooling across racial lines which emerged as a result of the case of *Brown v Board of Education* in 1954 (Bell, 1980). Bell argued that while desegregation as a product of legal precedent was presented as a move which was taken in the interests of advancing African American interests, in reality and over time, African Americans did not realize the promise of substantive gains which were implied through desegregating schooling (Bell, 1980: 519). Furthermore, the US as a nation taking the decision to desegregate schooling across racial lines reflected positively on its wider global image in the context of the Cold War (Bell, 1980: 524). The decision helped to provide immediate credibility in the political struggle between the US with the Soviet Union, and helped to 'win the hearts and minds of third world peoples' (Bell, 1980: 524), while also suggesting to African Americans that the principles of freedom from oppression manifested in the Second World War effort was being advanced for them within the US. The political and economic gains for American interests both globally and domestically presented a far greater value to white policy makers in the US compared with the actual outcomes and falsely promised gains of desegregating education for African Americans at home (Bell, 1980: 524).

However, while interest convergence is often read solely in terms of conventional social policy, it also can be read as a means of supporting discursive facets of systems of racialized injustice (Breen and Meer, 2019: 11). To return to the case of the transition from Obama to Trump, interest convergence can be used as a useful tool when considering its application outside of formal social policy, as well as a process which also informs sustaining white interests more discursively. Within this line of understanding, and against a backdrop of Bell's analysis discussed earlier, it is possible to see how Obama's electoral success might be seen as an indicator of progressive politics which reflected positively for the US in the wider global political climate. Through Obama, the US would again have the opportunity to demonstrate on the global stage just how progressive its political system was, securing political and economic gains which would inevitably benefit white interests over African-American groups domestically (even if only taking into account the relative proportions of each group within the US population). Furthermore, a wider discursive process could also be inferred from the severity of the political shift from Obama's Democratic administration to Trump's Republican reign. Obama's leadership might merely have been tolerated, safe in the knowledge that history had consistently dictated that the chances of securing an African-American successor (either Democrat or Republican) would be extremely slim. The backlash manifested in the turn to Trump is also an interesting phenomenon here. There is a popular conception that part of Trump's electoral success was due to him ironically successfully playing to the frustrations of mainly white, blue-collar, 'less educated', predominantly male voters in non-urban areas (Ben-Shahar, 2016). However, a more detailed analysis of the votership reveals that a significant part of Trump's victory resulted from a significantly smaller number of traditionally Democratic voters exercising their right to vote in the election (Ben-Shahar, 2016). Put simply, Trump did not win because he secured more voters, but rather because traditional Democrats did not resonate with Hilary Clinton in the same way they did with Obama previously. A significant factor in this might be the history of Hillary Clinton's connection with her husband's presidency, and not least his role in sustaining and advocating for mandatory minimum sentences in the context of the 'war on drugs'. Mandatory minimum sentences had their origins in the 1986 Anti-Drug Abuse Act, an Act which played out with massively racialized outcomes in the conviction and sentencing of African Americans, and which as a result had been repealed by Obama in 2010. Trump's victory then was at least partially the result of a lower than expected turnout of the Democratic vote (Ben-Shahar, 2016), and probably due to the fact that *there was no equivalent to Obama for Democrats to vote for.* This is an important point which presents us with two opposing readings of the transition from Obama to Trump. The first takes account of the lower-than-expected turnout in the Democratic vote which resulted from a lack of options in the way of being able to sustain the kind of leadership the US had experienced under Obama. But the second opposing interpretation, arguably held more prominently among Republican cohorts, would suggest that Obama's presidency had to be considered a failed experiment in progressive liberalism, which America had kindly entertained, but to no substantive political end. The irony here is that the postracial fallacy manifested in Obama's success resulted in facilitating a set of circumstances which both practically (through a lower level of connectivity with Clinton as a candidate) and discursively (through the reading of his presidency as a failed experiment in liberal progressivism) ensured a return to conservative politics as the only available way forward for American politics. The convergence of interests manifested in this process are such that the US saw both a benefit from the image of progressivism in having Obama as President, while steady undercurrents ensured a dramatic shift in the political waters towards the end of his leadership which would allow for a return to a more overt prioritization of white interests in the American public political sphere. This is the postracial state in action, whereby the appearance of progress becomes weaponized as a tool for sustaining not only the privileging of white interests but also the wider political and discursive rationales for doing so.

The UK, postracialism and the multicultural project

If the *notional* postracial state is the current archetypal endgame for race relations in the context of liquid modernity, then the 'multicultural project' was the process by which this had been pursued in the UK from the 1970s to 2010. Multiculturalism in the UK is a term which has many different meanings based on the context in which it is used. In its most simplified form, multiculturalism has been used as a label to describe the presence of ethnic and cultural diversity in various contexts from national to regional and local levels. At the other end of the spectrum, we have complex academic bodies of work on multiculturalism as theory, and a series of premises and strategies around how to achieve race equality in contemporary society (see Modood, 1994; Meer, 2016; Modood, 2017). Tariq Modood's (1994) seminal work on multiculturalism presented a series of arguments around the inability for anti-racism to effectively combat the cultural forms of racism experienced by South Asian groups in the UK. The argument was based on a critique of the commitment to mobilization through a sense of political Blackness which had sat at the core of anti-racist activism and academic scholarship. What follows is a simplification of Modood's contribution, but it laid out a rationale for thinking about how the nuances of minority ethnic identities result in differential experiences of racism. Addressing racism as experienced by South Asian groups in the UK would require a different strategy from that which might be sought in the fight against racism as experienced by Black British groups. While there is not the space to replicate the bodies of work which distinguish multiculturalism from anti-racism, it is important to acknowledge that there had been something of a political struggle for power in the late 1970s. The Labour government would lose the 1979 election to the Conservative Party, which partly secured votes through reiterating sentiments consistent with Enoch Powell's 'Rivers of Blood' speech over 10 years earlier, emphasizing the perceived perils of immigration, with party leader Margaret Thatcher recounting rhetoric appealing to nationalist movements such as the National Front. This context is significant, not least because of the wider tensions of the time, but also because an inquiry into racism in education had been initiated by the then Labour Secretary of State for Education, Anthony Rampton, prior to the election in 1979. The inquiry identified that racism had been significant in the experiences of Black Caribbean groups in education and society more widely (Rampton, 1981). The language and message appeared to align itself to anti-racism, and outlined a notion of racism which would be consistent with the kind of institutional racism later identified in the Macpherson Report (see Macpherson, 1999). While an interim report was eventually published in 1981, this was under a new Conservative government which had demonstrated anything but sympathy for anti-racist ideology in its election strategy. Subsequently, then Prime Minister Margaret Thatcher appointed Lord Swann to lead on the ongoing inquiry, and the final report reframed the findings diluting the conviction expressed in the interim report in 1981. When the Swann Report was finally published in 1985, the language was more closely aligned with 'cultural pluralism', a notion which was synonymous with multiculturalism. It is through the recommendations of Swann Report that 'state multiculturalism' came to be the favoured strategy for responding to increasing ethnic and racial diversity in schools, but also other public institutions.

While 'multiculturalism' became the preferred language utilized by the state on issues of diversity in subsequent years, this incarnation of multiculturalism lacked any of the critical nuance which was developing in academic discourse. Instead, 'state multiculturalism' leaned more closely towards being a label describing the presence of ethnic and cultural diversity, loosely suggesting that the celebration of diversity would inevitably be an effective strategy for achieving equality for minority ethnic groups in institutional settings. Perhaps unsurprisingly, progress was slow, and this was documented in the Parekh Report 15 years after the Swann Report (see Parekh, 2000). By 2010, almost immediately after securing office as Prime Minister, David Cameron declared that 'state multiculturalism had failed' (Helm et al, 2011). This marked an end to the 'multicultural project' in the UK, which had amounted to a series of promises and premises that were superficially manifested in state strategies for achieving 'cultural pluralism' dating back to the Swann Report (1985) and concluding with Cameron's declaration of the failure of this iteration of 'state multiculturalism' in 2010. This resolute declaration that state multiculturalism had failed raised questions as to what would have served as indicators of unequivocal success for the multicultural project. The political rhetoric of multiculturalism, which 'state multiculturalism' at least presented itself as aspiring to emulate, was inevitably based on a simple premise – that celebrating diversity results in increased cultural tolerance and integration and eventually the complete absence of any discrimination along cultural or ethnic lines. This would not necessarily mean becoming a 'raceless' society, but rather a society which 'embraces the diversity of racial affiliations and is not threatened by the presence of and interaction between people of colour and various ethnic heritages' (Choi, 2011: 83). Based on these premises, we can consider that – at least rhetorically – the aspirations of the multicultural project were to deliver a strategy for managing ethnic and cultural diversity which in its most possible incarnation would facilitate a postracial state closer to that defined by Choi rather than a society absent of 'race'. Instead of drawing on the voluminous body of critical and nuanced academic work on *theorizing* multiculturalism (such as Modood, 1994; Parekh, 2000; Meer, 2016), 'state multiculturalism' provided a very simplistic observation of the presence of cultural diversity with an oversimplified 'solution'. As such, it is the 'state' rather than academic incarnation of multiculturalism which most closely fits what has been conceptualized by Bygness (2013: 126) as 'ambivalent multiculturalism'. Such an 'ambivalent multiculturalism' would lack the ability and intention to achieve ideals relating to ethnicity and equality, much less deliver on the more absolute ideals manifested in notions of the postracial state. This whole process presents a confusing contradiction, whereby some iterations of multiculturalism are promoted in the public space under the premise of a commitment to progressive politics around 'race', while ensuring little action is actually taken to achieve these ends.

The failure of the 'multicultural project' informed a wider resistance to anti-racist praxis in the public political arena evidenced elsewhere in this book, and in particular around the resurgence of nationalistic ideologies that accompanied Brexit and the vote to leave the European Union (EU). The accumulation of this resistance has converged with economic and political narratives on austerity to solidify resistance to critical discussions relating to 'race' in the public-political arena after 2010. The resultant prophylaxis has ensured that seminal work in the field of critical race studies has been contained and confined to academic spaces. The resultant scholarship which has emerged in this wider social, political and economic context has been dammed in, with reservoirs predominantly taking either the form of university libraries with access mediated by high stakes and ticket prices via tuition fees, or paywalls which only economically affluent citizens are realistically able to permeate. The consequent sediments of this legacy have been highly problematic, and we will return to this point shortly.

The year 2010 marks a significant moment in the UK nation state actively distancing itself from any interest or responsibility to pursue the promise of the state multicultural project, in doing so stemming aspirations to become a postracial state. It is worth returning to the example of the US, which saw a more marked U-turn than the UK in relation to public political attitudes on notions of post-'race'. Prior to Trump's election, and in spite of 'repeated contestations and people of colour's everyday experiences to the contrary, the idea that the US had become a postracial society enjoyed significant popularity' (Speed, 2020: 77). Against this illusory representation of the ideal postracial moment manifested in the election of Obama, public debate following the 2016 election has been informed by political discourses which saw the election of Trump as a turning of the tide against the assumed progress of postracial society (Speed, 2020: 76).

We can draw parallels here with the EU referendum result in the UK as marking the culmination of sediments having settled following the failings of state multiculturalism. The public political markers for this shift can be identified in relation to David Cameron both as the figurehead to mark the death of multiculturalism and as the architect for the EU referendum (albeit against his own political convictions). However, the multicultural project failed, primarily in its efforts to construct notions of postracial social dynamics in the wider public consciousness. Not only were the implicit promises of state multiculturalism elusive for many racialized minority groups, but the persistent notion of an impending postracial state became reconfigured in the public consciousness against notions of political correctness, identity politics and notions of a 'left behind' white working class. As we will see in Chapter 4, the conditions around Brexit provided a perfect storm for a resurgence in both explicit ethnocentric English nationalisms, amid more thinly veiled and nuanced articulations of white resistance and viscosity in relation to the postracial project manifested in concerns around the implications of immigration for employment. Against this backdrop, the transition to austerity Britain exacerbated and intensified the marginalization and inequity of racialized minority groups; however, it also eroded coherent iterations of social class identity subjecting socioeconomically deprived white groups to the mercy of uber-free-market economic conditions. This displaced a working-class identity from recognition in the public political space, leaving only identification by way of reference to material deprivation, fragile employment status and resentment towards the falsely perceived gains of the multicultural project for racialized minority groups. The collusion between the falsehood of the postracial 'ideal' and the iteration of uber-neoliberialist state politics has laid the foundation for a resurgence in ethnocentric nationalist ideologies. While these mobilizations exist at the extreme end of white identification, their coming to fruition has invariably been informed by far more subtle, tacit and nuanced flows of racist discourses which have occupied a parallel stream alongside the murky uncertainties around state multiculturalism as a strategy for reifying an illusion of postracial inevitability.

Implications of notional postracialism: what about the 'white' working class?

Academic and public political debates on 'race' in the UK have in recent years come to be played off against those relating to socioeconomic marginalization as experienced by white groups. This has created a perceived dichotomy in the ability to resolve the two issues. Such an academic turf war has been characterized by convictions which have effectively seen a fundamental perception of a divide in studies on 'race' and those on socioeconomic status. This division has seen attempts to reframe and refocus work on social class on to the experiences of the most socioeconomically marginalized white groups, in an effort to bring 'race' into studies on the white working-class experience. There are two problems here which need to be addressed before we can progress. The first is that this has been done in response to misunderstandings around bodies of work in critical race studies and, in particular, with the increasing influence of CRT in studies on race inequities in the UK context. With narratives on white privilege assuming primacy in CRT, it perhaps is not surprising to anticipate that the most economically marginalized white groups in the UK might have some resistance to the notion of being 'privileged'. In fact, these groups have been referred to frequently as the *left behind*, a working class facing high levels of socioeconomic deprivation exacerbated by the austerity politics applied as the national strategy for economic recovery in the UK post-2010.

This leads to the second problem that needs addressing. This is that the economic oppression of the most marginalized white groups has *not* resulted from power being exerted against their interests *by* racialized minority groups. In order to understand the nuances of these two problems, they will need to be unpacked and their premises deconstructed so that a clear illustration of these two positions can be presented.

One of the more dangerous mechanisms in recent years whereby 'race' has been consistently eroded in public political debates has been the repeated assertion of the white working classes as the 'new racially oppressed'. The framing of this notion in the UK context in recent years is important. It suggests to casual observers that part of the failing of the multicultural project arose from actually *exceeding* postracial ideals and advancing the rights of racialized minority groups to the disadvantage of white marginalized groups. This notion has been constructed through various discursive formations which have obscured the realities of the position of white working-class groups in relation to 'race' and which have played off a wider ignorance on the specifics of terminology around whiteness used in critical race scholarship – most notably that of *white privilege*. It is important to unpack the apparent tension around these positions to provide a rigorous deconstruction and transparent illustration of how these discourses have been constructed, and how terminology relating to whiteness has been distorted and applied for the purposes of advancing racialized falsehoods concerning the white working class. It is important to acknowledge that these issues are complex, and a simplification is probably useful before we start to delve into the necessary complexities. In short, the problem can be reduced to the conflation of *race* privilege with *economic* privilege. For example, a dramatic simplification of the notion of white privilege would equate to the notion that being perceived of as 'white' in a white majority society normally means that individuals are rarely subjected to discrimination because of their being perceived of as 'white'. This is *not* the same as saying that all white individuals have a measurably privileged economic position in comparison to racialized minority groups. In short, being white does not mean that an individual cannot be economically destitute and/or exploited in many and various ways which constitute marginalization. But being white does mean that the origin of this oppression is not a direct result of racist experiences. In this context, the dissolution of 'race' as a potential factor in the oppression of white groups constitutes a privilege when compared with experiences of racialized minority groups that are able to evidence that their oppression *has* been directly impacted by resistances and viscosities around their racial identities. In short, carrying 'race' privilege does not necessarily mean always having access to economic privilege. Furthermore, the commitment to emphasizing racial whiteness as a factor in the oppression of the white working classes is dangerous for reasons which have an impact for both racialized minority groups and 'white' working class groups in equal measure. The first of these impacts is more obvious, in that the notion of the white working classes as the new racially oppressed is clearly a strategy to weaponize social class for the purposes of eroding critical considerations regarding 'race' within the public political pool. The outcome is an ongoing erosion of racial realities in the mainstream, and the bifurcation of critical scholarship on both 'race' and social class. We contend that the false *racialized* victimhood of the white working class is indicative of a *state of postracialism* only possible due to the conditions of *liquidity*, within which the apex of knowledge weaponization in a *postracial state* (of being) can be operationalized. The second of these impacts is dangerous for a very different reason, in that the misguided emphasis on racial whiteness obscures the reality that the foundation for the oppression of the working classes is and has always been *economic* as well as social. The effort to opportunistically racialize whiteness in the context of discussing oppression relating to social class draws accountability away from those responsible for their oppression – predominantly other white people with more economic power and social influence in the public political sphere. It is acknowledged that this discussion has been based on premises rather than practical examples. We will revisit this, giving a full breakdown and analysis, when considering the case study of education in Chapter 5.

Conclusion

This chapter suggests that liquid modernity has consistently served to ensure that notions of racial difference are not only sustained but also that these serve as the foundations for differential relationality to flows of power, and their implications for racialized marginalization in the context of the postracial 'state' of liquid modernity. Furthermore, it has considered how the postracial ideal has manifested across multiple or concurrent modernities, as well as considering specific examples of claims to postraciality. The 'state' of race relations in liquid modernity has faced a novel challenge in recent decades in the form of claims to postraciality which have served to facilitate ongoing racialized flows. These flows are experienced differentially because of the culmination and settling of sediments across tributaries of race, socioeconomic position, gender identification, sexuality, employment status, immigration status, and space and place. The nuanced intersections of these dynamics of identity result in sedimentary accumulation which filters racial flows differentially, with the interests of white, male, straight, cisgendered, economically successful citizens being most shielded through the resultant prophylaxis of this filtering process. For white groups, exposure to racial flows do not result in marginalization and, over time, the resultant accumulation of sediments from this experience further reinforces notions of racial progress. The consequent sedimentary accumulation results in a process which colludes with whiteness to obscure the full reality of racial flows as experienced by racialized minority groups. Consequently, notional perceptions of progressive flows regarding race inequities have frequently masked the realities and extent of the sedimentary legacies of coloniality. These flows are experienced differentially because of how the sedimentary legacies accumulate. This process allows for differential readings of the state of race relations at any given public political moment. In the context of white majority societies with colonial histories, for the vast majority, sedimentary deposits accumulate in ways which divert racial flows, meandering them away from white experiences of late modernity.

The sedimentary legacies of postcolonialism also serve to filter exposure to racial flows where they cannot be diverted. For instance, without question the most significant example in the last four years would be the death of George Floyd, the trial and conviction of Derek Chauvin for his murder and the sustained media attention relating to the Black Lives Matter movement. In this kind of context, sedimentary accumulation shields white experiences in ways which distort the full realities of race relations in late modernity. It is important to clarify that these processes are ongoing features of modernity, not processes which begin and end over the life course of the individual. As such, many individuals in white majority societies with colonial histories are born into a state of late modernity within which these processes are already longstanding. By way of contrast, sustained and unshielded experiences of racial flows would invariably see the murder of George Floyd as another example of the most extreme effects of systemic racism in contemporary policing in the US. Between 2014 and 2020, there were 7,680 recorded cases where an individual died because of force used by police in the US, with 25 per cent of those individuals being Black (*Al-Jazeera*, 2020). The fact that African Americans make up only 12.2 per cent of the US population would suggest that there is something systemic happening with the use of lethal force in policing and that this is resulting in Black Americans being proportionately overrepresented by more than double in deaths caused by police force. In this context, the murder of George Floyd cannot be considered an isolated incident. Nor can the deaths of Trayvon Martin, Tamar Rice, Philando Castille, Atatiana Jefferson, Breonna Taylor and the many other African Americans which have made up the 25 per cent of deaths resulting from police force in the US since 2014. Sedimentary filtering has resulted in many Americans emphasizing concerns about racist *individuals* in police forces as a preferable and more palatable conviction than acknowledging or entertaining that more systemic processes might be responsible. From this filtered position, incidents of racialized police brutality are individual-level phenomena arising from encounters with racist individuals who *happen* to be police officers. Part of the filtering which informs this reading is derived from the conviction that 'All Lives Matter' – a statement which is presented as a reasonable, inclusive and nondivisive alternative to Black Lives Matter. We argue here that it is the fluidity with which racial flows move in the context of liquid modernity that results in the redirecting and sedimentary filtering, and shields white groups in ways which distort the realities of race relations in late modernity.

It is via this process – of the liquidity of racism – that the critical mass of experiences relating to racial flows are redirected and filtered for the majority of individuals in white majority societies. The cumulative effects result in discourses on postracial idealism coming to dominate main*stream* narratives around the state of race relations and racial progress as a 'state' which ensures the ongoing racialized marginalization and unfiltered exposure to racial flows for racialized minority groups. These flows are not contained at the national level for white majority societies which have colonial histories; they have gradually extended to infiltrate oceanic tides, initially transferring patterns of ideological postracial sediments *to* the Global South, but subsequently transferring racial flows in an *exchange* of mutually affirming postracial discourses with the Global North. The following chapters will explore in detail how these dynamics are manifested across political, institutional and cultural spheres.

4

Liquid Racism and Brexit

Introduction

Racism played a central role in the UK's decision to vote to leave the European Union (EU) on 23 June 2016. Following the outcome of the 2016 EU referendum in which a narrow majority of 52 per cent voted to leave the EU, a number of academics have engaged critically with the ways in which racism got bundled up with its outcome. Sivanandan (cited in Burnett, 2017: 85) claimed that 'whatever else Brexit means or does not mean, it certainly means racism', and Virdee and McGeever (2017: 1802) in their now-seminal paper on racism within the Brexit debate articulated that 'Brexit and its aftermath have been overdetermined by racism, including racist violence'. This literature has focused on the ways in which racism became mobilized through the rise of racial violence and abuse in the aftermath of the referendum and how discourses of empire 2.0 and historical legacies of British colonialism fed into the 'Leave' and 'Remain' campaigns. However, within these racist registers of the Brexit debate, there is scope to see how Zygmunt Bauman's (2000) liquid metaphor can be used to flesh out new, contemporary understandings of how racism was deployed and mobilized during and after the UK's vote to leave the EU. Notions of sedimentary colonial legacies, viscosities, glaciation, soaking and filtering all play a role in the way in which Leavers and Remainers positioned their case to leave or remain in the EU. The praxes of liquidity also become integral to understanding the wider social and political condition that led to the EU referendum.

In this chapter, we explore how liquid racism operates as a concept in specific ways that contributed to the racialized discourses and set of circumstances that led to, and occurred during, the EU referendum. The Brexit conjuncture began much earlier, before the dominance of Eurosceptic narratives and demands for a referendum gained prominence in public discourse in the 2010s. It was the consequence of wider sociopolitical conditions concerning the liquefaction of daily lives. This process of liquefaction produced multiple risks including, a volatile neoliberal marketplace (resulting in the 2008 economic crash), time-space distanciation of people through increased global mobilities and technological developments, and the diminution of social and national infrastructure (for example, the welfare state and the NHS) through privatization and a corresponding shift to an individualized 'life politics' (Giddens, 1991). We argue that these wider social and political conditions resulted in what Zygmunt Bauman (2006a) calls a 'liquid fear' of the 'migrant other'. Brexit – or more accurately, the decision to vote to leave the EU – was the result of such fears, risks and insecurities (Beck, 1992), which themselves were the result of liquid racist discourses of previous governments (for example, New Labour and David Cameron's Conservative Party) that promoted transformationalist ideas of globalization that would benefit the UK. It was a strategic performance that sought to manage these associated risks, fears and insecurities to avoid becoming what Bauman (2003b) calls the 'wasted lives' of liquid modernity – a strategic performance that resolidified racism through increased anti-migrant sentiment while also mobilizing a liquid racist narrative of empire 2.0 by presenting the UK as a global project that sought to reclaim its position as the dominant hegemon of the world. It is the wider social and political conditions that led to Brexit and facilitated liquid fears associated with migration to which this chapter first turns.

Globalization, liquid fear and the migrant 'other'

Under the conditions of late modernity, the scale and intensity in terms of which the world has become globally interdependent have increased. There are no *terra nulla* or unknowable lands and peoples (Bauman, 2006b: 7). The quotidian lives and activities and events of distant places and individuals – both of human prodigality and suffering – can now be shown through advancements in technological communications, the internet and digital revolution, the use of cheap air travel and the encountering of superdiversity (Giddens, 2003; Vertovec, 2007). Electronic images of distant individuals, activities and events are shared through mobile phones, tablets and digital communication platforms, and in the routine propinquities with difference and diversity while going about daily lives. No longer are the immediate life worlds (Habermas, 1981) of urban or rural areas of one country disconnected and isolated from the urban and rural life worlds of people in another country somewhere else in the world. The distanciation of time-space has seen the world become increasingly relational and interdependent. with different spaces and places imbricated into a dynamic and ever-changing globalized networked society (Castells, 1991). Such global interdependence is best captured by Bauman (2000: 11) in *Liquid Modernity*: '[T]he advent of cellular telephones may well serve as a symbolic "last blow" delivered to the dependency on space; and so, consequentially, the distance and exoticism of faraway lands become immediately accessible.'

The intensity of time-space compression (Harvey, 1989) – or, simply put, globalization – in late modernity is based on the scale of the circulation of capital and commodities. The activities and exchanges by individuals in one place have an impact and influence on people living in other places throughout the world. No individual or country can operate outside of the global, neocolonial capitalist marketplace. All actions and routines are relationally affected (Massey, 1994), demonstrating globalization's ability to unite humankind while simultaneously raising awareness of there being 'nowhere one can escape to' (Kundera, cited in Bauman, 2006b: 9). Such processes of globalization do not benefit everyone homogeneously. The accumulation of wealth and power by countries in the 'Global North' has has had an impact on the economic marginalization and deprivation of those countries in the 'Global South'. Contemporary global economic conditions reveal stark inequalities and systemic modes of oppression, domination and subjugation imbricated with a historicized 'role of state violence' and the 'expansion of colonialism' (Carrington et al, 2016: 3). As the mobility of goods, capital and services as well as the concentration of economic influence from transnational corporations based in the 'Global North' increase, the 'Global South' is severely impacted by the most intense racialized and socioeconomic problems (Ciocchini and Greener, 2021) – for instance, the exploitative labour migration practices of temporary worker programmes by world governments (for example, Canada and some EU Member States) to extract surplus labour from sending-receiving destinations to work across industries of the 'Global North' (for example, agribusiness, health and social care sectors, tourism industries and so on) (McLaughlin and Weiler, 2017). There are also thousands of migrants working in unfree labour conditions in the fishery industries across East Asia (Jones et al, 2019), to produce goods and commodities to be sold and distributed across countries of the 'Global North'. There is financial extraction through tax evasion, offshoring and illicit flows of money out of the 'Global South', with more than US$1 billion leaving countries of the 'Global South' through illicit monetary flows every year and ending up in tax-free spaces (Kar and Spanjers, 2015). According to Hickel (2017: 51), because of these neocolonial practices by countries in the 'Global North', extreme poverty and forms of systemic or state-led violence sustained by globalized capitalism are defining features of existence in many regions of the 'Global South', with global poverty estimates around 4.3 billion individuals being from these regions. There is no sight of damming effects or viscosities to slow down global flows of racialized and economic polarization and marginalization. The oceanic tides (Deleuze and Guattari, 1988: 479) of late modernity have dismantled, disembedded and dislocated the once solidified national boundaries of modernity. All societies are now fully set afloat on the ocean of liquid modernity, with late modern capitalist processes of deprivation, exploitation and subjugation the sedimentary deposits, compounds and accumulations of historical colonial flows.

Countries in the 'Global North' are not immune to the sedimentary effects of globalization. The liquefaction of state insurance has meant individuals are now having to attend to their and their own social networks' socioeconomic and cultural concerns (for example, (un)employment, health and wellbeing, and education) while simultaneously being powerless to make decisions to decide their own futures without the certainties and protections of 'solid modernity' once the chosen itineraries of the future have been selected (Bauman, 2000; Bauman, 2006b: 7). The liquefaction of society and the unpredictable openness in which it brings produces a society based on fate and necessity, of unplanned and unanticipated consequences of globalization; that is, of the risks (Beck, 1992) associated with living with the uncertainty of the oceanic tides of late modernity – risks of trade and capital, surveillance, and the monitoring of information using big data, violence and warfare, crime and terrorism, and the increased mobility of people from one cartographic point to another. Under 'solid modernity', these risks were bounded by the fixedness of place. They did not move outside of the boundary of the nation state. However, in contemporary liquid times, they assert an active disdain for any sort of territorializing of state boundaries.

This unpredictable openness – while affording transformative possibilities of identification and belonging – brings with it a sense of ontological insecurity for 'host' populations who are now confronted with, and possibly overwhelmed by, a range of risks (Beck, 1992) that they can neither control nor fully understand (Bauman, 2006b). This has led to what Zygmunt Bauman (2006a) has called *liquid fear.* Fear, according to Bauman (2006a: 2), is the name given to affective feelings of distress when faced with uncertainty and threat, and what is to be done – or what can and what cannot be done – to prevent such uncertainty and/or threats. Modernity – or, more accurately 'solid modernity' – under the philosophical premises of the Enlightenment project suggested that the more individuals got to know the world through advancements in science and technology, the more the uncertainties, threats and risks of 'solid' modern society could be rationally controlled and tightly ordered. However, under the conditions of liquid modernity, the world is not tightly ordered or rationally controlled; it is the antithesis, a 'runaway world' (Giddens, 2003) marked by fragmentation, division, dislocation and generalized feelings of uncertainty. The hazards of late modernity, according to Beck (1992), are unlike the hazards of modernity which were bounded to certain localities or limited to specific groups. Late modern hazards span across time and space. Whereas certain risks (for example, crime, war and conflict, disease and illnesses, and migratory flows) were once bounded to certain nation states or regions of the world, under the conditions of a modernity that is liquid, not only can these same risks reach far beyond the boundaries of their place of origin and into new and different parts of the world, but the scale and intensity of such risks has also increased. Consequently, the fears now experienced by individuals are no longer based on 'real dangers' as they were in the past; they are more 'diffuse, scattered, unclear, unattached, unanchored, free floating' (Bauman, 2006a: 2), with no clear cause or anchor point. The spectres of existential and ontological threats are ubiquitous and ever-present in the lives of individuals, groups, communities and even whole societies. They are everywhere, but nowhere to be seen; it is only when such threats occur that they are noticeable. Because of this, fear too is always present and everywhere – a constant presence in people's everyday lives as they attempt to manage the unpredictable uncertainties of liquid modern society.

One of the central perceived risks and 'threats' of liquid modern times is migration. The 'opening up' of society has seen the scale and intensity of migratory flows increase. The diminution of employment markets globally has expedited international labour migration facilitating anti-immigrant sentiments among 'host' populations about migrants taking the remaining employment opportunities from 'host' citizens, ignoring how the liquefaction of local labour markets within sending destinations necessitated migrants to move elsewhere to find work and security. The paradoxical confluence between the disappearing of local employment opportunities and the expansion of the labour market globally has also meant that the skills in which 'host' citizens have are losing their utility, becoming outdated and old-fashioned in light of the rapid flows of change characteristic of late modernity, and thus having to adopt strategies of flexibilization (for example, learning new skills) as a way of maintaining security within an ever-changing and insecure global labour market. International labour migration thus becomes the source of intense anxiety and fear because of the liquid conditions of such migration (Bygnes and Erdal, 2017) characterized by temporalities, liminal legal status, unpredictability and the 'migrant habitus' (Engbersen, 2013: 7) of open options due to *the tacit intentionality* of the global capitalist marketplace which is rooted in logics of extraction. These 'liquid migration' flows (Engbersen and Snel, 2013) merge with the liquefaction of state insurances in the lives of individuals living within the 'Global North' (Bauman, 2006b) facilitating a confluent effect, leading to the solidification of anti-immigration rhetoric.

Thus, with rising national and global inequalities, majoritized white, working-class groups – those deemed *left behind* by globalization – aided by the media and politicians have attributed their declining standards of living to an increase in migration. Although there are structural issues at the national and global levels that have impacted on white, working-class groups' lives, it is migration that is often made a visible scapegoat for these other structural concerns: for example, economic austerity and cutbacks, the gig economy, and the precarity of work that white working-class groups experience (Seidler, 2018). These structural issues are of legitimate concern because the liquefaction of the solid-modern welfare state model (Bauman, 1998) has meant that the system that was supposed to protect them against the fast globalizing and increasingly extraterritorial labour market by mitigating fears of loss of social security has been washed away and replaced with an emphasis of individually managed 'life politics' (Giddens, 1991: 209). The confluence of the diminution of the 'traditional' welfare state and (since New Labour) the government's advocation of a global, corporate multiculture which sees wealthy nations such as Britain benefiting from the employment of migrant labour has facilitated waterfalls of resentment towards migrants by white-working class groups. White working-class groups are unable to see the racialized flows impacting migrants under the conditions of liquid modernity; restrictions to the types of employment opportunities afforded to migrants, with most often working in low-paid, low-skilled jobs in a wide range of sectors such as tourism, health and social care, agriculture, manufacturing and construction (de Lima and Carvajal, 2020). This is because while white working-class groups do suffer due to the increased liquidity of contemporary society, they are filtered out of experiencing the most extreme accounts of vulnerability as their whiteness affords them protection from certain risks and insecurities. Thus, when racialized flows do wash over white-working class groups, they are not soaked in the same way in which racial minoritized groups are, leading to specific racialized minorities (for example, migrants) being subjected to alterity.

Consequently, migrants and refugees have become the raison d'être of 'host' populations' existential and ontological uncertainties and fears. According to Bauman (2006b: 43), migrants and refugees have replaced the 'evil-eyed witches and other unrepentant evil doers, the malignant spooks and hobgoblins of former urban legends' in which the rapidity of global mobilities has situated the 'host' population as victims to planetary outcasts (see also Bauman, 2003b). Under this pretext, migrants and refugees are 'othered'. They are constructed as a 'threat' to their place of arrival, worked up as potential criminals looking to harm long-term citizens or perceived to have no intention to fully 'integrate' into the place of arrival, instead seeking to claim state-sanctioned insurances (welfare) to the detriment of long-term citizens. Moreover, the fears aimed at migrants and refugees also relate to the loss of community under liquid modernity. Coming from a range of 'somewheres' and 'everywheres' (Goodhart, 2017) and settling into local communities, long-term residents fear migrants and refugees turning their communities into 'non-places' (Auge, 1992) or 'nowhere villes' (Garreau, 1991), facilitating the diminution of (a perceived) community life – resulting in a call for arms to long-term residents of such spaces to mobilize community discourses in search of security (Bauman, 2001b) to resist their own communities becoming a 'place without a place, that exists by itself, that is closed in on itself and at the same time is given over to the infinity of the sea' (Foucault, 1986: 27).

The problems with mitigating against such fears and insecurities of 'host' populations is that the fears that are born out of such ontological insecurities and uncertainties towards migration often relate to the perception that individuals can no longer control and manage such risks – whether individually or as a collective effort – as the tools that are used to mitigate against risk (power) and the ability to decide which risks ought to be addressed (politics) are separated and pending divorce (Bauman, 2006b). The power to manage migration and refugee crises is held firmly at the level of supranational governance, while the politics to decide what can and cannot be done concerning migration is nationally and locally situated. Take, for example, the EU. At the level of the supranational, the EU constructs an ambivalence of uncertainty out of migration, seeing migrants – especially from Eastern Europe since the 2004 and 2007 enlargements – as valuable labour for low-wage sectors such as agribusiness, factories and service industries, while erecting strong bordering practices which lock migrants out of citizenship, settlement and rights. Such extractive logic to enact favourable trade terms from other countries while simultaneously policing external borders to keep people from those countries out (Klein, 2003) manifests a liquefaction of racism. The practices used to maintain the fortressification of Europe are anchored in the sedimentary accumulation of colonial flows through which Europe was constructed – especially the acts of expansion which are articulated as positioning Europe as being open and inclusive.

The global, supranationally situated power to manage migration unwittingly prevents the politics of nation states from deciding how to address the concerns migration and the increased mobility of peoples has for its citizens. As an attempt to address such concerns and a lack of control, political figures in countries such as Britain have used migration as a political 'hot potato', calling for tighter border controls and regulatory caps on migration as proactive actions in addressing citizens fears. David Garland (2018) would observe that this repositioning of the rhetoric towards migrant 'others' marks a shift from welfare and support to penal and control modalities, echoing Loic Wacquant's (1999) redefinition of the state's mission as one of reducing its social role and strengthening of its penal intervention. Thus, redrawing the Cartesian lines between 'us' and 'them' is more important than ever before, as it allows for the temporary rekindling of the marriage between power and politics at the level of the nation state. The state can be more selective and diverse in the ways in which it regulates and controls its borders, allowing inward flows of migration into its borders to facilitate continued competition of global labour markets while also viscously restricting racialized flows by protecting against 'undesirable' migrant categories. This is often done to stop the fears of its citizens from flowing out onto migrants and resulting in glaciating and resolidifying concerns around migration into overt moments of hostile and racialized violence. However, this was not the case with Brexit. According to Goodwin and Heath (2016: 13), the vote for Brexit was delivered by those *left behind* by globalization – all those 'pensioners, low-skilled, less well-educated blue-collar workers and citizens who have been pushed to the margins'. This can be seen in the higher voter turnout rate (72.2 per cent) for the Brexit referendum than for the 2015 UK General Election (66 per cent) a year earlier (Electoral Commission, 2021). The vote for Brexit was constructed as an act of resistance towards not only continuous migrations, which were perceived as eroding British nationhood, but also politicians, who were perceived as advocates for globalized multiculturalism (Habermas, 2016; Kerrigan, 2018: 141). Some sociologists who have examined the narratives of the white, working-class 'left behind' in relation to Brexit have suggested the resonant claim that Brexit was delivered by a majoritized, 'left behind' white, working-class had been largely overstated and driven by a distorted 'methodological whiteness' of some social scientific research on Brexit (see, for instance, Bhambra, 2017; Mondon and Winter, 2020; Begum et al, 2021). Brexit could therefore be understood as a shorthand for the management of fears produced by feelings of a postcolonial melancholia (Gilroy, 2004) within liquid modernity brought about by the need to return to an imagined, retrotopic past (Bauman, 2016). It is this argument to which the next section now turns.

Brexit, retrotopia and the management of fear

In the previous section, concepts of globalization, fear and othering were explored to provide a wider context for the sets of circumstances that led to Britain's decision to withdraw from the EU on 23 June 2016. Drawing upon Zygmunt Bauman's (2016) concept of *retrotopia* – or the imagining of the past as utopia – this section will explore the connection between Brexit and nostalgia to premise the enactment and mobilization of Brexit as a way of managing fear against the potential risks created by globalization – especially around the presence of the migrant 'other' – and of providing security in an insecure world.

Bauman (2016: 2) defines the concept of retrotopia as moving towards a '[p]aradise of the past (as, probably, it is retrospectively imagined after it has been lost and fallen into ruins)'. Retrotopia was a central element of populist discourses concerning Brexit. Notions of a romanticized and nostalgic past – an imagining of a lost time and culture – were drawn upon by populist right politicians and advocates of the 'Leave' argument to safeguard against the more protean cultural forms (for example, diversification of the British population) of the present and to mitigate the (perceived) threat of strangers arriving at the borders of Britain, bringing with them criminality and further diversifying and therefore eroding British – or, more precisely, English – national identity. Retrotopia can therefore be seen as a damming response to the uncertainties of which the liquid modern world has created to maintain a sense of security and national identity.

Underpinning this retrotopic frame around Brexit was the concept of nostalgia. Nostalgia was a significant theme in Brexit discourse. It was essential to the constructions of 'home' in the populist narratives around Brexit. After all, 'home is the centre of the world – not in a geographical, but an ontological sense … the place from which the world can be founded' (Back, 2007: 69). It was these imaginings of 'home' that were drawn upon throughout the EU referendum by those on the populist right to protect and defend what it meant to be British and/or English in a liquid modern world – which disembedded the nation state from its 'solid' sense of identity – and to establish the 'other' as the source for such loss of national identity (Taggart, 2000: 3). Nostalgia was a constitutive feature of the lexicon of the 'Leave' campaigns, which connected both English and British nationalisms to expressions of postcolonial anxiety (Gilroy, 2004), anti-globalism and anti-immigrant sentiment. Such discursive strategies were based on emphasizing sedimentary legacies of colonialism by representing a social space flooded with 'others' in need of damming to safeguard against future racialized flows (we will return to these points later on in the chapter when mapping out the liquid racist dimensions of the 'Leave' campaigns).

The concept of nostalgia and the diminution of contemporary societies within the oceans of late modernity is well documented in the academic literature. Wheeler (2017) maintains that histories (of whatever kind) are always bound up in romantic nostalgia – understood as inaccurate forms of remembering, as all forms of remembering are contingent on the cultural and political contexts in which such memories are recalled (see Said, 2000; Cubitt, 2007). There is no escaping the fact that in the context of Brexit, the nostalgic narrative accounts used during the 'Leave' campaigns were inaccurate reflections of the past. They were drawn upon as an attempt to resolidify the sedimentary compounds of a colonial history, resulting in a resolidification of historical manifestations of racism (as in the case of Leave. EU) or reinscribing the remnants of a lost empire through tacitly intentionally mobilizing the rhetoric of a 'global Britain' to create *empire 2.0* (as in the case of Vote Leave) (Virdee and McGeever, 2017). Eatwell and Goodwin (2018) argue that the sort of romantic nostalgia used in the discourses around Brexit was a restorative nostalgia. Bonnett and Alexander (2013) elucidate that restorative nostalgias seek to reconstruct and preserve the past (see also Boym, 2001). Thus, restorative nostalgia is the type of nostalgia evoked in nationalism and national populisms, of which Brexit was one. Dorling and Tomlinson (2019: 281) described the 'imperial mindset' in the UK behind much political thinking on Brexit and nostalgia. Similarly, Zappettini (2019: 141) outlines how 'the British government indulged in post-imperial nostalgia' (see also Gilroy, 2004), while Seidler (2018: 57) detailed the ways in which 'post-imperial nostalgia' was tied up with the demand for sovereignty in discourses around Brexit. Wheeler (2017: 471) would go further and argue that Brexit was not just a restorative form of nostalgia; rather, it was productive in Britain's – or, more precisely, England's – nostalgic imaginings of longings for a forgotten past to escape the turbulences and sea changes of late modernity. In other words, the nostalgic narratives surrounding Brexit were constantly mobile, always changing and always on the move, with different romanticized histories being remembered for different purposes, but all to mitigate against the (perceived) 'threat' of different diverse individuals and processes. Moreover, the nostalgic discourses on Brexit are reminiscent of Benedict Anderson's work (1983), who linked nationalism to the notion of the 'imagined community'. Anderson argues that '[a]ll profound changes in consciousness, by their very nature, bring with them characteristic amnesias' (Anderson, 1983: 204) and thus implies retrotopia, which is described by Bauman (2016: 32) as gratifying 'the yearning for belonging and the obligation of self-formation, inescapable and staunchly non-negotiable under liquid-modern conditions. Instead of being at loggerheads, the two demands intertwine and are (or at least appear to be) amendable to being answered concurrently, side by side, in one fell swoop'.

What this discussion has evidenced is that Brexit is clearly bound up with resolidification processes of colonialism through nostalgic narratives that have a damming effect on the racialized flows of diversity and difference as well as a viscous moment for racial progressivism. In the following section, we will unpack the ways in which these notions of nostalgia, retrotopia and the (re)production of populist nationalisms manifested through the liquid racist dimensions of the 'Leave' campaigns.

Liquid racist dimensions of the 'Leave' campaigns

There were two distinctive campaigns in favour of Britain's withdrawal from the EU during the Brexit referendum. *Vote Leave* was the official campaign of the 'Leave' argument and consisted of mostly right-wing libertarian Conservative politicians (for example, Chris Grayling, Michael Gove, John Whittingdale, Boris Johnson and Priti Patel) and those on the right of the Labour Party (for example, Frank Field, Graham Stringer, Kelvin Hopkins, Katie Hoey and Roger Godsiff). There was also the unofficial referendum campaign in favour of exiting the EU – *Leave.EU* – primarily made up of United Kingdom Independence Party politicians Nigel Farage, Aaron Banks and Richard Tice. The constitutive feature of both Vote Leave and Leave. EU was their emphasis on reinstating sovereignty and protecting borders from encroaching migrant 'others' (Virdee and McGeever, 2017). However, they were different in terms of how they constructed narratives around migration, exemplifying the liquefied ways in which racism gets mobilized as a performative strategy of control, resistance and protecting the British public interests and national identity against the ontological insecurities that migration – as a globalized process – raises.

In the case of Vote Leave, advocates – both professional-political and public-political – maintained that by restoring democratic control and sovereignty of the nation state, the UK could move away from the EU trading bloc and begin trading with other countries around the world to secure its own political economic future as an independent sovereign state. Such narratives and arguments were continually put forward by Vote Leave during the campaign. Vote Leave frequently maintained that by withdrawing from the EU, Britain could once again reclaim long-standing (colonial) ties with other Commonwealth countries such as Canada, Australia, New Zealand and India, as well as non-Commonwealth countries (but which did have colonial ties) such as the US. However, these arguments denoted by Vote Leave were less about the desire to become a sovereign state with hopes of trading all over the world and more about returning to a nostalgic past of empire (Gilroy, 2004).

'Race' and racism were imbricated in the rhetoric of the nostalgic past and empire in the Vote Leave campaign. Discourses of the nostalgic past and empire highlighted how the sedimentation of colonialism and imperialism, bringing with them legacies of racialized violence, marginalization, exploitation and exclusion, which were brought into being through the arguments constructed by advocates of Vote Leave. For instance, the then Prime Minister, Theresa May, and the then-Secretary of State for Exiting the European Union, David Davies, made countless references to notions of a 'Global Britain'. The framing of a 'Global Britain' in the Vote Leave campaign could not have happened without the sedimentary flows of Britain's history of colonialism and imperialism. In other words, the rhetoric of a 'Global Britain' was based on suggestions about how Britain could be in the future through invoking warm collective memories of an imagined past where 'Britain was the hegemon of the global economy, with everything from ships to spoons marked with a Made in Britain stamp' (Virdee and McGeever, 2017: 1805).

What was interesting in relation to Vote Leave's mobilization of a 'Global Britain' narrative was the absence of the darker side of colonialism (Mignolo, 2011). The absence of acknowledging the most extreme vulnerabilities of the colonial project – racialized violence, marginalization, exploitation and subjugation, both physically and emotionally – that racialized minority groups experienced throughout the African slave trade and the ways in which the legacies of colonialism and imperialism continue to shape the uneven development of contemporary global neocolonial capitalism, facilitating migratory patterns to Western economies as a racialized reserve army of labour (Virdee, 2014) was a strategic performance. It facilitated racialized meandering. There was an interest convergence between Vote Leave politicians and the wider British public that allowed the racialized flows of the sediments of colonialism to become symmetrical with those (sentiments) of the past. The increased risks, (perceived) threats and (imagined) fears of migration for the British public and the need on part of Vote Leave politicians to appear electable and in support of the plight of (predominately) white working-class communities meant that there was space for promoting a narrative of control and regulation to stop the racialized flows of migration. This could be why the British public decided to come out and vote in the Brexit referendum and not the 2015 UK General Election, with the EU referendum having higher voter participation than 'any UK general election since 1992' (Dempsey and Johnston, 2018: 10). The British public were not politically passive as previously understood (see Amnå and Ekman [2014] for a wider discussion on political passivity); under the conditions of liquid modernity, they have become 'monitorial citizens' (Schudson, 1996, 1998). Monitorial citizens do not formally engage in politics; rather, they become politically involved when ontological insecurities are experienced. They avoid 'any routine-based or institutionalized forms of political participation' (Hooghe and Dejaeghere, 2007: 250). They were the 'everyday makers' (Bang, 2005) whose lives had become increasingly fluid as a result of the liquefaction of the solid social welfare state, the shift towards a 'life politics' (Giddens, 1991) and the diminution of trust among 'expert citizens' (Bang, 2005) and elitist politicians who were perceived as supporting the expansion of a global, corporate multiculture to the neglect of the interests of the British public, Thus, the meandering of a 'Global Britain' sentiment that attempted to whitewash Britain's colonial past through promoting a racially progressive, outward-looking forward of Britain to the wider public while still maintaining a staunch stance of controlling and regulating the racialized flows was an attempt on the part of the Vote Leave campaign to promote a vision of the future that was based on an imagined version of the past that would encourage political participation through claiming to resolidify the risks and insecurities of the British public regarding migration.

Ultimately, this meant that Vote Leave could circumvent having to confront the horrible legacies of the colonial project and legitimized the racism enmeshed in anti-migration discourses through positioning migrants as an *ambivalence of uncertainty*. Vote Leave made the racist narratives of the 'Global Britain' rhetoric palatable through employing economic and individual liberalism (Bonilla-Silva, 2013)– that is, they could claim they were not against migrants per se, but rather migration needed to be controlled, suggesting they were welcoming of migrants who contributed economically and individually participated in civic life. Not only does this visioning of a 'Global Britain' invisiblize racism, but it also allowed for accusations of racism by those of the political left to be viscously resisted.

While Vote Leave campaigners emphasized the 'aching loss' of empire (Gilroy, 2004: 95) through reinstating Britain as the dominating politico-economic force at the centre of global neocolonial capitalism, the advocates of Leave.EU championed a more overtly racist narrative around British nationalism. The central argument of Leave.EU was that Britain needed to withdraw from the EU to control concerns relating to migration. This can be seen in the way in which Nigel Farage, the leader of Leave.EU, positioned migrants as impacting the lived realities of the British public: 'Open-door migration has suppressed wages in the unskilled labour market, meant that living standards have failed and that life has become a lot tougher for so many in our country' (Farage, cited in Virdee and McGeever, 2017: 1806).

This positioning of migration as an economic 'threat' was bundled together with constructions of migration as a security 'threat' to British borders. It is important to note the sociopolitical context at the time as providing a reason why such mobilization of anti-migration and a 'migrant threat' discourse was successful. During the lead-up to and during the 2016 EU referendum, there was a cooling effect with regard to attitudes towards migration, resulting in visible accounts of racism and racialization. One factor that played a role in this cooling effect was the growth of the alt-right (see Hawley, 2017; Wendling, 2018; Johnson, 2019), globally, which saw a return to ethnonationalism, particularly European nationalism, viewing culture and national identity as being inherently primordial (see the works of Barth [1969], Geertz [1973], Banton [1983], Rex and Mason [1986], Jenkins [1997] and Fenton [1999] for a review of how primordialism has been applied to understand national identity in sociology and anthropology). The mobilization of such 'born and bred' understanding of national identity and culture was used to justify the anti-globalism stance of the alt-right and the need to retreat from a globalizing world with the pervasive 'contaminants' of difference, diversity and strangerhood. Thus, when coupled with the terror atrocities that occurred in France and Belgium and the European refugee crisis in 2015 and 2016, Leave.EU was able to present a 'rational' argument for controlling and regulating British borders – that is, by withdrawing from the EU, they (Britain) could also restrict entry of those constructed as 'undesirable' to make Britain safe again.

Mobilizations of anti-migration sentiment were strategically used by Leave.EU. It produced a moment of stickiness facilitated by the viscosities of Leave.EU to slow down the racialized flows perceived to be coming into Britain. This resolidified racism, producing worse and more hostile conditions for migrants to settle and experience a sense of belonging as part of the British nation state, resulting in moments of racial tension, conflict and violence (we will explore the resolidification, or glaciation, processes of Brexit later on in the chapter). The viscosity of the Leave.EU argument was most prominent in the now infamous 'Breaking Point' poster. Such racialized viscosities led to anti-migrant performativity becoming an act of damming to circumvent the migrant 'other' arriving from a range of elsewheres and turning up on our shores (Bauman, 2017). The Powellite narratives of retreat from a globalizing world that was no longer recognizably 'British' – a 'island retreat' narrative (Winter, 2016) – promoted an act of damming whereby if Britons voted to leave, they could successfully keep migrants from coming into the country.

The reason why the viscosity and damming of the Leave.EU campaign worked as well as it did is because it filtered into the pre-existing and often historically embedded cultural repertoires (Swidler, 1986: 273) of the British public which are often drawn upon when negatively evaluating an othering presence. This was particularly the case with how Leave.EU was able to continue the ongoing racialization of Muslim communities (Meer, 2012). While the central claims of the Leave.EU campaign were about withdrawing from the EU to secure sovereignty and Britain's right to control its own borders, the problematizing of the 'other' was rarely geared towards white European groups. Constructions of Leave.EU's anti-migration sentiment concerning the break away from the EU and taking back control of borders was a sleight of hand to stem the flow of Muslim individuals coming into Britain. Leave.EU was successfully able to racialize Muslim groups through buying into and reflecting the cultural repertoires that the wider British public have drawn upon when voicing their anxieties towards racialized minorities (specifically, Muslim groups) since 2001 (for example, 9/11 and the precipitating 'race'-motivated riots in Oldham and Bradford). These waterfalls of resentment the wider (often white, working-class) British public have towards Muslim groups were because of their visible markers of culture and racial identity. White European groups were not subject to the same levels of racialization – or often considered when drawing upon pre-existing cultural repertories – because their whiteness filtered them out of receiving the worse accounts of racism and racialization during the EU referendum.

The Leave.EU campaign was able to tap into the cultural repertories of the wider British public and racialize Muslim communities because they tacitly intentionally avoided 'race' talk; that is, no mentioning of 'race' was ever present throughout the Leave.EU campaign. This made its argument to control borders appear sensible, rational and pragmatic in response to growing economic and political insecurities and risks. A liquefication of racism was achieved through the production of such coded and concealed language about immigration. That is, Leave.EU was able to adhere to the formal rules of postracial thinking (Lentin, 2016) by promoting to the British public an abstract liberal discourse (Bonilla-Silva, 2013) that was about ensuring British sovereign power and rights in a globally aligned world.

Liquid racism and the 'Remainer' argument

Dimensions of liquid racism were not only bounded up within the arguments of *Vote Leave* and *Leave.EU*. They were also present in the case to remain in the EU. The Remain campaign – *Britain Stronger in Europe* – provided a moral justification for Europe. It advocated that being part of a wider social European project would mitigate the fears and concerns of its citizens by providing greater freedom, equality, peace and security in an increasingly insecure world (see Habermas, 2016). This was a deliberate rhetorical move to publicly position themselves (Remainer politicians and public-political advocates) as being antithetical to the 'thick' overtly politicized racism espoused by the 'Leave' campaigns. However, it is not difficult to disentangle the ways in which the 'Remain' argument can also be read through a racialized lens.

The central argument of the 'Remain' campaign was that given the pervasiveness of globalization, it was crucial to stay in the EU in order to promote change from within and continue to have a political 'voice' to benefit British citizens, while also protecting them from the broader negative consequences of globalization (for example, economic recessions, the risk and threat of terrorism, and rising social and spatial inequalities) (Crouch, 2017: 103). However, such globalist sentiments underpinning the 'Remain' campaign were not driven by temporal and situated concerns by political experts around the set of economic, social and political dangers resulting from change to the political norm, but rather had been made much earlier under Tony Blair and Gordon Brown's New Labour. Through globalization, there has been a diminution of jobs available, but an increase in the labour to fulfil the jobs that were available. New Labour was keen to draw upon highly skilled international labour migration and saw the role of international labour migration as one of the inevitable (and desirable) benefits of living in a globalized world (Findlay, 2006). This embrace of international labour migration to meet labour demand was a performative move on part of the New Labour government, which understood contemporary society as protean and risk-laden. In order for Britain to remain a competitor in the global marketplace, New Labour knew it needed to recruit labour and skills from a range of 'elsewheres', while also reforming local labour demands through skills redevelopment (Cressey, 1999), with an emphasis placed on the 'life politics' (Giddens, 1991) of the individual to retrain should their previous skillsets be no longer sufficient for the jobs available.

This policy reorientation became a cornerstone on which the 'Remain campaign' was fought. New Labour's economic reforms to maintain

Britain's position in the global economy as well as the 'Remain' argument's justification for the need for migration (and thus to remain in the EU) during the referendum were constructed around a similar process of meandering that the 'Leave' campaigns drew upon. While the 'Leave' campaigns articulated a process of meandering that advocated for a 'Global Britain' that was reminiscent of empire building through seeking new trade arrangements with Commonwealth nations (for example, Canada, Australia and India), the 'Remain' campaign meandered around a European history coterminous with colonial violence and theft (El-Enany, 2020: 73). Proponents of the 'Remain' campaign – along with New Labour politicians before them – espoused a racialized meandering through advocating for a political institution which allowed minoritized groups conditional inclusion based on the economic interests of the dominant group. The rhetoric surrounding the 'Remain' campaign was one of embracing diversity and difference through international labour migration by constructing migrants as contributing to the wider British economy, thus being within the EU-facilitated routeways to open democracy, equality and security. However, a closer inspection can see that this embrace of international labour migration was simply a repackaged version of the colonial logics that Britain and other European empires have historically done to reinscribe privileges of white dominant societies through the extraction of labour of minority groups from other countries elsewhere in the world.

It is no surprise that proponents of the 'Remain' argument were supporters of multiculturalism and superdiversity. The political geographies of those in support of 'Remain' often overlapped with geographies of superdiversity and multiculturalism (Neal and Cochrane, 2022). Neal and Cochrane (2022) concluded in their study of the lived realities of multiculturalism in high 'Remain' areas of the UK that a possibility of a politics of hope is possible. However, this argument fails to identify the ways in which the 'Remain' campaign mobilized discourses of multiculturalism and superdiversity as a damming attempt to resist the overly politicized, racialized flows of anti-migrant sentiment from the 'Leave' campaigns. For instance, 'Remainers' wanted to promote difference and diversification through policies of embracing international labour migration. This was an attempt for the political main*stream* (see Virdee and McGeever, 2017: 1812) to be seen as championing difference and diversity (principles at the centre of European and global integration) by moving beyond discourses of 'race' and difference when it came to recruiting those with the highest skillsets. However, these policy frameworks that advocated for migration and to remain in the EU were less about being competitive in a global marketplace and more attributive to deracializing the use of cheap labour for the growth and development of the UK, thus reinscribing colonial practices of extraction and exploitation.

This mixophilic position championed by 'Remainers' was diametrically opposed to the lived realities of how 'Remainers' experienced difference and diversity. 'Remainers' tended to live in the most culturally and socially diverse cities in the UK and be among the wealthiest people (Neal and Cochrane, 2022). Their experiences of the issues created by globalization, of which increased diversification is one, soaked differently to economically disadvantaged white groups. This is because their economic positionality allowed them 'connected withdrawal and selective social engagement' (Atkinson, 2016: 1306) that enabled their contradictory embrace of both mixophilia and mixophobia. They could advocate for diversity and difference to support the growth of the UK economy because their economic and social position allowed them to not have to sit alongside the 'other', unlike that of economically disadvantaged white groups. This social insulation from diversity and difference (see Atkinson, 2006) meant that 'Remainers' could maintain a globalist position pertaining to migration and the UK's position in Europe because their relative or absolute affluence afforded them the possibility of becoming what Bauman (1997) termed the *tourist*. Tourists perform nonbelonging to place; they occupy liminality between being in and out of place at the same time. They exist within their own tightly controlled 'bubble' where the only things that may leak in are the things that they admit. Inside their 'bubble', the tourist feels safe; whatever risks are experienced within the oceanic tides of late modernity, however perilous and threatening such risks may be, the tourist is secured.

Thus, given the widening gap of social and spatial inequalities, it is unsurprising that economically disadvantaged white groups voted to leave the EU. Unlike the majority of 'Remainers', economically disadvantaged white groups were structured into a set of experiences in which they could not avoid embracing difference and diversity while simultaneously facing some of the worse socioeconomic issues. However, because the 'Remain' campaign had positioned its case for Britain's future in Europe on the economic losses around the curbs to international labour migration, it is clear why this group was among one of the highest to vote to leave the EU, and thus exhibit mixophobic attitudes as its members conflated their socioeconomic marginality with the racial marginality of minority groups who were perceived as getting 'preferential treatment'. However, it is not the case that racialized minorities are preferred over economically disadvantaged white groups; it is simply that jobs are disappearing. The liquefaction of the global labour market has meant that British individuals – much like individuals elsewhere on the other side of the world – are continuously under threat of losing their jobs. But it does not follow that this is a direct result of international labour migration. International labour migrants were forced to move to countries such as the UK because their own jobs and social security disappeared. Both racialized minorities and economically disadvantaged white groups are the collateral damage; the 'wasted lives' – or vagabonds – of late modernity (see Bauman, 1997, 2003, 2011), groups that are victims of a world made under the neocolonial and liberal logic of the tourists (for example, all those Remainer politicians). However, when economically disadvantaged white groups come into contact with such racialized flows they do not experience the same levels of marginalization and disadvantage that racialized minorities do. This is because their whiteness filters them out of the most extreme accounts of vulnerability – indeed, they are vulnerable based on economic marginality, but international labour migrants are both racially and economically precarious in relation to global socioeconomic forces – leading to the perceived preferential treatment of racialized minorities and thus resentment towards racialized minorities more broadly. Such resentment led to a resolidification of racism in the direct aftermath of the EU referendum. It is this process to which the discussion now turns.

Brexit, glaciation and the resolidification of racism

In the immediate days and weeks following the EU referendum, incidents of racist hate crimes began to be reported and recorded (Burnett, 2017). Muslim individuals and communities reported being spat at and received verbal abuse in the street, Polish cultural centres were attacked and had racist graffiti daubed across Polish people's homes and public property, and other racialized minorities were told to 'go home' by their neighbours (Wilson, 2016). This rise in racist hate crime demonstrated no signs of slowing down, and the subsequent weeks were marked by continuous reports of violent attacks and racist abuse, most of which took place in urban areas as opposed to rural areas (Williams et al, 2022). In the first four days after the EU referendum, the Metropolitan Police recorded 85 racist hate crimes compared to 57 similar incidents in the same period four weeks earlier (Burnett, 2017). Likewise, 6,000 racist hate crimes were reported to the National Police Chiefs Council (NPCC) in the four weeks after the EU referendum result was declared (Komaromi, 2016). According to Komaromi (2016), in 51 per cent of the racist incidents reported to the NPCC, perpetrators referred specifically to the referendum in their abuse, with the most common phrases including 'Go Home' (74 stories), 'Leave' (80 stories) and 'fuck off' (45 stories) (see also Virdee and McGeever, 2017: 1808).

While the scale of such increase in racist hate crime is notable, these incidents did not occur in a vacuum and nor were they entirely new. Racism occurs through a process of solidification-liquefaction-resolidification – or, in other words, racism goes through periods of cooling and heating, moments of time which make it more or less visible contingent upon a range of public-political, institutional and sociocultural factors.

The resolidification effects of racism that were successful in the aftermath of the Brexit referendum result were not ahistorical. The racialized violence that appeared to characterize much of the postreferendum racism – for example, racialized narratives expressing that minorities should 'go home' and 'leave' – have sedimentary compounds in the social and political policy in the decades leading up to the EU referendum. For example, New Labour's neoliberal (and racially liquefied) embrace of international labour migration (and thus its policy agenda of multiculturalism) to reform Britain's position in the global economy and respond proactively to the liquefaction of jobs and skills at the national level fuelled the solidification (or resolidification) of older manifestations of racism built on racialized nationalisms. This resulted in the 'race' riots in northern English towns such as Oldham during the summer of 2001, as well as the rapidly changing geopolitical situation in the aftermath of 9/11 and the war in Iraq that solidified 'Muslims' as a new racialized threat (Kundnani, 2007). Consequently, the Conservatives moved away from discourses of multiculturalism, with the then-Conservative leader David Cameron (cited in *The Independent*, 2011) declaring 'state multiculturalism has failed'. The Conservatives argued that state recognition of cultural and ethnic diversity perpetuated feelings of separation and racial division. However, their solution to state-led multiculturalism was their own liquid racist narratives of assimilatory nationalism (Back et al, 2002). The Conservatives anticipated that racialized tensions would dissipate through greater civic engagement. They envisioned the more racialized minorities became more involved in local community life the greater sense of local and national identity and thus establish cultural and social diversity and integration without the need of state recognition. This was equally as problematic in creating the social and political conditions that facilitated the resolidification of racism following the EU referendum.

Therefore, the racial violence that had intensified – or, more accurately put, had become resolidified – following the EU referendum result would not have manifested without the complicity of New Labour and the Conservative Party in manufacturing the social and political conditions for Brexit. The resolidified racist violence that followed the EU referendum was not just a temporal, thickly racialized and politicized moment, as the main*stream* consensus had us believe. It was the result of a manifestation of the political climate that acted as a cooling process that made racism explicitly visible and politically acute. The growth of racist hate crimes in light of a pro-Brexit victory was the affirmation that a country that was not the public's is now 'theirs again'; there was a sense of history being corrected and of historical wrongs – for example, multiculturalism, specifically in its state-authorized way – being righted.

Sociologists such as Outhwaite (2017) have maintained a narrative of shock and outrage at the 'unprecedented' nature of such racist hate crime and have recast the consequences of such postreferendum racism as exceptional, with the role of academics to make what Habermas et al (2003: 88) call an 'impression of a major event'. The wider literature (see, for example, Benson and Lewis, 2019; Pitcher, 2019; Rzepnikowska, 2019; Abranches et al, 2021; Mintchev, 2021) has presented incidents of racial harassment and violence after the EU referendum as anomalies rather than something that exists in quotidian life in Britain and occurs in moments of liquefaction-solidification. Our argument in this section has been that racism goes through periods of cooling and heating. Racism is never wholly visiblized (and thus solidified), but nor is it purely fluid, motile and liquid either. Instead, racism needs to be understood as a process of glaciation. Much like how glaciers melt away or become solidified under atmospheric conditions, the racism(s) that happened because of Brexit were the result of social and political conditions which made racism more or less solidified or liquefied. It was policies under New Labour and the Conservative Party which aimed at reforming Britain's position in the global economy through embracing diversity and difference to fulfil demands or gaps in the labour market that reinscribed processes of liquid racism via the logics of extraction present in the African slave trade. These heating effects that made racism increasingly liquefied, fluid and motile, allowed for the conditions of cooling effects to happen by those groups left behind by the flows of globalization, which solidified the concerns of 'host' white majority groups – leading to a glaciated, cooling period for 'solid racism' to occur – manifested through anti-immigration and 'island retreat' (Winter, 2016; Virdee and McGeever, 2017) narratives around Brexit and the growth of alt-right politics nationally.

Conclusion

Brexit highlights a specific conjuncture in our contemporary thinking around 'race' and racism. On the one hand, it denotes yet another example of the ways in which racism has become liquefied, fluid and ever more mobile. This occurred through the ways in which the concepts of difference and diversification got mobilized in social and political policy. This was evidenced both in the risk-mitigation strategies of acknowledging the liquefaction of labour markets and thus the need to embrace international labour migration, and also the ways in which Vote Leave sought to articulate Empire 2.0 narratives by presenting themselves as being outwards looking and embracing difference and diversity through a sleight of hand that positioned the UK as the global hegemon of the world once again. On the other hand, these liquid racist practices were not wholly fluid. This chapter has noted how liquid racism operated through a process of glaciation: that is, Brexit represented the heating and cooling effects of racism. The 'Remain' campaign perpetuated a solidification of racism in the aftermath of the EU referendum. The growth of hate crimes, the ever-more hostile language towards migration this characterizes, and the landslide victory of a Conservative Party that has edged slightly more to the political right are just a few examples of how racism(s) under the New Labour project, which was seen to represent a period of racial progressivism, have become resolidified and saw the emergence of older historical manifestations of racism brought to light.

Public attitudes towards issues of migration, 'race' and racism have remained highly politicized since 2016, and the country remains socially and racially divided, perhaps more so than ever (Curtice, 2019). This calls for a renewed discussion about the ways in which racism get mobilized in discourses on the EU referendum. This chapter has demonstrated that 'race' and racism matters in relation to Brexit needs to be grounded in what we have identified as liquid racism; a racism that is ever more fluid and mobile, but is not completely without solidifying effects. Through an application of the concept of liquid racism, we have highlighted the ways in which both the 'Leave' and 'Remain' arguments can be interpreted as using racialized narratives in ways which visiblize racism in each account to varying extents. However, both liquid racist accounts can never purely contain the liquefied nature of racism. Liquid racist flows can become cooled and can lead to a resolidification of racism. We saw this in the emergence of racist hate crime, violence and abuse in the aftermath of Brexit. This surge of racialized violence and abuse was the consequence of liquid racist narratives by previous governments (New Labour and David's Cameron's Conservative Party) that attempted to embrace the liquefaction of daily life through mobilizing international labour migration at the national level in order to stabilize the UK's position in the global marketplace. Yet, the rise of racialized violence and abuse was not wholly contingent upon the social and political condition of previous governments. It was also the response to wider risks, fears and insecurities (Beck, 1992) that living in a liquid modern society has created, with the decision to leave the EU a management strategy to such risks, fears and insecurities.

This novel approach to studying contemporary sets of racism is crucial in helping to understand the social and political future of a post-Brexit Britain and its toxic polarization in the public-political arena. Therefore, racism, under the conditions of liquidity, needs to be seen as a social and political reality, expressed as processes of glaciation, where racism oscillates between 'solid racism' (for example, hostility, violence, and anti-migrant and exclusionary rhetoric) and 'liquid racism' (for example, using diversification for political means that reproduce extractive logics and to rearticulate Britain's colonial past as a form of racialized progressivism, as in the case of Vote Leave). This has effects on reproducing new structural inequalities and systems of racism and racialization. In fact, since the EU referendum result, we have already seen two oscillations in the solidification and liquefaction of racism; from Priti Patel and Suella Braverman's migration policies of suspending foreign bodies in *bare life* (Agamben, 1998) in Rwanda and on Bibby Stockholm (a refugee and migrant holding barge) while waiting for their asylum claims to be processed (and thus resolidifying racism) to Liz Truss and Rishi Sunak's claims to tighten migration laws while simultaneously attempting to prop up a the current precarious state of the British economy by creating routeways into the UK labour market for 'skilled' migrants and refugees (for example, liquid racism through the extraction of labour to support the British economy).

5

Liquid Racism and Education

Introduction

The liquidity of racism and racial flows in the context of late modernity has served to obscure the realities of race relations and the persistence of colonial legacies. Having discussed these concepts at the macro (societal) level, this chapter will explore education as a site within which their effects might be manifested at the meso, institutional level. Education represents one of the key sites within which differential viscosities in utilizing education as a site for negotiating social mobility are manifested across highly racialized lines. In the context of late modernity, education is presented as an entity which aspires to egalitarianism, whereby meritocracy supersedes social inequalities, and represents a site of the investment of progressive politics in policy and practice. Nowhere more substantively have we seen the embedding of the multicultural project than within education policy in the UK. This chapter will develop themes introduced earlier on around 'race' and postracialism to provide a critical account of the extent to which racist outcomes persist in education. This book is focused on demonstrating how relationships between structure and agency, which characterize late modernity, manifest through persistent racialized inequities across political, institutional and cultural spheres. It draws upon various processes – both active and passive – to demonstrate how apparently unrelated phenomena collude to ensure the sustaining of highly racialized inequities in educational outcomes and displacement from education itself. Furthermore, we also demonstrate how racialized inequities are facilitated and sustained through public policy in the absence of any clear or discernible agenda with regard to 'race'. The continued implementation of strategies which have a proven record of disadvantaging particular racialized minority groups (Gillborn, 2005) is important. Education demonstrates racial flows through a range of phenomena, including emergent global/international knowledge economies, national education strategies and policy, institutional processes, and social factors such as space and place, socioeconomic position, gender, race and immigration status.

Race and education in liquid modernity

Race inequalities have been a consistent feature of the educational system in the UK. It is not the purpose of this book to replicate well-established bodies of work on race inequalities in education. Instead, it will focus on education as an example of how racial flows and the dynamics of race in the context of liquid modernity can be observed. In the context of the New Labour governments (1997–2010), and the Coalition and Conservative governments from 2010 to 2024, there have been a range of significant shifts from wider ideas about the purpose of education, ongoing policies and longstanding educational strategies and emergent shifts in assessment and expectations in relation to what constitutes educational success. All of these factors have had impacts on education which can be used to denote the liquidity of racial flows and how these disadvantages marginalized racialized groups.

The case in context: politics, education and race

Even before the New Labour administration assumed power in 1997, the mantra 'education, education, education' was already a significant feature of the Labour Party's political rhetoric. Education would continue to be a focal point for New Labour, and this was informed by a particular perspective on the changing nature of employment markets, both nationally and globally. New Labour's rhetoric around public sector reform can be seen as an active effort to encourage growth and productivity so that Britain could compete on the global stage. In this context, the predominant strategies for education were initially manifested in the 1997 White Paper *Excellence in Schools* (DfE, 1997), and characterized the education sector for at least a decade (Ball, 2008: 90). Several priorities were set out in the White Paper, including positioning education 'at the heart of government', designing policies that 'benefit the many, not the few', access to technology for all and raising standards for all on the premise that 'standards would matter more than structures' (Ball, 2008: 90). The intention here was that New Labour's education sector would provide the skills required to compete within the wider emerging global knowledge economy. Allied with this vision was the widening participation agenda in Higher Education, with the 'target of 50 per cent of young adults going into Higher Education in the next century' (Blair, 1999). This context assumed two premises, the first being that this standard of education in the UK would be at a globally competitive level 'for all', and that in achieving this, young Britons would be equipped to compete as individuals in the global knowledge economy.

Thus, New Labour's education strategy was predicated on the emergence and continued development of an increasingly global employment market characterized by flows of economic migrants competing for jobs based on the quality of their educational skills and qualifications. As we have seen in Chapter 4, Brexit along with the return to nationalistic sentiment has meant that the New Labour vision of the relationship between education and the global knowledge economy has not yet been fully realized. Furthermore, it is important to set out the political landscape against which education has been positioned as a way of demonstrating variances in racial flows and how these relate to shifts in the political landscape across which their trajectories travel. Similarly to the 'multicultural project'(see Chapter 3), while there have been variations in the extent to which racial flows in education might have represented progress around race relations, this is met with two main problems. First, regardless of what the surface suggests in terms of the state of race relations under New Labour, the Liberal Democrat-Conservative Coalition, or the Conservatives, deep below that surface, racial flows have persisted in ways which play out with consistent racialized outcomes for stakeholders in education. Second, we contend that this is another feature of the postracial 'state' facilitating ongoing racialized inequities in education. There are complexities, and this chapter will endeavour to unpack such complexities, but in simple terms, the second problem is enabled through a legacy of educational policies which appear to be progressive, or at least politically neutral on race, but which facilitate racialized marginalization. It is important to acknowledge here that the arguments informing this conviction are in part derived from insights gained through bodies of work on interest convergence and tacit intentionality in critical race scholarship. It is important to acknowledge that these *apparatuses* are utilized because of what their insights contribute to understanding what the wider theoretical developments are attempting to achieve around demonstrating the liquidity of racism in the context of late modernity.

Where New Labour represented progressive party politics centred around educational empowerment for all, the contrast of austerity politics since 2010 has been coupled against a backdrop of increasing anti-immigration sentiment, ultimately culminating in the Brexit vote of 2016 (see Chapter 4). The multicultural project (including the conditions relating to its failure) was coupled with the emergence of a notional 'left behind' – a forgotten working class whose interests had been eroded away from any meaningful representation in mainstream politics (Winlow et al, 2017: 145). This notion opens up an interesting dynamic, particularly with regard to how the working classes have been presented as stakeholders in education towards the end of New Labour's second term of office. The notion of the *white* working class as a new *racialized* marginalized group started to emerge shortly after the events of the London bombings in 2005, and from 2007 onwards, there were increased media reporting around the white working classes as the 'new underachievers' in UK schools (Gillborn, 2009: 17). This media reporting followed the publication of GCSE results from 2006 which showed that only 24 per cent of white boys who qualify for Free School Meals (FSM) achieved five GCSEs at grade C or above, compared with 33 per cent of Black African boys who also qualified for FSM, a disparity of nine percentage points (Gillborn, 2009: 18). Initial media responses that reported white working-class boys were the new underachievers in British schools provided more than enough ammunition to condemn the multicultural project, several years prior to David Cameron declaring its failure (see Chapter 3). This was played out through media reporting focused on pitching the interests of the white working class against those of other ethnic minority groups at a time where mobilizations of the British National Party (BNP) and the United Kingdom Independence Party (UKIP) had resulted in questions of ethnic citizenship becoming particularly heated (Bottero, 2009: 7). There are several problems with the ways in which these figures were presented in the media, and the subsequent arguments which were made on this basis on the white working classes in education. Some of the confusion lay in the technical criteria for qualifying for FSM, and there are some critical questions to ask about the relationship between these criteria, who it applies to and working-class identity more generally.

At the time of the emergence of the white working class as the 'new underachievers' in schools, 13.2 per cent of white British groups qualified for FSM in 2006 (DfES, 2006), with this increasing to 14.5 per cent by 2019 (DfE, 2020) and to 17 per cent in 2020 (ONS, 2020). We can clearly see some marginal increase in the eligibility for FSM among white British groups in recent years, and this number is likely to fluctuate in the future. However, we can also consider that a fair estimate based on the information above would be to suggest that around 14 per cent of white British pupils have qualified for FSM during the period where we have seen the notion of the white working classes as the 'new underachievers' emerge. This group can most meaningfully be identified in socioeconomic terms as the 'precariat' in Savage's model of social class (Savage, 2013), a cohort which make up around 13 per cent of the population. The underattainment of those children is a legitimate cause for concern. But this naturally leads us to ask another question: what proportion of the wider population consider themselves to be working class? The British Social Attitudes Survey (Department for Transport, 2015) identified that 60 per cent of Britons self-identified as working class, whereas the Social Mobility Commission the following year recorded 49 per cent of Britons identifying as working class (Social Mobility Commission, 2016). If we proceed with the more conservative figure here, we still find a disparity whereby the experiences of 14 per cent of the population are being conflated with those of 49 per cent of the population. It is important to be clear in acknowledging the substantial impact that socioeconomic position has on educational inequities for those children included in the 14 per cent of white families which qualify for FSM. However, this has consistently been presented *as if* these impacts now apply to a far bigger proportion of the population through the simple slippage of substituting those who qualify for FSM with those who self-identify as working class (Gillborn, 2009: 21). One final factor to consider is that according to the same dataset which identified the nine percentage-point gap between Black African boys who qualify for FSM and white British boys, a far more significant disparity was present between white groups who qualify for FSM and white groups who do not. The difference in attainment between white Britons attaining 5 A*–Cs at GCSEs who did not qualify for FSM and those who did was 32 percentage points, more than three times the gap between white boys who qualify for FSM and Black African boys who qualify for FSM (Gillborn, 2009: 18). Clearly, socioeconomic factors appear to be a far more significant indicator of educational success than race for white groups in education. The media reporting on the white working class as the new educational underachievers was laden with a subtext which politically spoke to a notional 'left behind', as was discussed earlier. It is important to acknowledge here that we entertain this term not to suggest that the 'left behind' is an accurate depiction of those most socioeconomically disadvantaged white groups. While we do not have the word-space to replicate existing work here, valuable critical perspectives on this are presented elsewhere (see Bhambra, 2017; Mondon and Winter, 2020; Begum et al, 2021). However, it is important to acknowledge that much political messaging around far-right mobilizations and influential individuals intends to appeal to a *notional* audience fitting the description of the 'left behind'.

Racialized flows of misinformation, or at least reporting without rigour, have resulted in and contributed to shifts in the tides around race and stakeholdership in education in the public political space. This process allows for a perception of reality which is highly filtered by the sedimentary deposits of racial flows, whereby the left behind find themselves drowning in flows of immigration and progressive politics around 'race'. The murky and turbid distortion of the truth has invariably informed the kinds of tensions between class and race-based debates in the public political sphere, which have seen the socioeconomic oppression of working-class groups reframed by notions of racial white victimhood (Gillborn, 2009). What this example demonstrates is that while a small proportion of those who possible identify as working class may be underachieving relative to other minority ethnic groups who also qualify for FSM, a far more significant disparity exists *within* white groups which are demarcated across *economic* lines (Gillborn, 2009: 18). This more accurate perception has become obscured because of the cumulative meandering legacies of racial flows which have shielded white interests and the accompanying sedimentary filtering of racial realities. Furthermore, we contend that this is a key feature of the postracial state (see Chapter 3). The racial marginalization of the white working classes can only be meaningfully considered against the backdrop of a perceived reality which has seen the eradication of the racialized marginalization of minority ethnic groups. While the postracial 'state' is being used here the refer to the UK as a politico-spatial context, its ability to obscure the realities of race relations also leads us to question how far the postracial state can also be considered a 'state' of perception. This perception takes the form of a civic reality within which the priorities of racialized minority ethnic groups and immigrants have indeed eroded away those of the white working classes in the public political arena. Postraciality in the context of social class has been achieved through the overflowing of minority interests into the mainstream, with the left behind flailing in newly formed creeks, lacking the paddles afforded through economic and social status.

Clearing the waters around the notion of the white working classes as the 'new underachievers' reveals that the oppression of the most socioeconomically marginalized white British groups as stakeholders in education has happened because of power being exerted against them at the hands of *other more affluent white people*. Thus, the power dynamic in the marginalization of the 'left behind' does exist, but *without* a racialized component. Their socioeconomic marginalization is not a consequence of how they are racialized, but rather a consequence of their socioeconomic position. For race to be the main source of their marginalization, they would have to be subjected to power being exerted over them *by* racialized minority ethnic groups. Given that this is not the case, the term 'white' can only ever be meaningfully applied as an ethnic label to describe one section of those who are *socioeconomically oppressed* in contemporary Britain. As we have seen, this (possibly inadvertent) sleight of hand has resulted in the frequent mispresentation of the 'white working classes' as the 'new educational underachievers'.

Immigration and education in liquid modernity

The construction of the white working class as the new racialized underachievers in education is not possible without the wider public political shifting tides around education, economic migration and political representation. The Blair-inspired vision of an education system fit for a global employment market invariably represents a key moment of postracial idealism, characterized by flows of economic migrants (see Chapter 4 for a critical analysis of how the exploitation of cost-effective labour at least partially informed the 'remain' argument in the context of Brexit). The premises underpinning New Labour's vision for education are characterized by an inclination towards *mixophilia*, or a sense of attraction and tolerance (Bauman, 2007) towards economic migrants. However, as argued by Bauman in *Liquid Times*, in the context of liquid modernity, mixophilia exists in tension with its counterpart *mixophobia*, a sense of fear and uncertainty ultimately arising from more liquid ways of living (Bauman, 2007). This implicit tension between mixophilia and mixophobia is useful as it helps us to understand shifting public political narratives around economic migration. The postracial idealism of New Labour's education strategies clearly represents a sense of mixophilia regarding economic migration in the context of a competitive global knowledge economy. However, there is a key caveat here – the emphasis on *economic* flows which would accompany immigration within this model. *Economic* migrants are welcome owing to their ability to contribute 'brain gain' and *economic* growth to offset any 'brain drain' incurred through Britons migrating to compete for jobs elsewhere. However, through the very mixophilic nature of this idealistic vision, the realities for the precariat or 'left behind' is a perception of increasing competition with economic migrants for employment, a prospect met with anxiety and mixophobia, especially with the proliferation of job losses and redundancies as a consequence of economic restructuring and the liquefaction of work under the neoliberal 'gig' economy It is this process that inevitably fuelled the shifting tides in wider public political discourses on economic migrants. In the context of a competitive political system, this afforded opportunities for rival political parties such as the Conservatives, but also BUKIP and the BNP, to court the mixophobia around economic migration held by traditionally conservative groups but now also held by the new left behind, the new racialized underachievers in education – the white working class. The consequences of these shifting discourses would ultimately lead to the Coalition government introducing the Academies Act (2010) in the context of a wider programme of austerity, the implications of which for race inequities in education will be discussed later on in this chapter.

The preceding example demonstrates the significance of three related phenomena in terms of how far racial flows distort perceptions of contemporary race relations which can then potentially increase in viscosity or even solidify in the wider public consciousness, or rather perhaps *publics' consciousnesses*. The example of educational underachievement among white groups in socioeconomically marginalized positions and, more importantly, how racial flows saturated news media discourses on social class demonstrate the significance of *audience*, *stakeholders* and *positionality* in terms of how messages concerning race relations flow into the public political space, and also the ways in which dynamics of identity along with cumulative lived experiences can combine, reified through sedimentary filters which selectively and differentially alter both the potency and viscosity of flows around 'race', race relations and racism. Shifting flows in public political discourses on immigration are also key here, as we see the construction of white racial marginalization in education coincide with tidal shifting from the pro-economic migration model which fuelled education policy under New Labour to the anti-economic migration sentiment that invariably informed the 2016 Brexit vote, and subsequent resolidifying and damming which has restricted immigration under the Conservatives (see Chapter 4 for a full discussion of how attitudes around immigration fed into Brexit).

However, in addition to the larger scale, more tidal political flows which have informed misreadings of racial disadvantage in education against a backdrop of mixophobia on immigration, the sediments of these flows have trickled down to impact on policy and practice in educational institutions. The notion of *tacit intentionality*, a concept developed and applied in CRT, is particularly useful to consider how the sediments of the larger public political flows around 'race' and immigration have settled at the institutional level. The ways in which education policies in the UK have functioned are embodied with a latent intentionality which disadvantages racialized minority groups and reproduces racialized educational inequities. Policies and strategies, as well as guidelines on educational standards and practice, are informed by a *tacit intentionality* on the part of policy makers (Gillborn, 2005). Breen (2023) has considered how this type of intentionality can take two main forms, namely that of being *actively* or *passively* embedded. The first form would see *intentionality* as something which is *actively* embedded in policy and practice, with the clear intention of maintaining racialized inequalities. Even though the intentionality is *active* here, such policies and strategies operate in ways which obscure the racist processes embedded within them. The second form of tacit intentionality would see *passivity*, or the overlooking of potentially racist outcomes leading to race inequalities because of how a given policy or strategy functions. In both scenarios, policies are presented as politically neutral and appear to have no implications in relation to 'race'.

Traditionally, *tacit intentionality* has been applied through exploring policies and legal structures to identify the ways in which they reproduce racialized inequities while masquerading as being egalitarian and neutral. The mixophobia relating to immigration flowed into education policy as an embodiment of *tacit intentionality.* This can be demonstrated with the introduction of the monitoring of pupil nationality in schools in England and Wales in 2016 under point 5.3.5 of the School Census guide issued by the Department for Education (DfE) (DfE, 2016: 65). The monitoring of pupil nationality from 2016 until the summer of 2019 raised a series of concerns regarding the purpose of nationality monitoring in schools. In fact, for many who were not directly affected, awareness that the monitoring of nationality was even taking place in schools did not come to public attention until news media reports that it was to be abolished for the 2019–2020 academic year. The decision to repeal the practice followed concerns raised by charities and nongovernmental organizations (NGOs), with efforts being made through legal channels to contest the practice. The practice of monitoring pupil nationality and country of birth was 'quietly introduced' through Parliament as a new law during the summer recess of 2016 (Whittaker, 2018). It was reported that these measures were actually a compromise negotiated by the DfE, which managed to restrict more extreme measures proposed by the then Home Secretary, Theresa May, which included teachers carrying out immigration checks and schools 'deprioritizing' places for children of (currently) illegal immigrants (Elgot, 2016). Following this compromise, it was also subsequently reported that a number of schools had taken the approach of targeting minority ethnic children and requesting to see their passports (Whittaker, 2018).

The preceding case represents an example where data collection and access to that data are highly controlled, but also how the intentionality behind government and legal mandate on practices can collude to ensure that the interests of highly vulnerable minority ethnic groups are marginalized *within* and even displaced *from* mainstream education. There are two main points to carry forward here. First, the period of time where pupil nationality was being recorded as a moment where public political flows around immigration cooled to the point at which we see their solidification, manifested through public policies which directly targeted marginalized racialized groups in ways which reflect the older, more solid racist systems of modernity (see Chapter 2) Second, the *rationale* behind collecting data on children and nationality had insisted that the data would not be passed on any other government agencies for immigration control purposes (DfE, 2016), but would rather be used to help support schools with large numbers of pupils where English is a second language (Whittaker, 2018). However, rather than utilizing this data to identify where inequalities could be addressed, concerns that the strategy is a thinly veiled attempt to monitor immigration status have resulted in legal action being taken by charities to block the practice (Bulman, 2017). The fallout of this process would invariably impact migrants who might be only suspected to be living in the UK illegally through their children being denied school places. The subsequent potentialities for deprioritizing school places for children represent a hidden mechanism for excluding children of parents with uncertain immigration statuses. Given the relationship between exclusions and pathways into the criminal justice system, this tacit intentionality has significant implications. These implications are not confined to the informal exclusion of children. Protecting the interests of those groups most affected through the courts has incurred the cost of legally mandating against tracking nationality for any purpose in schools. This includes gathering or using that data as a strategy for identifying and addressing educational inequalities where they might be most present for minority groups where English is a second language. The tacit intentionality has directly resulted in a lose-lose scenario, and one which has ultimately guaranteed that the initial premise of gathering data to support pupils within vulnerable migrant groups can now never happen at the state level unless there is a further legal precedent which opens up the possibility for doing so. The tacit intentionality behind 'deprioritizing' school places for children of (currently) illegal immigrants based on data of nationality is troubling. The outcome has led to an educational system which has ensured that children with uncertain immigration status cannot be tracked for the purposes of *improving* their educational opportunities, thus again leaving them open to the vulnerabilities regarding barriers to attainment, exclusions and wider educational disenfranchisement.

Voluntary sector advocates are taking up legal action because of a government initiative driven by tacit intentionality manifested in a focused attack on families where immigration status is currently ambiguous. In many ways, this represents something of a perfect storm embodying tacit intentionality, whereby the drivers (or, intentionality) behind monitoring nationality have been actively obscured, yet ensured highly racialized outcomes for groups at the extreme end of economic and civic vulnerability within minority ethnic communities in the UK. While these *potentialities* in policy were facilitated through the solidification of wider flows around anti-immigration which coincided with Brexit, the assurances around how data would (not) be used along with inconsistencies in actioning policy at the institutional level resulted in a more intangible and uncertain sense of vulnerability for families whose immigration status might be called into question. The coexistence of states of solidification, and more liquid and intangible vulnerabilities, can be understood as embodiments of glaciation, whereby racist sentiments solidified in policy through tacit intentionality are surrounded by more ambiguous possibilities for racist outcomes in the flows immediately surrounding them.

Tacit intentionality and the displacement of Black British groups from compulsory education

A more *passive* form of tacit intentionality is in the form of the practice of school exclusions in education in the UK. Exclusion embodies one of the formal pathways through which pupils can find themselves displaced from schools, and the implications are not simply confined to disparate educational experiences. A total of 63 per cent of people in prison in the UK were temporarily excluded from school and 42 per cent were permanently excluded (Timpson, 2019: 103). This latter figure should not be overlooked, particularly given that only 0.06 per cent of the general population were permanently excluded from school (UK Government, 2021). As with many features of the educational system in the UK, exclusion is presented as an egalitarian process, one which is intended to operate without prejudice and as a last resort in circumstances where all other available measures have been unsuccessful. It has been argued elsewhere that the logic underpinning exclusion draws on Charles Murray's moral underclass discourse (Kulz, 2019: 94), adopting a punitive approach to 'combating' educational disengagement by removing the opportunities afforded *in principle* in the compulsory education system from pupils who are deemed 'problematic' (Christian, 2005: 327) or 'hard to reach' (see Clegg et al, 2009). Intersections across gender and age are important here, as boys are three times more likely to be excluded than girls (UK Government, 2021), and the most common age at which pupils are excluded is 14 (UK Government, 2021). With the regard to 'race', patterns of exclusion have indicated a picture which indicates that, as a practice, it is far from egalitarian. Black British groups have been consistently overrepresented in school exclusions, and this is a phenomenon that persisted throughout the late 20th century and into the 21st century (Hamilton, 2018: 578). For example, permanent exclusions for Black Caribbean groups in 2017–2018 were almost three times higher than those for white British groups, dropping only marginally in 2018–2019 (UK Government, 2021). While there has been an apparent and significant drop in exclusions for Black Caribbean groups in 2019–2020 (0.14 per cent, down from 0.25 per cent the previous year), this is likely due to the impact of the COVID-19 pandemic and extended periods of school closure. A comparable reduction can also be seen in permanent exclusions in general and specifically in white British groups, whose rates of exclusion dropped from 0.10 per cent in 2018–2019 to 0.07 per cent in 2019–2020 (UK Government, 2021).

There are nuances to the representation of minority ethnic groups in school exclusions, but against the national average of 0.06 for 2019–2020, there were significant disparities and overrepresentation in groups including dual heritage white and Black Caribbean (0.15 per cent), traveller of Irish heritage (0.14 per cent) and Gypsy Roma (0.23 per cent). It also should be noted that travellers of Irish heritage also experience identical vulnerabilities in relation to exclusion to Black Caribbean groups. At 0.23 per cent, Gypsy Roma groups are clearly the most overrepresented, and the ways in which Gypsy Roma and Irish traveller groups experience racism and discrimination in education has been documented extensively elsewhere (see Bhopal, 2011). The traditions and lifestyles of many travellers of Irish heritage and Gypsy Roma groups, most significantly in relation to mobility, mean that proportions of these groups can experience interruptions in schooling and movement between schools (Jordan, 2001: 117). Furthermore, 'interrupted', or nomadic learning, is a process which has not been effectively accommodated in the UK education system, and traveller and Gypsy Roma group continue to experience educational marginalization because of misunderstandings around their history and culture (Bhopal, 2004: 61). The institutional processes regarding attendance monitoring and educational engagement assume an absence of this history and culture, and, as such, significant proportions of travellers of Irish heritage and Gypsy Roma groups may find themselves excluded as a result of having a nomadic approach to education and learning.

There are also some interesting phenomena around exclusions when looking at dual heritage groups. For example, dual heritage white and Black Caribbean children are overrepresented in almost identical ways to Black Caribbean children, which suggests that the racialization effects that lead to disparate school exclusions do not include any measurable privilege deriving from whiteness. This is a significant point. Prior to the introduction of 'mixed white and Black British Caribbean' as a specific ethnic category in the 2001 Census, most children who would fall into this group were politically and ontologically classified as Black (Hamilton, 2018: 578). The almost identical overrepresentation of Black Caribbean and dual heritage white and Black Caribbean groups in school exclusions is the sedimentary legacy of the 'political and ontological' classification of the latter group as Black prior to 2001. There are significant differences between Black British groups with regard to permanent exclusions, with the rates of exclusion for Black African pupils being 0.04 per cent for 2019–2020. This is not only far lower than the rate of exclusion for Black Caribbean (0.14 per cent) and dual heritage white and Black Caribbean groups (0.15 per cent) the same year, but is also lower than the national average of 0.06 per cent (UK Government, 2021). Exclusion rates for dual heritage white and Black African groups matches the national average at 0.06 per cent, and the rate for 'any other Black background' is only slightly higher at 0.09 per cent (UK Government, 2021). These variances are important for understanding the racialization of Black groups in liquid modernity. They demonstrate that the old categories used to demarcate racial differentiation in modernity are not playing out in prescriptively uniform ways for Black British groups. Processes of liquification see social identities begin to leak, seep, spill and fill from and out of their previously solidified states in liquid modernity, and so maybe these variances between Black British groups with regard to school exclusions represent an example of this. Perhaps these variances resemble a slow liquification of old binary racial notions of 'Black' and 'white', with groups of Black Caribbean heritage facing more intense racialized flows in the context of school exclusions compared with other Black British groups. The emphasis on *exclusions* specifically is important here, and this liquification cannot be assumed to be present with regard to Black British groups more widely.

The variances in *exclusions* between Black British groups might be explained to some degree by the impact of socioeconomic factors, as 30.6

per cent of Black Caribbean pupils qualify for FSM compared with 22.9 per cent of Black African groups (UK Government, 2020). While the proportion of Black African groups qualifying for FSM is not insignificant, the national average for children who qualify for FSM was 20.8 per cent for 2020 (UK Government, 2021b). Interestingly, the proportion of dual heritage white and African pupils who qualify for FSM is almost identical to that of Black African groups at 22.8 per cent. Furthermore, the proportion of dual heritage white and Black Caribbean groups who qualify for FSM is 31.7 per cent, again almost identical to Black Caribbean groups at 30.6 per cent (UK Government, 2021b). The final piece of the picture here is also revealing, in that the proportion of pupils of 'any other Black background' who qualify for FSM is 24.9 per cent, a figure slightly higher than the national average of 20.8 per cent (UK Government, 2021b). The variances in qualifying for FSM in each of these groups clearly align to some degree with rates of exclusion for each group, and so it is likely that socioeconomic factors are intersecting with race to inform variances between Black British groups in school exclusions. Government data on ethnicity and type of residential area suggest that there is little to no difference in the proportions of Black British groups living in spaces defined as 'urban' in the UK Census – for example, 97.9 per cent of Black Caribbean groups live in urban areas compared with 98.2 per cent of Black African groups and 98 per cent of those with any other Black background (UK Government, 2018).

However, perhaps confusingly, it has been found that exclusion rates for Black Caribbean boys in some local authorities are up to six times higher than white groups in the same local authorities (McIntyre, Parveen and Thomas, 2021). This would suggest that space and place is a factor in exclusions, but at specific local authority levels rather than the distinction between 'regional' and 'urban' locales. There were 348 local authorities at the time of the 2011 UK Census, and 49.5 per cent of Black Caribbean groups lived in just 12 of them (UK Government, 2019). These authorities and the respective proportions of the UK Black Caribbean population living within them were Birmingham (8 per cent), Croydon (5.3 per cent), Lewisham (5.2 per cent), Lambeth (4.9 per cent), Brent (4 per cent), Waltham Forest (3.2 per cent), Hackney (3.2 per cent), Haringey (3.0 per cent), Enfield (2.9 per cent), Newham (2.5 per cent), Ealing (2.2 per cent) and Wandsworth (2.1 per cent) (UK Government, 2019). The data for school exclusions in Birmingham are problematic. The broader category of 'Black British' is used, which does not allow for any nuanced picture of how school exclusions are impacting for Black Caribbean groups specifically. This also prevents us from being able to explore any variances within the category of 'Black British', or nuances around impacts of school exclusions for Black African groups. Where there is more nuanced data, Brent, Haringey and Wandsworth were among the local authorities with the highest risk of exclusion for Black Caribbean boys, with pupils in this group being 5.8 times, 5.1 times and 4.5 times more likely to be excluded than their white peers respectively (McIntyre et al, 2021). In the case of Croydon, in 2018–2019, Black British pupils made up 43 per cent of fixed term exclusions, with 60 per cent of Black pupils excluded of a Caribbean background and 40 per cent Black African (O'Connor, 2020). In 2015–2016, Lewisham had the highest rate of secondary school exclusions in London at 0.5 per cent, and Ealing (0.33 per cent), Enfield (0.21 per cent), Hackney (0.19 per cent), Lambeth (0.14 per cent) and Newham (0.14 per cent) all had exclusion rates above the national average of 0.08 per cent for the same year (DfE, 2017). This is a serious concern, especially given that the representation of Black Caribbean groups across these wards constitutes 35.3 per cent of all Black Caribbean groups in England and Wales. As such, a significant proportion of Black Caribbean pupils are living in wards with the highest exclusion rates in London, and exclusion practices impact on Black Caribbean boys more than almost every other ethnic group.

The emphasis on Black Caribbean groups is significant not least because of the ways in which they have been so consistently disenfranchised throughout the history of secondary schooling in the UK. From its inception, it is evident that secondary education never considered allowing capacity for minority ethnic communities arising from postwar migration to be equitable stakeholders in the 'equality of opportunity for all' promised in the Butler Act of 1944 as part of the state guarantee against personal misfortune embedded in the welfare state. Nevertheless, the relationship between immigration and education was framed in very specific ways at this point in the epoch, within which state secondary education was in its infancy, represented through much more solid institutional forms, processes and practices. Those arriving from the Caribbean in the postwar period were met with a public political response advocating for their assimilation into a pre-existing and solid vision of British culture, an incarnation which had hardened following the domestic hardships of the Second World War, and the national spirit which accompanied them. In this context, children of families from Black Caribbean backgrounds were 'bussed' or distributed across schools to ensure assimilation into British culture and, where the education system failed to facilitate their learning effectively, found themselves disproportionately allocated to schools for the educationally sub-normal (see Coard, 1971). The solid structures which enforced both assimilation and educational displacement on Black Caribbean pupils were part of the wider provision for secondary education concurrent with the establishment of the solid-modern welfare state and the state-guaranteed insurance against individual misfortune (Bauman, 1998). We have seen the slow liquification of this educational system, from the neoliberalization facilitated through standardized assessments and national league tables facilitating parental choice through the Education Reform Act 1988 to the erosion of Local Education Authorities in the governance of education following the Academies Act of 2010. State schooling under Local Authority control gradually liquified through the neoliberalization of quasi-education markets in the 1990s, with governance eventually flowing from local state to academy trust jurisdiction after 2010. Yet even in the light of all of these changes, the racialized outcomes for Black Caribbean groups as stakeholders in education have persisted, with there being no apparent benefit to them arising from the liquification of the old structures which so forcibly disempowered the children of the Windrush generation.

Government data on the representation of Black African groups by local authority are not available, and so it is not possible to draw direct comparisons with the representation of Black African groups in local authorities within which Black Caribbean boys have such elevated risks of exclusion. There are also wider inconsistencies with other datasets which might be used to indicate ethnicity by local authority area. Figures often only report on a broader ethnic category of 'Black British'. What can be identified is that 58 per cent of Black African groups and 57.9 per cent of Black Caribbean groups living in the UK live in London (UK Government, 2018). While it is not yet possible to identify whether there are comparable representations of Black African and Black Caribbean groups in specific local authorities, the inference can be made that there is at least a racializing effect occurring for Black Caribbean boys which is not impacting on Black African boys to the same degree in the local authorities with the highest overrepresentation in exclusion rates. While there is data for Croydon which raise some serious concerns for Black African groups in that local authority, access to more detailed data on the representation of Black African groups by local authority is needed in order to gain a more substantive picture of how locality impacts risk of school exclusion for these groups. The almost identical trends in exclusions more generally between Black Caribbean groups and pupils of dual heritage white British and Black Caribbean backgrounds means that the inference can also be made that the impact of space and place on risk of exclusion is likely to be the same for dual heritage white and Black Caribbean boys as it is for Black Caribbean boys living in these local authorities. In this context, boys with a Black Caribbean background or dual heritage white and Black Caribbean background in their years 9 and 10 of secondary schooling and who live in the most problematic local authorities identified previously have the most elevated risk of exclusion.

The preceding analysis demonstrates a *passive* form of tacit intentionality which ensures racist outcomes, but without any clear declaration of an agenda. By way of contrast, the active efforts to monitor pupil nationality were laden with a latent intentionality characterized by increasing anti-immigration narratives in the wider public political arena. However, school exclusions have no clear or apparent racialized agenda. The ability to permanently exclude pupils came into effect through amendments to the processes around exclusions in the Education Act of 1986 (Kulz, 2019: 94). The amendments were focused on the procedure for appealing an exclusion and saw a change from appeal panels having the power to reinstate a pupil where they ruled in their favour to being able to only direct governors who sanctioned the head's decision to reconsider (Kulz, 2019: 94). Where there is no clear or definitive focus on any racialized minority group, racist outcomes have consistently impacted Black Caribbean groups over time (Hamilton, 2018: 578). *Passivity* highlights how an apparently passive process devoid of any discernible focus on racialized minority groups can be considered to bear any *intentionality*. The notion of *passive* tacit intentionality demonstrates that the ways in which school exclusions have persistently displaced Black Caribbean and dual heritage white and Black Caribbean pupils, yet school exclusions continue to be used as common practice. This is not a simple matter of identifying a problem which has been overlooked in education policy and practice – the very evidence drawn upon has most substantively been published by the UK government and its affiliated agencies such as the DfE. How far can we then suggest that policy makers could not possibly know of the racist outcomes that have persisted because of allowing school exclusions to remain common practice in the UK education system? And why, in light of this evidence, have exclusions been allowed to continue? The implicit answer to these questions indicates the absence of an agenda concerned with addressing these racialized inequalities even in the light of clear evidence which constitutes passive tacit intentionality. *Passivity* in the light of *evidence* effectively demonstrates an *intentionality* to allow existing racist processes to continue unchecked. As argued by Gillborn (2005), it is the continued implementation of strategies, which have a proven record of disadvantaging specific racialized groups, which constitutes tacit intentionality on the part of policy makers. The decision to disengage or the failure to act to rectify these inequalities is a political act in and of itself (Preston and Chadderton, 2012: 92), and an act of allegiance with the reproduction of racism in liquid modernity.

We contend that passive tacit intentionality represents a process of ensuring the endurance of racialized outcomes which is difficult to easily identify, owing to its apparent lack of any agenda relating to 'race'. In this context, identifying apparently neutral practices as racist can easily be dismissed as paranoia, readily met with second guessing and demands for evidence that these outcomes are not derived from other factors. Racism in this form is a far cry from the more tangible or solidified forms which characterized racism in the context of modernity. Rather, we see racisms that are ubiquitously present but not clearly delineated, and such 'liquid racisms' – unlike 'solid racisms' – are not easily noticeable. The ambiguity around intentionality constitutes one of the ways in which racism has become more difficult to detect, while simultaneously continuing to facilitate observable racist outcomes in the context of liquid modernity. These processes indeed collude with the wider sense of always being on the move in liquid modernity, under threat and experiencing feelings of ontological insecurity. This has clearly been realized for Black Caribbean groups and dual heritage white and Black Caribbean groups as stakeholders in education. However, this sense of ontological security also applies within educational institutions and may inform adopting routines and strategic performances as coping mechanisms against the fear of the unknown and specifically against perceptions of strangerhood (Giddens, 1991). Perhaps it is this fear and uncertainty around how to accommodate Black Caribbean boys as a long-constructed 'stranger' in educational settings, a reminder of the educational failures of the past, which fuels a sense of ontological insecurity resulting in their disproportionate exclusion in the context of liquid modernity. Liquid modernity is open to structural amnesia and reinvention, and the tacit intentionality around school exclusions arguably represents one of the ways in which the education system has embodied this as a way of sustaining the racist intolerance and the displacement of groups who have historically been most marginalized within it.

School exclusion represents one of the processes in contemporary education in the UK whereby racialized outcomes have become differentiated within the wider racial categories which informed more solidified racist processes in modernity. With regard to school exclusions, we appear to see a slow liquification of the broader racial categories of modernity which has allowed for differential and nuanced vulnerabilities around school exclusions for Black British groups. There are variances in the viscosities of racial flows, to the extent that some groups *do* continue to experience educational displacement as a result of more solidified processes. For travellers of Irish heritage and Gypsy Roma groups, educational institutions respond to nomadic learning with high levels of viscosity and resistance to accommodation to the point of immovable solidification around protocols around attendance, the prerequisite for permanent enrolment in access to education. Concurrent to their exclusion via solidified institutional resistances to the cultural nuances that inform nomadic learning, the fact that these groups occupy such a liminal relationship to whiteness, while also broadly being perceived of as white groups, further demonstrates the ambiguity around racist flows in liquid modernity.

Liquid racism in action: opening the dam on attainment benchmark measures

So far, this chapter has considered how wider public political flows have impacted on perceptions of the state of race inequalities in education, and what this meant for the monitoring of migrant groups in education through active tacit intentionality. It has also considered school exclusions as a more passive form of tacit intentionality which has impacted long-established Black Caribbean groups in education. Attainment within education represents another interesting site for discussion, not least because persistent racialized inequities in educational attainment highlight one of the clearest examples of how wider racialized barriers to social mobility are maintained. As has been argued by Breen elsewhere, the implications of racialized inequities in education do not stop at educational failure for individual children (Breen, 2023). Problems relating to attainment gaps for Black students are not confined to compulsory education, with Black students being found to be more likely to engage in their studies, but only 53 per cent graduating with a first or 2.1 compared with 78 per cent of white students (Busby, 2019). The reproduction of such race inequalities has wider implications for the social positioning of individuals over the life course, one of which is likely to be increased viscosity in achieving social mobility through legitimate employment markets. It is important to identify the state of race inequalities relating to attainment in the UK education system. For the year 2020–2021, the national average for pupils achieving a level 5 in English and maths was 51.9 per cent. Against this figure, groups which had attainment levels below the national average were Pakistani (50.3 per cent), Black Caribbean (35.9 per cent), Black other (45.1 per cent), mixed white and Black African (50 per cent), mixed white and Black Caribbean (39.1 per cent), white British (50.9 per cent), Gypsy Roma (9.1 per cent) and Irish traveller (21.1 per cent) (UK Government, 2022). Many other ethnic groups have attainment levels substantially higher than the national average, with British Indian (72.4 per cent), Asian other (67.1 per cent), Chinese (83.8 per cent) and mixed white and Asian (62.1 per cent) all attaining more than ten percentage points above the national average. If we consider the attainment of Pakistani, white British, Black African, and mixed white and Black African groups, while attainment levels are below the national average, the difference is marginal, being within two percentage points of the national average – a figure which will have been influenced by the significantly high rates of attainment in groups performing above the national average. The groups where we see the most substantive inequalities in attainment are identical to those overrepresented in school exclusions: Black Caribbean, mixed white and Black Caribbean, Gypsy Roma and Irish traveller. This suggests that, even for those who are not excluded, the education system facilitates comparable disenfranchisement through the medium of inequities in attainment. Considering attainment more widely, similar patterns are revealed. Attainment 8 scores measure pupil attainment at state-funded schools in England across eight GCSE-level qualifications including English and maths (UK Government, 2022b). The national attainment average by this measure is 50.9 per cent, and British Indian (62 per cent), Asian other (58.6 per cent), and Chinese (69.2 per cent) all substantially exceed this (UK Government, 2022b). It is not possible to draw direct comparisons as attainment for English and maths is measured as a percentage, whereas attainment 8 scores are an average of pupil scores out of 90 across eight subjects. Nevertheless, the same trends in attainment can clearly be seen, with Black Caribbean (44 per cent), mixed white and Black Caribbean (45 per cent), Gypsy Roma (22.7 per cent) and Irish traveller (30.7 per cent) having attainment 8 scores which indicate the most substantive educational inequities against the national average (UK Government, 2022b).

These differences in measured attainment, along with the fact that these groups map directly onto those most displaced from educational opportunities through school exclusions, paint a very different picture to the image of the white working classes as the new racialized underachievers – a product of postracialism and casualties of the multicultural project. This represents one of the key conditions of racism in liquid modernity – the ability for the postracial state to not only mask but also facilitate the persistence of racial flows (see Chapter 3 for a full explanation of this process). Tacit intentionality certainly seems like an effective strategy for maintaining the persistence of these flows while maintaining a façade of public political commitment to political progressiveness in relation to 'race'. Evidence of this can also be seen regarding how the kinds of inequalities on educational attainment are sustained. Gillborn and colleagues (2017) provide an interesting analysis on the ways in which 'dominant benchmark measures of attainment' have been adjusted over time, and what this has meant for disparities in educational attainment between Black Caribbean and white British groups. Following the introduction of GCSE examinations with the 1988 Education Reform Act, the dominant benchmark measure for attainment was generally understood to be five GCSEs at grade C or above in any subjects (Gillborn et al, 2017: 12). By this benchmark of five 'good' grades across *any* subjects, by 2013 the gap in attainment between white British and Black Caribbean had narrowed from 22 percentage points at its widest in 1993 and 1996, to just two percentage points (Gillborn et al, 2017). However, this original benchmark was adjusted in 2006 with the introduction of a 'tougher' new 'gold standard', which required 'good' grades in English and maths to be among the five subjects which students should demonstrate a grade of C or above (Gillborn et al, 2017: 14).

The impact of this change affected attainment for Black Caribbean groups severely, and disparities with white British groups grew from 12.8 percentage points under the original benchmark in 2005 (a gap which history would eventually show was well on its way to closing) to 15 percentage points under the 'gold standard' (Gillborn et al, 2017: 14). Following some adjustment, attainment overall improved, with Black Caribbean students benefiting, such that by 2010, disparities in attainment compared with white British groups narrowed from 15 percentage points in 2006 to 11.4 percentage points in

2010 (Gillborn et al, 2017: 14). The shift to the Coalition government in 2010 saw new steps taken to establish a new benchmark (Gillborn et al, 2017: 14) – the English Baccalaureate – to include five GCSEs at grade C or above in English, maths, two sciences, a humanities subject and a foreign or ancient language (DfE, 2010b, para 61). Against the new English Baccalaureate benchmark, attainment fell dramatically for all groups (Gillborn et al, 2017: 15). A total of 84 per cent of Black Caribbean students who met the gold standard failed to meet the new benchmark, compared to 73 per cent for white British groups (Gillborn et al, 2017: 15). The shift was substantial and saw a gap of 9.4 percentage points under the gold standard, with 58.2 per cent of white British groups hitting the benchmark compared to 48.6 per cent of Black Caribbean groups. This amounts to a 7.7 percentage point gap, but whereby only 7.6 per cent of Black Caribbean pupils achieved the E.Bacc compared with 15.3 per cent of white British groups (Gillborn et al, 2017: 16). This effectively meant that in terms of proportionality, under the new benchmark Black Caribbean groups were now half as likely to achieve the English Baccalaureate than white British groups. While there has been considerable improvements in the achievement of Black students over time, relative to their white peers and attainment against shifting dominant benchmarks, educational disparities have remained remarkably consistent (Gillborn et al, 2017: 2).

The extent to which the persistent changes in what constitutes dominant attainment benchmarks for attainment in secondary schooling are active or passive is perhaps more ambiguous than the examples we have considered. However, based on the racialized outcomes of these changes, it is clear that the constant shifting of goalposts (Gillborn et al, 2017) bears all the hallmarks of tacit intentionality. Gillborn and colleagues' analysis demonstrates not only uncertainty around progressive gains with regard to race inequalities in education which is consistent with the nature of racism in liquid modernity, but also demonstrates 'the speed with which they can be rolled back by apparently technical changes in how "standards" are measured and debated' (Gillborn et al, 2017: 2). Changes in 'dominant benchmark measures of attainment' (Gillborn et al, 2017) appear to constitute a cycle which resets racialized inequities in education insofar that it appears they may start to close. This process flows from policy makers downwards, with each change to attainment expectations representing points in time where dams are momentarily opened, and surges in flows of racist, yet tacit, intentionality, ensuring that educational equity remains ever elusive for the *real* racialized casualties of education. In the context of liquid modernity, it is important to consider how educational failure has become reformulated by the erosion of societal accountability for social inequalities. Educational outcomes become framed by individual accountability for successes *and* failures, with society being devoid of all responsibility. Against this backdrop, racialized educational inequalities become situated as the product of individual under-investment in education rather than of systemic, albeit liquified, processes of racialized marginalization.

Conclusion

This chapter has argued that education presents an almost perfect feature of the postracial state – an institution which on the surface advocates for equality of opportunity, but in practice utilizes seemingly neutral processes and strategies which actually consistently reproduce racialized outcomes. The ambiguity and uncertainties that policies characterized by tacit intentionality raise in relation to racialized inequities represent new challenges concerning even the acknowledgment of the presence of racism in the context of the more liquified racist processes which characterize education in late modernity. We are not only able to identify that racialized outcomes occur, but also *how they are able to occur in plain sight in the apparent absence of any clear or active racist agenda*. Through the tacit intentionality embedded within educational policy and practice, the cumulative outcomes of reliably racist processes results in a swelling, whereby racialized groups which are most marginalized are displaced, flowing into liminal spaces, and contained by increasing viscosity when attempting formal and accepted pathways to social mobility.

The prospect of contending with racisms such as those demonstrated through the example of education in the context of liquid modernity is an unstable process. While there has been a liquification of the more solidified structures which characterized racism in modernity, we do not suggest that racism has in any real way become less present in the context of liquid modernity. Furthermore, we also contend that moments of solidification in the educational institutions of liquid modernity will replicate racisms in the forms in which they existed more consistently in the older educational structures of modernity. What we have been able to observe is that racism, while consistently at work in the educational institutions of liquid modernity, functions in ways which are fluid and elusive, posing ambiguous and nuanced risks of highly racialized outcomes. Variances in exposure to racialized flows in educational settings are evident in the ability for many groups to succeed and even excel in education, while other groups are consistently faced with not only greater exposure to racialized flows but also greater viscosities in navigating access to education and educational attainment as a pathway to social mobility. As we have seen with Black British groups, variances in the viscosities of racialized flows are apparent, with higher and lower levels of viscosity impacting on educational inequities, at least with regard to exclusion and educational attainment. In addition, we have seen degrees of intersectional solidification, with gender, space and place, socioeconomic factors, and immigration status intersecting alongside race in a confluence around dynamics of identity. Within such confluences, we find nuanced and varying viscosities and degrees of glaciation, whose forms are informed by the cumulative build-up of sedimentary compounds arising from flows around multiple dynamics of identities. With regard to race, educational spaces occupy many states and forms in relation to the solidity of their structures, with many concurrently existing states being simultaneously present, informing dramatic variances in educational opportunities and outcomes. The liquid school is an uncertain space, capable of adopting many and varied forms with varying degrees of viscosity and even solidifications according to the intersectional dynamics of educational stakeholders.

We have also seen how liquid racism in the context of education embodies and reflects the principles and premises of the postracial state. The embodiment of anti-immigration narratives in the wider public political sphere and their implications for the damming of access to educational spaces for minority ethnic groups with questionable immigration status represents a clear backflow against perceptions of postracial idealism having gone too far under New Labour. Tacit intentionality has been key for understanding how policy facilitates and even ensures more elusive forms of racisms which flow below the surface, hidden from view in the educational and public policy mainstream. Racism in this context is for the most part elusive as an identifiable flow for those not directly in the path of its flow, yet embodies a consistency which ensures enduring viscosities in access to education, educational qualifications and social mobility. These processes collectively see 'race' constituted in ambiguous ways, resulting in uncertainties about when racialized flows will increase in their intensity, when waters might be calmer, and moments where transient serenity might fleetingly indicate that the flow has finally passed. This uncertainty exists concurrently with perceptions that a state of postraciality has solidified enough to protect those previously subjected to racialized flows, damming and channelling them away as a feature of the educational past. However, as we have seen in Chapter 4, and as we have explored through the examples in education considered in this chapter, these moments never exist in any meaningful way other than in the false perception of their reality.

6

Liquid Racism and Road Culture(s)

Introduction

In this chapter we will seek to develop the liquid metaphor to help aid our understanding of an issue which has received consistent media attention in recent years in the UK; that is, the recent popular panic linking drill music to violent crime. To understand how contemporary racism operates in a liquid society (Bauman, 2000), we have to conduct analyses which offer nuanced and intricate ways of understanding social problems. Drill music is a subgenre of rap which has its origins in the southside of Chicago, where artists like Chief Keef leveraged their gritty street sounds to launch themselves to global celebrity status. Sonically, drill and trap music have comparable sounds, using stripped-back ominous beats and borrowing heavily from the panacea of gangsta rap. Forrest Stuart (2020: 58) describes them thus: 'Both trap and drill embrace dissonant minor keys played on electronic synthesizers – something like Jaws, Psycho and suspenseful horror movies. The booming 808 drum machines provides percussive punch. The kick drums, snares and hi-hats are often layered in rapid sequences that simulate the sound of an automatic machine gun.'

Both subgenres (but drill in particular) have become well known for specific kinds of provocative street aesthetics. Accompanying music videos tend to have a DIY feel, commonly filmed within the physical spaces of the artists' neighbourhoods and usually featuring groups of people (predominantly young men) presenting some affinity to one another and the space(s) depicted. Artists like Chief Keef and their associates have been known to brandish automatic firearms in videos, along with balaclavas and masks. Lyrically these subgenres tend to match the provocative visual, with lyrics pertaining to drugs, violence and some of the grittier realities of life in the American ghetto.

It is hard to pinpoint exactly when drill and trap began being produced in the UK context, but some commentators claim it began in the south

London neighbourhood of Brixton around 2012, before spreading to other surrounding areas and being produced nationwide (Children's Society, 2021), with the varying regional accents becoming a feature of the UK scene. These subgenres have contributed to the growth of UK rap in terms of chart success. In recent times rap and hip-hop music have achieved exponential growth in terms of consumption in the UK (BPI, 2023). For example, singles consumption of titles classified as rap and hip-hop have increased from 3.6 per cent in 1999 to 22 per cent in 2020 overall, with UK rap and hip-hop artists responsible for around 7.3 per cent (BPI, 2023). BPI themselves cite well-known UK rap artists like Nines, Headie One, Stormzy, Dave, Digga D, Tion Wayne and Little Simz, some of whom have at least featured on drill or trap-type beats, as being the driving force behind the growth of the consumption of UK-based artists in this category, citing various top 10 singles released from UK rap and hip-hop artists.

This UK-based success has not come without significant controversy as the anti-establishment sentiment and allusions to crime and violence have caught the attention of authorities. 'Drill music' in particular has been singled out by Cressida Dick, the former Commissioner of the Metropolitan Police, as inciting real-world violence (Waterson, 2018). However, others have been critical of the response of authorities, claiming that the music is an expression of the realities experienced by marginalized communities and that their punitive attitudes towards it is an indication of institutional racism predominantly targeted at Black communities (Fatsis, 2019a). This chapter will seek to work through the complex, historically routed and contemporarily ambivalent relationship between racism(s) and the responses to drill music.

It is an interesting coincidence that rhythm and poetry is at the centre of this analysis, as Bauman (2000: 203) himself advocated for the 'art of sociology', breaking with methodological convention and following the 'true poets' to 'pierce the walls of the self-evident' offered by the dominant ideological thinking of the day – in this way hoping to find insights into the 'yet hidden human possibilities' made most perceptible through the arts. This irony is not lost on us. Approaching street culture and its connections to rap music in this way will hopefully help to draw out some of these qualities inherent in the art form, allowing them rise to the surface and making them knowable in a slightly different way, by placing them within the context of the sociological imagination (Mills, 1959).

Each of the authors of this book has different specialist interests which have been explored here. These contribute to our 'cognitive a priori' (Bauman, 1967). Central to Bauman's artistic approach to sociology was an epistemological perspective which accepts the subjective nature of human experience. This itself can be challenging for contemporary researchers; it is still common for academics to aspire to positivistic methods and scientific framings of the knowledge they produce. While it may be a stretch to suggest previous work relating to life on road (Bakkali, 2019, 2022; Bakkali and Chigbo, 2023) sought scientific status in its epistemological aspirations, that body of work was still largely written using data collected via various, widely recognized research methods/methodologies. Bauman's approach to sociology as an art involved incorporating a range of cultural sources into his sociological imagination – largely rejecting more main*stream* methods of data collection (Jacobsen, 2013). He did large-scale thinking using this range of cultural resources to paint vivid images of his analyses of society.

We will work to embrace aspects of Bauman's way of thinking and writing about the social world. Yusef Bakkali has a personal connection to communities where road life as well as drill music are a part of social life, where friends and family have themselves traversed both the roads and the music industry, allowing insights perhaps outside of the traditional focus of academic enquiry. In addition, academic research into both rap music and road life (Bakkali, 2019, 2021; Bakkali and Chigbo, 2023) have informed these understandings further. This chapter is a reflection which draws together various sources of knowledge in what might be considered nontraditional ways. Drawing inspiration from Bauman, this analysis seeks to help elucidate some of the ways in which race and racism(s) are pertinent to this specific area of social life and the framing of perceived social problems.

To do this, we will examine the ways in which flows of racism(s), which are influential in producing conditions in specific contexts, subsequently flow into one another, leading to sometimes more intense instances of structural violence and racism. This is a complex and often uneven process, making it especially challenging to analyse. This will involve examining the historical damming of Black cultural flows through the historical policing/restriction of Black music and cultural expression. We will then consider the role of racism and structural violence in forging the hardened masculinities which are commonly depicted in street cultural settings. This is complicated as this work does not seek to establish truth in stereotype, but instead the ways in which stereotypes and other aspects of marginality and exclusion resulting from racism leave sections of those from Black and other minoritized backgrounds vulnerable to the processes which would cultivate hypermasculine responses, in a sense demonstrating that where this does occur, racism is a feature in its development, affecting minoritized people. Next, we will consider the role of the market in further exacerbating aspects of street masculinities, with racialization and fetishism features in constructing markets whereby particular kinds of hypermasculine performativity might be consumed. The final part of this analysis will examine the state responses to new cultural flows of UK rap music by trying to resurrect their dams in the digital age, seeking to clamp down on the hypermasculine performativity and allusions to violence featured in drill and trap music – yet this response is blinkered in its inability to view the role of racialization/racism in these processes, failing to address many of the causal factors and instead potentially deepening processes of marginalization.

These processes lead to deeply ambivalent outcomes, as while the success of UK rap music is laudable and deeply meaningful for those whose life possibilities it has changes, as well as many more who find representation and joy in the music; it also illustrates deep social problems in terms of social deprivation, the continued survival of problematic racialized tropes and the limited sympathy and/or understanding policy makers and law enforcers are willing/able to demonstrate for those experiencing these difficulties. At times it appears that the performativity those wishing to change or provide commentary on their situations through music provides the ammunition to those in power to perpetuate the marginalization, and so musical subgenres like drill can lead to suffering for many.

Road culture and street masculinities

Road culture (Gunter, 2008, 2010) is a U-based variation of 'street culture' with discernible cultural connections to the Caribbean and the US. Commonly road life in the UK is strongly associated with symbols of Black Atlantic popular culture (Gilroy, 1993) embodied in fashion, speech and musical tastes, with rap music being a particular mainstay. UK rap music is examined as a kind of case study demonstrating wider processes of social change and liquefaction. It is important to emphasize that the connections between UK rap and road life are particular and not universal, as it is predominantly specific subgenres like drill and trap which are closely associated with street culture in the UK. Indeed, youth worker and social critic, Ciaran Thapar (2021) observed that despite drill music emerging in the 2010s in Chicago, it is a subgenre which communicates via a personalized, explicitly digital wavelength, which young people living in proximity to road life can recognize and relate to. This sensitized connectivity echoes other observations around the mobility of concepts like 'ghettoness' which are able to become itinerant, articulating themselves to identities in spaces far from their origins due to their shared axes of marginality (van Hellemont, 2012).

Indeed, 'road life' is itself not an unproblematic space/grouping, existing both in physical reality and online spaces as well as exteriorly at the level of representation (Hall et al, 1978). Thus, definitively drawing cultural or spatial borders in relation to road life is problematic, as it contains multiple, complex and often contradictory sets of meanings and modes of being – something shared with other street cultural spaces (Ilan, 2017). We can see this even within the limited literature on road culture in the UK. Layers of differential representation coexist, with accounts depicting it as a youth culture particularly involving teens (Gunter, 2010) as well as one involving somewhat older people (Glynn, 2014; Bakkali, 2019). Commonly in criminological studies, it is depicted as a volatile and spectacularly violent space (Hallsworth and Silverstone, 2009) while in other studies it is described as predominantly being about mundane activities focused on leisure, passing time and economic survival (Gunter, 2010). Similar contradictions emerge when it comes to gendered possibilities, with some studies portraying a violently patriarchal street space where young women face victimization (Young and Trickett, 2017) and others highlighting the ways in which women themselves can successfully negotiate and embody aspects of hegemonic masculinity becoming agentic actors on road (Choak, 2021). Our position is that to an extent, all these representations reflect situated (Bakkali, 2021) aspects of life on road, making it a diverse, hybrid, deeply ambivalent and liquid culture and concept.

This ambivalence has potentially been underexplored, particularly in relation to race and racism. In recent years, use of the term 'road' and associated representations have repeatedly surfaced in popular discourse and culture, through news, social media, drama series, comedy, politics and music, to name but a few. Throughout dominant representations of road culture, there are a consistent set of associations with Blackness, as well as criminality, policing and inner-city council estates. Many of the tropes associated with the 'roadman' follow trajectories of popular Western racialization which include depictions like the 'bad buck' (Hall et al, 1978), 'Black macho' (Sernhede, 2000), 'gangsta/rapper' (Hall et al, 1978; bell hooks, 2004) and 'mugger' (Hall et al, 1978), among others. Indeed, it is not a stretch to claim that road culture is often (mis)cast as an exclusively 'Black thing' or 'problem', in many senses representing how many of the signifiers associated with it are clearly racialized. Yet, these same signifiers also intersect or are appropriated in more main*stream* forms of 'popular culture', making them slippery to dissect in terms of their relationship to race and racism. Perhaps the promise of intellectual fluidity and mobility offered by Bauman's liquid metaphor can help to capture these inconsistencies and confluences.

The concept of ambivalence is of particular importance in this chapter. In his book *Modernity and Ambivalence* (1991a), Bauman views ambivalence as the 'permanent companion' of language, as its naming/classifying function seeks to help make meaning of the world we inhabit. As language seeks to render the world knowable by classifying entities and situations, it creates categories which depend on inclusion and exclusion. Ambivalence occurs when entities do not neatly occupy assigned classifications and have multiple and even often contradictory sets of meanings. Resisting ambivalence through further, more meticulous naming and classifying also gives rise to further possibility for ambivalence, thus making it seemingly inevitable in Bauman's thinking, though this does not prevent actors from waging a 'bitter and relentless war against ambivalence' (1991a: 3).

We have already witnessed ambivalence in action relating to studies of road culture, as different sets of meanings are applied to one concept/category. It is the relationship to 'race' and racism with which this chapter will be specifically concerned, though the interconnected nature of concepts may at times draw on intersecting concepts like social class. We will engage with the recent main*stream* traction of UK rap music and subsequent controversies. There is a sense at times that these controversies are dehistoricized as culturally, geographically and temporally isolated issues, with efforts to re-embed them into their social context essential if one wishes to have any hope to better understand them. This process involves intellectual journeying through both time and space, attempting to account for the shifting consistency of the social world. We will continue with our analysis by exploring further the 'street' or 'hyper' masculinities associated with road life, trying to understand how processes of race and racism have a role in forging hardened dispositions among marginalized people.

Street masculinities and road life: a confluence of causes

The section is included to help the reader to understand some of the ways in which the hardened masculinities on show in rap lyrics and performance, currently under state scrutiny, are at least in part a response to racisms in the UK and beyond. It is difficult to analyse the UK in isolation due to parallels and cross-cultural flows, particularly between the UK and the US. The shared histories of colonialism and slavery also cause overlaps and blur lines.

Street masculinities have been well documented worldwide, with many studies as well as media content examining the formation of masculinities at the margins. It is not the authors' position that even a majority of minoritized people in the UK hold such values or comportments, but more a demonstration of the ways in which racisms mean that minoritized people are made vulnerable to developing them as a defence against the hostilities of a society permeated by racisms, as well as being seduced by the ontological security offered by stereotypical identity performance in the context of structural inequalities and other social pressures. The socializing effects of racism vary across a continuum which on the one hand disproportionately leads minoritized groups to come into contact with hardship and structural violence and on the other hand utilizes high-profile industries like sports and music to give an artificial impression of opportunity (Orelus, 2010), promoting stereotypical dispositions and qualities among marginalized groups which might offer possibilities in specific social settings and popular culture, but disadvantage them in other main*stream* institutions.

Despite the range of perspectives on road culture, many studies agree on the importance of toughness to everyday life and survival on road (Hallsworth and Silverstone, 2009; Gunter, 2010; Glynn, 2014; Bakkali, 2018, 2019, 2022; King and Swain, 2023; Reid and Ilan, 2023). Even a cursory look will reveal similar literature on masculinities in street spaces from diverse locations such as the US (Bourgois, 1996; Anderson, 2000); the Nordic region (Sandberg and Pedersen, 2009; Kalkan, 2022) Brazil (Salem and Larkins, 2021) and Trinidad (Baird et al, 2022), for example. It would be a mistake to fall foul of any 'assumed similarity' between these contexts, as distinctive histories and social processes led to their formation on the margins in each context; however, often they are preceded by racisms, patriarchy, social exclusion, poverty, actual and/or structural violence and instability. So, while we have seen earlier on that general concepts and street representations are able to travel and cross-pollinate in other areas experiencing marginality (van Hellemont, 2012; Thapar, 2021; Kalkan, 2022), these spaces are still distinct with their own historical, ethnic and structural-make up.

Street masculinities are often regarded as a response to the harsh conditions of marginality combined with the pressures of patriarchy (Miller, 1958; Bourgois, 1996; bell hooks, 2000), serving those occupying such spaces as an 'armor [*sic*] against their world' (Coates, 2015: 14). Protest masculinity (Connell, 1995) is a term coined to help understand the development of hypermasculinities which borrow themes from hegemonic masculinities, but recontextualize them into the limits of lives on the margins. When men become strongly disadvantaged in the labour market and other areas of society, they adopt exaggerated styles of masculinity to enact a sense of power which compensates for their social dislocation from 'factory floor'-style working-class masculinities (see Willis, 1977). Interestingly, protest masculinity as proposed by Connell (1995) has its intellectual roots in the work of psychiatrist Alfred Adler. Adler's idea of 'masculine protest' is a condition demonstrated by both men and women against feminine weakness in a society as a way of devaluing the feminine. Protest masculinity does not refer to an individual condition, but is more of a sociological formation operating across a society of inherent contradictions. The basic idea is that capitalism does not offer the possibilities for the realization of hegemonic masculinity across society and some men who are surplus to or have a marginal stake in the labour market are unable to embody dominant forms of masculinity, and subsequently are vulnerable to feelings of impotence and emasculation, leading to hypermasculine forms of performance, with Connell (1995: 110) listing behaviours like 'violence, school resistance, minor crime, heavy drug/alcohol use, occasional manual labour, motorbikes or cars, short heterosexual liaisons'.

Poynting et al (1998: 78) highlight Connell's (1995: 80) observation that 'race relations' as well as social class influence the formation of masculinities. In their study on Lebanese young men living in Australia, they highlighted the ways in which these men were disadvantaged and discriminated against, with the repeated experience of being called 'wogs' by Anglo-Australians leading to them engaging in violence and anti-authoritarian attitudes in response. Poynting et al emphasize that 'race' and ethnicity is an axis along with class and gender that informs the formation of masculinities in society:

> It is important to stress that this is a gendered, a masculine, reassertion of dignity in the face of racist affront … It is as if, in experiencing diminution as humans, through racism, these young men are experiencing diminution as men; offence to their humanity is an affront to their manhood. (Poynting et al, 1998: 88)

While it would be wrong to attempt to explain the formation of street dispositions or violent masculinities as exclusively the products of racism in the UK, disproportionality and various forms of racism(s) have been influential factors among others (Gunter, 2010; Bakkali, 2019). In Chapter 5 we saw how supposedly neutral policies and educational processes disproportionately disadvantage specific populations. Considering that Connell's notion of protest masculinity is intricately connected to situations of social exclusion and powerlessness, one can begin to see how racial discrimination and disadvantage could contribute to the formation of such dispositions.

Working in the US context, Pierre Orelus (2010) made explicit the links between specific kinds of hyper-masculinities displayed by Black/brown men and slavery/colonialism. He argues that white upper-class Western men have established the norms of masculinity for other men since the colonial period, both in the West and globally. In the colonial encounter and subsequent years of slavery and exploitation, white masculinities were responsible for acts of extreme violence against both Black/brown men and women. Stories/stereotypes attempting to legitimize Western domination cast people from these places with what in the West would have been considered socially repressed characteristics like hyperviolence, low intelligence and hypersexuality. These dynamics have persisted, leaving in Baumanian terms 'sedimentary effects' in Western societies like the US and UK. It is impossible to 'fully understand' the masculinities of Black/brown men without incorporating knowledge of these histories of injustice. While acknowledging that patriarchy and other harmful masculinities existed in many places before colonial encounters and that there are many different kinds of masculinities exhibited by Black/brown men, Orelus (2010: 78–79) argues that Black/brown men displaying hyper/street masculinities are heavily influenced by socializing processes stemming from racism in white supremacist societies:

> The violent demonstration of masculinity of young black/brown men through gang violence and drug selling activities stems from

> having learned a false concept of masculinity from the media, the white patriarchal system … that is, men always have to be financially stable, strong, aggressive, powerful and in control of women. Being deprived of the resources, which could have enabled them to fulfil this male role, many black/brown men feel powerless in the eyes of their families and other men and women. To regain their maleness and masculinity, many of them, unfortunately, resort to what is available to them, including selling drugs in their communities … we need to understand the socioeconomic, historical and political root causes that lead many young black/brown people to become involved in drug selling. In my view the root causes, including unemployment, despair, hopelessness, and marginalisation, often derive from institutionalised racism. (Orelus, 2010: 78–79)

While there is evidence of non-white populations in the UK for a long time, the period after the Second World War saw a rapid growth in migration in Britain. Britain turned to its colonies and Europe to help fill labour shortages and rebuild a war-torn nation. The 1948 British Nationality Act legislated for the free movement of people from within the Empire to Britain, classifying them as Citizens of the United Kingdom and Colonies (Byrne et al, 2020), with schemes/recruitment drives set up to encourage those in the colonies to come to work in the 'motherland' (Sutcliffe-Braithewaite, 2018). These schemes recruited people from former colonies to work in the National Health Service (NHS), transport infrastructure and other industries, meaning that in large part, migrants were being attracted to large urban centres like London and Birmingham.

The reception to migrants from the former colonies, and subsequently the Commonwealth area, was often unwelcoming, with non-white migrants facing many inequalities in work and housing as well as overt forms of state and interpersonal racism. Subsequent revisions to immigration law sought to restrict the settlement of migrants from these groups. Acts like the 1962 Commonwealth Immigrants Act and the 1968 Commonwealth Immigration Act introduced quota systems and patriality respectively, with the former initially restricting flows of people who previously held freedom to move to the UK and the latter further limiting this by requiring those wishing to settle in the UK to prove they had a parent or grandparent with British citizenship. This also represented a shift from citizenship based on place of birth to a genealogical model which favoured white Old Commonwealth migrants (Byrne et al, 2020). Subsequent laws like the Immigration Act 1971 and the Nationality Act 1981 further limited flows from the Commonwealth. More recently, the 2014 and 2016 Immigration Acts followed the 2012 'hostile environment' initiative cooked up by the UK Home Office. These policies made it a legal requirement for in-house immigration checks to take place within the labour market, housing and education sectors, as well as making it easier to remove people from the UK and reducing the channels available to people to appeal these processes (Byrne et al, 2020).

One of the combined effects of the introduction of patriality in 1972 and the creation of the 'hostile environment' was that it led to issues for Commonwealth migrants who entered the UK before 1972 in terms of being able to 'prove' their status. This was the case for people who did not establish their status with further documentation like a passport, as at this time it was not deemed necessary; this was a particular problem for those who may have travelled to and settled in the UK as children under their parents' passports. This was also the case in government. In October 2010 under Home Secretary Theresa May, the loss of thousands of landing card slips recording the arrival dates of migrants from the Commonwealth made it harder to provide evidence for their claims relating to their status and arrival in the UK (Gentleman, 2019). The posthostile environment, where people were now being asked to evidence their citizenship status more than 40 years after it was legally established, led to many people from the Commonwealth and subsequently their children and grandchildren being unable to work or access basic services like healthcare (Gentleman, 2019). In a sense, this was a kind of rug-pulling of the legally acquired citizenship status of predominantly non-white people. While it might not seem immediately apparent, what came to be known as the 'Windrush Scandal' serves as a reminder of the added precariousness non-white people experience in the UK and the ways in which they can be plunged into extreme hardship at the whims of policy.

Burnett highlighted the ways in which ethnic and religious differences are also played on in political discourse, showing how blame is shifted for social problems by powerful groups onto those they are able to discern as 'others', usually in the form of migrants who are regarded as 'parasitic', using up resources like healthcare and housing while also eroding national culture and identity: 'the particular economic, political, domestic and international policies adopted by governments, in the nineteen years since Stephen Lawrence was killed, have both underpinned and exacerbated the formation of new patterns of racism and racial violence' (Burnett, 2012: 6).

Policy approaches like the hostile environment highlight the extent to which racial, ethnic and cultural difference is still a divisive topic in Britain. There has been a long history of racially motivated violent incidents with non-white people being targeted. The racist murder of Stephen Lawrence in 1993 is among the most high-profile in the UK. Stephen was waiting at a bus stop in Eltham with a friend (Duwayne Brooks) when he was attacked by a group of white youths who shouted racist slurs at him before brutally murdering him. Police at the scene failed to give Stephen any first aid and repeatedly failed to properly investigate his death, with officers apparently adopting 'racialising categorisations', assuming the case to be involving young Black men up to trouble (Holdaway, 1999). After many years of struggle, the 1999 Macpherson Report declared the Metropolitan Police 'institutionally racist', in that they failed to deliver equal protection and level of service to people based on their race or ethnicity (Macpherson, 1999).

In the years between 1993 (when Stephen was murdered) and 2011, the number of racist incidents reported to the police increased fivefold to 51,187 per year, with this exponential rise explained as being down to an increase in reporting of this type of crime (Burnett, 2012). There is debate as to whether this represents a rise in actual incidents or whether better reporting methods mean this is more of a partial unveiling of the extent of an existing problem; however, either way, it demonstrates a significant number of incidents. According to the Institute of Race Relations (IRR), between 1993 and 2013, there were at least 105 murders with a racial element or suspected racial element (IRR, 2020). The majority of those killed in these types of incidents are males under the age of 30, but incidents also include children, one of which was a three-year-old child who was killed in an arson attack on their home (Burnett, 2012). These deaths, which rarely received large-scale media coverage, serve as a reminder that the physical safety as well as the wellbeing and legal/social status of minoritized people in Britain are in certain cases threatened by racism.

In a similar vein, Ta-Nehisi Coates evocatively reflected on the connections to the past in the forging of street masculinities in America. Writing about the American context, he vividly contrasts the hardened masculinities of young men on his block, whose comportment demonstrated 'a catalogue of behaviors [*sic*] … enlisted to inspire the belief that these boys were in firm possession of everything they desired', against the 'nakedness' or vulnerability they experience in the face of 'visceral racism':

> [R]acism is a visceral experience, that it dislodges brains, blocks airways, rips muscle, extracts organs, cracks bones, breaks teeth. You must never look away from this. You must always remember that the sociology, the history, the economics, the graphs, the charts, the regressions all land, with great violence, upon the body … I think back on those boys now and all I see is fear, and all I see is them girding themselves against the ghosts of the bad old days when the Mississippi mob gathered 'round their grandfathers so that the branches of the black body might be torched, then cut away. The fear lived on in their practiced bop, their slouching denim, their big T-shirts, the calculated angle of their baseball caps, a catalogue of behaviors and garments enlisted to inspire the belief that these boys were in firm possession of everything they desired. (Coates, 2015: 10)

The changes leading up to the eventual hostile environment policies in some ways follow the logics of liquefaction as they produce greater insecurity among multiple generations of migrant groups, increasing their precarity. However, this policy direction also represents the resolidification and increase in 'security' against the uncertainty of global flows of migration. This demonstrates the ways in which 'race' is one of the deciding factors during processes of glaciation, whereby groups are offered differential protections based on their locatedness and influence. The working classes in the West have all suffered in the wake of deindustrialization, yet they appear to offer those groups who have power at the ballots, and to potentially disrupt capital flows, a sense of inclusion and security. In some ways, migrant and non-white groups become a kind of proxy upon which Western populations project their fears and insecurities: 'we seek substitute targets on which to unload the surplus existential fear that has been barred from its natural outlets' (Bauman, 2006: 11).

Bauman rightly points out that such activity only serves to deepen the crisis of insecurity for all. As these actions are supposedly designed to ameliorate the insecurity faced by white Western populations, they simultaneously deepen the sense of crisis. Moreover, deepening the actual marginality and violence faced by the other plunges the world into deeper chaos and insecurity: 'Each extra lock on the entry door in response to successive rumours of foreign-looking criminals in cloaks full of daggers … makes the world look more treacherous and fearsome and prompts more defensive action – that will alas, add more vigour to the self-propagating capacity of fear' (Bauman, 2006: 11–12).

It is understandable how the violence of racism, combined with a variety of other axes of marginality such as social class and patriarchy, lead to the 'hardening' of people who have to tolerate relentlessly violent realities at the hard edge of our societies. Anderson (2000) observed how predominantly African-American communities living in proximity to poverty and social suffering had to become literate in 'the code of the street'. He differentiated between those who lived a street lifestyle full time and those who aspired to respectable/decent social status but, due to their proximity to the unpredictable circumstances which can occur in the lives of those living on the margins, had to be able to demonstrate the capacity to take care of themselves and, if necessary, mobilize violence or at least its threat. Other theorists like Sandberg and Pedersen (2009) also observed code-switching behaviours in their study of street-oriented (predominantly non-white migrant) men in Oslo. This adds weight to the notion that such masculinities are complex and adaptive responses to specific social circumstances, which themselves are impacted upon by racisms.

Racisms pervade institutions such as the welfare state, education, employment (McGregor-Smith, 2017), main*stream* media (Hall et al, 1978), housing (UK Government, 2017), policing, courts and prisons (Lammy Review, 2017) – impacting on both lived realities and representations of Black communities. This leaves Black communities disproportionately at risk of being vulnerable to the sets of social forces which produce hypermasculinities along with the added pressure of existing stereotypes which researchers have found also weigh heavy on young Black men/boys, in particular damaging their performance/experiences in institutional spaces such as school (Steele, 1997; Gillborn, 2008). These stereotypes are compounded by other social inequalities – for example, all Black ethnic groups are disproportionately likely to live in the 10 per cent of most deprived neighbourhoods, which also equates to a tendency 'to be disadvantaged across multiple aspects of life' (Lammy, 2017: 33). Black groups have more than double the youth unemployment (30 per cent) of the white group (13.3 per cent), and forecasts also show that Black and Asian groups are and will continue to be overrepresented in the low-paid and intermediate-earning sectors of society (McGregor-Smith, 2017). In the post-industrial British cities to which many people migrated, job opportunities for both white and non-white working-class people have been radically transformed, with most jobs created tending to lean towards highly precarious, non-unionized and highly casualized work (Standing, 2011).

In the UK context (as well as elsewhere), there are also disproportionate outcomes in policing and convictions along axes of race. The Lammy Review (2017) identified worrying trends in the British criminal justice system. Non-white groups tended to be overrepresented at many stages of the criminal justice system from detection to arrest and subsequently conviction. Rates of arrest were higher among most racial minoritized groups when compared to the white group, with Black men three times more likely to be arrested than white men. Black women and boys were also markedly more likely to be arrested than their white counterparts. Disproportionality in arrests is also reflected in the disproportionality of stop-and-search statistics, with 27.2 searches for every 1,000 Black people taking place, compared to 5.6 for every 1,000 white people (UK Government, 2023). Postdetection and arrest, the Crown Prosecution System onwards added a further 'degree' of disproportionality but less pronounced than those as the stage of arrest, suggesting that the relationship between the police and non-white communities is a strong exacerbating factor in disproportionate outcomes in the criminal justice system (Lammy Review, 2017).

These inequalities close the field of legitimate opportunities for minoritized people as well as representing a kind of closing in of the punitive arms of the state. This puts minoritized people more at risk of living on low incomes, in poorer neighbourhoods, receiving less positive experience and outcomes in schooling, and being disproportionately more likely to come into contact with the police and the criminal justice system. These figures are averaged out across the population, and when you consider experiences of those living in the poorest neighbourhoods, this situation becomes far more acute. When legitimate possibilities are blocked, people search for alternative possibilities, establishing value systems where survival and certain forms of recognition are possible to them, even if these possibilities do not match those offered in main*stream* institutional space in many cases.

Questions of identity become pertinent in these situations, whereby minoritized people experience devaluation and search for meaningful identity projects to seek meaningful lives. This is also often the situation where the pressure and allure of stereotypes come into focus. Histories of slavery and forced migration, as well as other forms of migration caused by poverty and instability rooted in Western domination, have also led to 'ruptures' in the sense of self of young, non-white people in the UK (Hall, 2015). These genealogical and epistemological ruptures in time and space lead to the creation of a 'race of angels' (Fanon, cited in Hall, 1989: 7) where some young people experience ontological insecurity in their sense of self, making them especially vulnerable to the fixities of stereotypes and harmful behaviours present in their environment, as these root them to some extent in the known (Bakkali, 2019). Phoenix (2013: 10) highlights the ways in which these realities weigh on young people, damaging their sense of self: 'These psychological and sociological processes operate simultaneously to produce a process of subjectification in which children from the (ex-)colonies are positioned in ways that necessitate their engagement with constructions of themselves as devalued.'

Ilan (2015) highlights the ways in which street cultures often offer ways to provide greater sense of meaning in these contexts. They offer tough repertoires of conduct made up of hybrid cultural forms created by a multiplicity of global flows of people and cultures into local spaces. These repertoires ground these 'glocalities' into specific local space, giving a basis for meaning which provides possibilities for individuals with diverse background to develop meaningful interactions and friendships. The global flows of 'street tropes' (Ilan, 2017) from countries like Jamaica and the US, which themselves have long histories of violent racism, are also cultural reference points in the UK context, influencing popular vernaculars and comportment (Gunter, 2008). We can see wider global processes, if predominantly Western ones in the aforementioned examples, flowing into national and local processes of marginalization, furthering the pressures and expectations on young Black men in particular (but not exclusively) to embody tough street/hypermasculinities. This is an example of confluence. Sedimentary legacies of solid racism from local and global genealogies flow together to create contexts whereby hypermasculinities form.

In both the US and the UK research indicates that young Black men are commonly viewed in some ways as 'super-masculine' (Majors and Billson,

1992). They are constructed as possessing attributes which are considered to be most masculine: toughness and authentically male style in talk and dress. Paradoxically, while they are feared and discriminated against because of these features, they are also respected, admired and gain power through taking on characteristics which are antithetical to good classroom performance (Mac an Ghaill, 1986). We can see here the ambivalent and pervasive nature of racism, as its victims work to mitigate its negative effects, with some success at times, but the sedimentary formations and emerging confluences muddy the waters, reinforcing racialized systems of meaning. Street masculinities are often viewed in this way as a kind of self-defeating adaptation which, while serving some limited purpose in marginal street spaces, ultimately results in deeper marginalization as the attitudes and comportments demonstrated are seen as incompatible with main*stream* society and its institutions (for example, Harding, 2014).

Bakkali (2019) highlighted how these shifts in political economy have permeated the lives of young men living in proximity to serious violence on road. He draws on a vivid reflection of one of his participants around the gendered humiliation he experiences attending the Job Centre, the organization responsible for some of the delivery of welfare service provision in the UK. Young men like these were acutely disadvantaged in the labour market due to the deprivation they experienced across housing, schooling and other areas of life. These newer changes in political economy melded with older forms of inequality, serving to transfer the responsibility for their struggles to the site of the individual, leading to them to performatively struggle to relieve the stigma of the pathological status assigned to them. Bakkali described the discomfort experienced as a result of these multiple sources of personal difficulty and social stigma as *the munpain*, a kind of malaise with its origins in structural contradictions in which these young men lived, experienced every day in deeply personal ways.

A liquid metaphor can be developed in the context of the munpain. Imagine most people in the course of their daily lives traverse environments to conduct their business. While some people are walking normally with only the friction of the group and resistance of the air inhibiting them, others are wading through water and some still are trying to walk through treacle or quicksand. These are the differential experiences of the munpain. The structural impositions which impose disadvantage onto particular groups delimit their agency and ability to satisfy their needs and desires, causing them to experience greater frustration and difficulty. However, those that must walk through treacle analogously speaking do not necessarily perceive their problems such as structural impositions resulting from problems like racism, meaning that they internalize their difficulties compared to others as being caused by some personal deficit, subsequently further devaluing their sense of self and deepening their desperation, leading to malaise and suffering.

This multifaceted complexity makes writing about street/working-class masculinities and life in general very challenging. Typically, in working-class spaces certain hypermasculine dispositions can be valued; classic studies like Willis' (1977) *Learning to Labour* demonstrate some of the reasons why this was historically the case for white working-class neighbourhoods too. In addition, urban spaces are shared with other minoritized and marginal groups with their origins in places like the 'orient' who themselves have had their own histories of colonial 'othering' (Said, 1978). Moreover, groups categorized as Black are not homogeneous themselves and have rich and diverse cultural heritage. This itself is quite a fluid cultural formation at a micro-level, yet still even in this context, we can see the sediments of older solid structures re-embedding themselves in social life.

We can see that street masculinities or hypermasculinities themselves have racialized components, both in reality and at the level of representation, flowing into one another. The experiences of marginality, to which racism contributes, are foundational in the forging of these hardened dispositions. Those occupying these marginal spaces struggle for security and self-respect. Racisms have also played a part in rupturing and undermining cultural identities, which are commonly connected to ethnic origins. Those growing up Black or non-white at the margins of a white-majority Western society can seek 'ontological security' (Bakkali, 2019) in their identities by adopting stereotypical dispositions which dominate at local and to some extent global levels. These stereotypical representations themselves feed into and are reified by these processes, further cementing these issues.

Controversies like those surrounding drill music, which involve hypermasculine performativity, supposed links to actual violence and bigotry, are indelibly linked to the conditions which produce these dispositions and canonical stories about specific communities across Western societies. We should rightly point out that not all those identifying as part of the Black community are vulnerable to these processes, and other groups sharing proximal marginality may find sections of their communities drawn into them, making the issue more complex. However, there is a sense that both due to reasons of stereotyping and representation, along with social realities/inequalities, Black men are disproportionately likely to end up in circumstances which would lead to more difficult and limited choices and stronger socializing factors in terms of ending up on road and susceptible to the adoption of street masculinities.

UK rap and genealogies of racialized exclusion

In recent years there has been much discussion in the British media on the possible connection between rap music, in particular the 'drill' subgenre, and violence. Influential members of the police, politicians, journalists, academics and prominent artists have all weighed in on the debate. This recent panic needs to be historicized around a longstanding process whereby there has been growing level of interest in UK rap music among academics, yet this is still relatively recent. Hip hop itself, the global panacea that much of UK rap falls under and draws from in terms of cultural heritage, is a relatively recent cultural phenomenon, dating back to the early/mid-1970s in the Bronx area of New York (Alridge and Stewart, 2005). The field of hip-hop studies is a growing one, with Tricia Rose's (1994) study being regarded as one of the most prominent texts in terms of historical and cultural understandings of hip hop and African-American life and culture. Hip hop studies is a discipline which has seen significant take-up globally across a range of disciplines, including: musicology/music studies (for example, Duinker and Martin, 2017; Kajikawa, 2021); linguistics (Cutler, 2007), sociology (for example, Kubrin, 2005; Harrison, 2008; Persaud, 2011), history (for example, Alridge and Stewart, 2005), criminology and legal studies (for example, Dixon and Linz, 1994; Schumacher, 1995; Greene, 1998; Dennis, 2007; Khan, 2022), along with countless others. At present, journals like the *Journal of Hip Hop Studies*, based out of Virginia Commonwealth University, have produced 145 articles published over nine volumes (VCU.edu, 2023).

Even among British thinkers and researchers, there have been a rapidly growing number of studies and publications relating to hip hop and rap music in recent years (for example, White, 2014, 2015, 2021; Boakye, 2017; Charles, 2018; Fatsis, 2019a, 2019b). While the focus of these publications varies, there is now an established level of interest both among fans of rap music as well as cultural commentators such as academics and authors (with potential overlap in between). However, probably some of the most prominent public discussions of rap music in the UK have focused on its purported connections to criminality and violence. For example, Cressida Dick, former Commissioner for the Metropolitan Police, called on social media platforms like YouTube to remove drill videos which contain 'lyrics that glamourise violence, serious violence, murder, stabbings' (Riley, 2020).

For a long time in the UK, Black music (or music of Black origin) has been viewed by those in positions of power as troublesome and has subsequently been policed, disrupted and suppressed in various ways since the early 1950s (Fryer, 1986; Fatsis, 2019a). This process pre-dates what is recognized by many as the birth of hip hop music across the Atlantic; DJ Kool Herc's end of summer party at 1520 Sedgwick Ave in New York City in 1973 (*The Source*, 2023), meaning that we need to understand UK rap as part of a longer genealogy of Black musical expression and subsequent state suppression. The *Small Axe* series, created by Steve McQueen and originally shown on the BBC, captured aspects of the suppression of Black joy and music endured by the British-Caribbean diaspora. The episode entitled 'Lovers Rock', which focused on a reggae house party, vividly depicted the ways in which

Black communities utilized spaces like private homes in order to be able to collectively enjoy music with its origins in the 'Black Atlantic' (Gilroy, 1993).

Early examples include police raids that targeted house parties ('blues dances' or shebeens), youth clubs and other venues where ska, rocksteady and roots reggae were played (Gilroy, 1987: 95–104; Gilroy, 2007: 152). This also extends to a lack protection under the law for Black leisure, with the New Cross Fire in 1981, the cause of which was suspected as being racially motivated arson, being dismissed by the authorities, leading to a mass demonstration in London (Howe, 2011), adding to a an already established sense of injustice for many.

In recent times, measures like Form 696, introduced in 2005 by the Metropolitan Police as a risk assessment for event organizers and venues, explicitly targeted events which featured DJs or MCs, as well as including questions about ethnic composition of guests and offered suggested genres like R&B, garage and Bashment (Hancox, 2009; Ilan, 2012; Fatsis, 2019b). The form was later revised by the Met, before finally being scrapped in 2017 by the Mayor of London, Sadiq Khan. Fatsis (2019a) argues that recent controversies and attempts to suppress subgenres like drill music are a part of the same trajectory in targeted policing of Black communities.

There have even been instances where the police have attempted to intervene in record deals. One well-known example of this came when 'road rap' (Thapar, 2021) artist Giggs' deal with record label XL was allegedly put in jeopardy by the Metropolitan Police's Operation Trident. After an initial effort to dissuade XL from signing Giggs failed, the Met proceeded to utilize the Form 696 to force the cancellation of his live shows and eventually his UK tour in 2010 (Wolfson, 2013). This attitude towards Black artists and culture is something which has also been seen emanating directly from government and other establishment figure.

The media and policy response to the 2011 riots was particularly illustrative of the ways in which 'culture' is central in the framing of the gang problem in parts of the state and the media. Famously, historian David Starkey was platformed on the BBC in the wake of the riots, where he claimed that the issues underpinning the national unrest were because 'whites had become Black' and that a 'destructive, nihilistic gangster culture … has become the fashion' (*BBC News*, 2011). Though Starkey's take was derided in the left-wing press and elsewhere, Scott (2020) points out that it is not an isolated perspective. She reflects on David Cameron's comments to the editor of *Good Housekeeping* during his time as leader of the Conservative Party, where he claimed 'that some of the stuff you play on [Radio 1] Saturday nights encourages people to carry guns and knives' (Day, 2006). Scott (2020: 59) goes on to expand upon Steve Goodman's notion of 'dub virology' whereby the metaphor of a contagious virus is applied to the growing influence of Black music. Scott identifies this as part of a cultural struggle responses like those of Starkey and Cameron, which are emblematic of 'white conservative fears about the growing influence of Black music … allow[ing] us to consider this expressed dread of sonic domination as the recurring fear of the Black man having "the whip hand over the white man"'.

These processes of limiting the spread and influence of music of Black origin in the UK can be viewed in two ways as part of this analysis. They demonstrate the movement Bauman (2006) identified from a solid society whereby the marriage of power and politics held at the level of the state was able to curtail cultural flows. Attitudes towards non-white people and their cultures have been tainted since the colonial period, with racialized sets of meanings and oppressive practices continuing into supposedly postcolonial times. The inability to recognize the harm racism does to communities leads to processes whereby these harms are repeatedly compounded by punitive interventions into social problems which have been characterized by the powerful because of pathologies in non-white populations such as violence and criminality, which following the epistemological logics of colonialism are inherent features of these populations. In this way, the powerful are able to 'alchemize culture into crime' (Fatsis, 2019b: 7). Of course, as anti-racist movements and technological innovations have taken a hold, these solid interventions have struggled to hold up. The next section will examine how the liquification of society through the development of new technologies and agility on the part of those in minoritized communities have helped them to gain a bigger presence in British popular culture.

The digital revolution: liquefaction and new flows

One of the key features of liquid times for Bauman was what he described as the gradual separation between 'power and politics' (Bauman, 2006). As the world becomes increasingly globalized, new intranational and supranational actors and forces are coming to prominence, filling the vacuums created by individual nation states' limited control of flows beyond the confines of their borders. The internet is a technological innovation which has contributed to this separation. Individual nation states have struggled to effectively control content and flows of information, along with the multinational corporations operating in the digital space. Corporations such as Facebook (now Meta) have not only become difficult to regulate due to their multinational legal structures (Skegg, 2017), but they themselves also have a vested interest in the governance of users as well as wider political issues. However, these shifts have opened up temporary possibilities for populations who previously found themselves locked out of and/or underrepresented in media spaces, as the digital world's impact on everyday life continues to be inconsistent across different spaces and contexts (Hayward, 2012; Miller, 2012).

The suppression of forms of Black music meant that for many years, artists struggled to gain main*stream* national and global success. However, the digital revolution created more fluid possibilities for artists to circumvent some of the limitations, reacting faster than policy makers and institutional actors in the industry. This undermined the control exerted by the 'solid' institutional actors which previously limited the possibilities of Black artists in the UK, now they had a new route to market that allowed new capital flows and encouraged those willing to platform this growing scene to benefit. In her study of grime artists in East London and Ayia Napa in the late 2000s and early-mid 2010s, White (2017) observed that the savvy and agile artists, along with those involved in the production and promotion of the music, were able to respond quickly and in innovative ways to the shifting technological landscape, helping to increase the profile of their music as well as streamlining the processes enabling the consumer to access it. Historically Black British music struggled to find consistent mainstream playtime and labels would often be reluctant to work with artists with a 'street' image, with the controversies which surrounded groups like the So Solid Crew serving as an example of the kinds of problems faced (Garcia, 2017).

Pirate radio was an initial means for artists to network and perform live sets, finding their origins in sound system culture emanating from the Caribbean. Later along with the growth of affordable DVD writing technology productions like Lord of the Mics and Streets Incarcerated, which would feature clashes and sets from different crews or groups of artists from various neighbourhoods, became well known among young people in London. Independent retailers in London's West End (and elsewhere) would often stock these along with some artists LPs. Bakkali (2018) highlighted how mobile phone technology aided in this process too, as infrared and Bluetooth as well as Walkman-like functionalities made the sharing as well as impromptu performance of rap music a common feature of many of London's playgrounds and youth clubs.

As the digital revolution took hold, sites like YouTube and file-sharing tools like Limewire made music even more accessible, and those seeking to promote UK rap took full advantage. YouTube channels like SBTV used a similar model to DVD productions, offering the opportunity for fans to view/listen to a range of artists as well as platforming artists to extend their reach by featuring on these platforms. The level of uptake surprised some artists themselves, as Bakkali (2019) highlights that some initially thought they were producing music for local audiences, only to be surprised themselves by the level of attention garnered, as demonstrated by the metrics offered by social media platforms. Gradually the levels of interest in the music snowballed to levels that main*stream* labels could no longer ignore. At the time of writing, UK rap is very much part of the main*stream* musical landscape; however, this process of social change caused by the digital revolution is one worth paying attention to. This melting of traditional business models as well as the reduced level of control legacy media agencies and record labels had in relation to which artists and genres are platformed could be regarded as a liquefaction providing those previously frozen out with new ways to access the market.

This heightened connectivity made possible by technological innovation has allowed for the circumvention of certain static limitations faced by those in marginalized communities. When we consider other central features of social change brought about by processes of liquefaction, this response is in keeping with life in the liquid age. These technologies have contributed to as well as layering atop of the 'collapse of long-term thinking' (Bauman, 2006: 3), along with the individualization of social problems and continuing atrophy of social safety nets (the welfare state, healthcare and so on). The ontological security provided by skills and careers which might last a lifetime has been eroded by the constantly shifting needs of a globalized economy faced with rapid technological and supranational change. This leads a 'splicing' of individual lives as people are disciplined to become mobile, adaptive and responsive to change and opportunity. For marginalized populations, this necessity for adaptability may well pre-date some of these structural changes, as while in the past society may have taken a more solid state, racial prejudice and exclusion often lead marginalized groups to have a precarious experience in the labour market. In the context of these social changes, we can see how rap careers could be viewed as especially desirable life projects, offering a greater sense of personal autonomy and authenticity, at least at a cursory glance.

This highlights a potentially more progressive element in the shift to more liquid social structures as groups that were held on the outside of a particular industry and/or society at large can renegotiate their terms of inclusion by gaining income, visibility and status via popular culture. Of course, while the digital revolution has created new possibilities for art, inclusion and capital, it has also had negative effects on the lives of young people in inner cities, particularly those growing up on the fringes of street cultures. In his book on youth violence in London, youth worker and cultural critic Ciaran Thapar (2021: 112) argued 'that social media was a key lubricant in the cycles of exclusion taking place'.

These concerns have been echoed by Irwin-Rogers and Pinkney (2017) and Irwin-Rodgers et al (2018), who view the online world as offering possibilities to 'amplify' the value systems, leading to violent encounters in street spaces. As we have seen in the previous section on street masculinities, in situations where people are devalued, they seek to attempt to cultivate value in the localities or other spaces, sometimes by inverting social norms maintained by the institutions which exclude them. This can lead to violent forms of conflict as issues relating to social status are highly sensitive and precarious. In situations where slights against a person's (and men's in particular) social status have been made, this can lead to incidents of violence conflict, though this does not always happen as there are other performative methods to manage such situations (Samanani, 2022). Irwin-Rogers and Pinkney (2017) argue that the larger audience provided by social media and the digital world increase the pressure on young people living in proximity to street settings to respond in kind, including with the use of violence. This also raises questions about the state of the marketplaces in which people wish to consume this kind of content (something we will develop later on in this chapter), but we can see that the liquification of society that afforded technological innovation is not unilaterally a positive process for marginalized communities.

However, the content of rap music, particularly of some of the most economically successful artists in, and genres of, rap has been widely criticized across the political spectrum. For a long time in the US, 'gangsta rap' has been criticized for violent and bigoted lyrical content, with subgenres which have found contemporary success in the UK, with drill and trap facing similar critiques. Understanding how themes such as these continue to appear in quite different moments and contexts (Wacquant, 2008) requires some dynamic thinking in terms of both the cultural locations of artists along with the conditions of the market – for example, what sells. In both spaces we can see the legacies of racism and their contemporary manifestations looming large.

The market

In contemporary times the market dominates aspects of social relations. Central to Bauman's thinking on liquid modernity was the globalization of neoliberal, more laissez-faire economic models, which favoured individualism and private ownership (Harvey, 2006). These processes have altered social and political relations, as nation states are less able to govern the multinational organizations which operate at the global level, with production and supply chains which straddle both the Global North and South, generally taking advantage of lower living standards, weaker currencies and infrastructure in the latter in order to minimize production costs and then benefiting from being able to 'sell' into wealthier nations where there are strong consumer cultures and higher average incomes.

These values broadly include the promotion of free-market fundamentalism with minimal state intervention aside from the maintenance of institutions working to secure private property rights and functioning markets, such as the police force and the judiciary (Harvey, 2007a). There is also a drive to create markets in spaces, which sees governments often attempting to actively initiate the creation of markets in sectors where previously none existed, such as healthcare, prisons and social welfare. This entails stripping back state social security services in favour of more limited private alternatives, often combining these with marketized security-orientated responses to social problems, often utilizing the criminal justice system as a solution to social problems (Bauman, 2006; Wacquant, 2009; Giroux, 2013). David Harvey (2007b) has described this as a process of 'creative destruction'. In the UK, an example of this would the Private Finance Initiative, which sources private investment for the building and increasingly the running of schools, prisons and hospitals (Dunleavy, 1994). Alkaraan and Floyd (2020) highlight some significant failures in the PFI, highlighting that the state can borrow at more favourable terms and does not require large profit margins, meaning that in general PFI offers higher cost and poorer service provision, something backed by the findings of the National Audit Office (2018), which claimed that PFI contracts often seem like a better deal for the private sector than for taxpayers.

Even in the richer nations of the Global North, such as the UK, social relations have been radically transformed by these directions of travel in political economy. Social safety nets have gradually been eroded and new punitive approaches to managing populations that exist at the margins of the neoliberal project have been implemented (Wacquant, 2009). In the context of the UK, we have seen a growing number of low-paid and precarious job roles saturate the lower end of the labour market. This usually involves individuals taking on a 'self-employed' status, similar to that of the entrepreneur, while really operating in a role that in the past might have been regarded as a job which should include various benefits such as sick pay and holiday. These include roles like delivery drivers, which were once the staple of the Post Office and Royal Mail, which operated with a unionized workforce, but now is an open market where many drivers work precariously in order to help fulfil the massive demand for the services of giant multinationals like Amazon. This liquefaction of once 'solid' state insurances has led to a prevailing ontological insecurity about the status and prospects of many people in society, leading to what Bauman described as *Unsicherheit*, a prevailing sense of insecurity: 'We live in a world of universal flexibility, under conditions of acute and prospectless Unsicherheit, penertrating all aspects of individual life' (Bauman, 2000: 135).

Those who fail to adapt and take on the new demands and subsequent conditions of the labour market are disciplined by a highly conditional welfare system. In the UK, a conditional system called Universal Credit operates, which seeks to pressurize individuals to take whatever opportunities exist in the labour market, regardless of whether they provide adequate income to support themselves, with the welfare services offering conditional possibilities to make up some of the shortfall. Essentially, this has become a benefit to employers, who no longer have to ensure jobs which offer sufficient possibilities for a decent standard of living. Wiggan (2012) highlights the ways in which this approach ignores the structural causes of unemployment, instead transferring the responsibility to individuals, who if they fail to overcome structural limitations are stigmatized as in some way pathological.

However, in this context, there seems to be space in the market for young men from these backgrounds to forge new kinds of careers for themselves, facilitated in part by the digital revolution discussed earlier. Conditions and possibilities now exist in the UK for some young people to subvert the socioeconomic conditions of their circumstances by leaning into the performance of the kinds of racialized and classed stereotypes applied to them, and selling them in the cultural marketplace – a marketplace which itself is strongly influenced by histories of racism(s) and other forms of domination. This is a process which needs to be picked apart carefully, but also needs to coincide with the acknowledgement that not all those who occupy these spaces do so.

Ove Sernhede (2000), in his study of white Swedish hip hop fans, puzzled over why white middle-class Swedes would find such a strong affinity with a Black diasporic art form, seemingly so far from their own set of experiences. Drawing heavily on psychanalytic concepts, he argued that there exists a collective fear and desire for the Other, which has long been suppressed. Colonial stereotypes of the other, which sought to dehumanize and to justify Western domination, played on repressed tropes in Western societies, like hypersexuality and violence. These sets of meanings were governed 'not simply by empirical reality but by a battery of desires repressions, investments and projections' (Said, 1978: 8, cited in Hall, 1997: 264), leading to Bauman's (2006) assertion of mixophilia in which consumer practices afford white groups the ability to buy into and consume the 'other', thus facilitating a racism through the jouissance of otherness and the creation of a racialized totality driven by market practices and an unconscious white desire to incorporate difference into mainstream society (see Chapter 2 for a more detailed discussion of this).

In psychoanalytic thought, the need to repress behaviours, experiences or characteristics is often necessitated by the common desire for them at some level, even if this is subconscious. This led to a relationship between the white Western world and the Other which was mediated by often simultaneous feelings of fear, repression and desire. Stuart Hall (1997) observed similarities between historical stereotypical depictions of Black men, such as the 'bad buck' identified by Bogle (1973), and more contemporary images of Black youth: 'for example, the "mugger", the "drug-baron", the "yardie", the gangsta rap singer, the "n★★★★s with attitude" bands and more generally black urban youth on the rampage' (Hall, 1997: 251), demonstrating a degree of continuity in the collection perception and projection of images. Sernhede (2011) indicates that, during a time in late modernity where transcendent lifestyles and experiences are highly sought-after, these stereotypes offer the possibility to experience 'intensity', breaking free from the restraints and monotony of middle-class Western cultures. This collective desire for the 'transcendent' and 'essential' quality of the Other, generally in the form of the Black man in this context, has created market conditions where new opportunities for those willing to perform racialized tropes appear. These young men can potentially gain attention and economic traction. As Sernhede (2000: 311) puts it:

> A paradoxical situation has arisen. While segments of the culture and consumer goods industries have an interest in de-stereotyping our images of the Other and working for ethnic equality, segments of contemporary ghetto culture are tending towards doing the opposite. This culture is partially developing its power of attraction through taking advantage of and using the ambivalence between fear and attraction that has long constituted the Western man's relationship to the foreign. Gangsta rap not least is playing upon classical stereotypes with its stylized overtones of sex and violence.

Essentially this commodity value of 'gangsta rap', or drill music in this context, creates a strong incentive in the current 'attention economy' (Stuart, 2020) for a variety of actors to become involved in creating this niche of content. It is important to remember that artists themselves are not the sole architects of the narratives of violence surrounding subgenres like drill and trap. Schwartze and Fatsis (2023) remind us that platforms reward a variety of creators, such as YouTube compilation channels that seek to develop the narrative of violence surrounding drill music in return for advertising revenue.

bell hooks (1994) expressed a similar perspective when discussing the presence of misogynistic language and imagery in gangsta rap. hooks observed that given the virulent nature of the expressions of misogyny in some gangsta rap, it is common to perceive these as a predominantly Black male problem; however, she highlighted how marginalized spaces produce the most acute manifestations of broader social structures like patriarchy, and that many are making the choice to participate in producing such content situated in this context. She analyses various high-grossing films of the day, observing content which 'eroticize(s) male domination via the exchange of women as well as the [violent] subjugation of other men' (1994: 142), yet these Hollywood blockbusters had not received the same degree of condemnation as gangsta rap. This dissonant critical response suggests an imaginary whereby young Black men who produce gangsta rap live in a 'cultural vacuum' where misogyny, nihilism and violence thrive, away from the gentile and civilized society. Concurrently, critics of rap music turn a blind eye to demonstrations of similar values which 'reflect bourgeois standards (no rawness, no vulgarity)'. Essentially, she is arguing that the values criticized in gangsta rap are manifestations of the values of wider white supremacist capitalist society, a society which provides the possibility for young Black men to make more money 'producing lyrics that promote violence, sexism, misogyny than with any other content' (1994: 136–137).

hooks' perspective further reminds us that the sedimentary racisms underpinning consumptive practices in the market provide possibilities for stereotypical dispositions to be economically rewarded, both for individuals willing to embody them and those corporations who platform and produce their outputs. This confluence between these liquid flows feeds into one another, creating complex and deeply ambivalent outcomes. On the one hand, this liquefaction has enabled a new generation of artists, many of whom come from the margins, to self-actualize as neoliberal subjects, leading lifestyles unimaginable to previous generations of Black and brown Britons. On the other hand, they represent a group of people taking on disproportionate risks in this process of capital accumulation. Those who publicly engage in conflicts and/or embody violent dispositions take on great personal risks, including the risk of being imprisoned or harmed via interpersonal violence, a situation which can also lead to great harm to the psyche. Artists are disproportionately taking on these risks in relation to the audiences which can safely consume their content anonymously online, particularly white audiences (Oliveira, 2018: 135), while brands and platforms are able to extract significant value from them both directly and indirectly, without taking on significant risk of the same kind.

This action is in keeping with Bauman's evaluation of the direction of both the labour market and wider society. He viewed society as increasingly lacking in social projects seeking to improve the conditions of humanity as a whole, but which instead had become saturated with individual 'involuntary nomads' trapped in a labyrinth of uncertainty and chaos. He argues that there is an absence of long-term planning and construction of desirable future outcomes; instead, there are short-term projects where individuals 'chase a chance' rather than building long-term sustainable projects. Work no longer represents a lifelong project which identities can 'wrap around'; instead, actors are lacking anchors and are suffering from ontological insecurity, leading to Bauman's (2000: 139–140) diagnosis:

> [W]ork has acquired – alongside other life activities – a mainly aesthetic significance. It is expected to be gratifying by and in itself, rather than measured by the genuine or putative effects it brings to one's brothers and sisters in humanity … Hardly ever is work expected to 'ennoble' its performers, to make them 'better human beings', and rarely is it admired and praised for that reason. It is instead measured and evaluated

> by its capacity to be entertaining and amusing, satisfying not so much the ethical, Promethean vocation of the producer and creator as the aesthetical needs and desires of the consumer, the seeker of sensations and collector of experiences.

Bauman is describing a structural context which facilitated the existence of the 'attention economy' (Stuart, 2020), whereby actors compete, not around a personal ethic and life project, but instead to garner as much attention and revenue as possible by shocking audiences with the most audacious and challenging content possible. In the context of drill music, this is often seen in anti-authoritarian attitudes and comportment, as well as 'authenticity' in terms of really being about street life, which leads to another confluence between their performativity and real-life experiences of marginality. In this context, this means living by street or 'road' (in the UK context) values, which put young people at risk, in their localities, where their performativity can be tested or be used as a touchstone for rivals to accrue road capital (Bakkali, 2018, 2021), while also attracting punitive attention from the state in the form of the police as well as the national media, which seek to help establish main*stream* values, using these artists as an 'othering' post upon which to construct their boundaries (Hall et al, 1978).

Dyson (2008) views the huge market draw for those willing to engage in gangsta performativity, arguing that, to a degree, it is a two-way street and that some artists are indeed sophisticated in their understandings of cultural representation. Consequently, in the clamour to access the market for gangsta rap, 'middle class blacks faking home boy roots', along with others, are able to serve up 'colourful exaggerations' of 'ghetto life'. It is worth noting that he also claims that there are artists who are able to provide 'compelling portraits of real social and economic suffering' (Dyson, 2008: 175). Similarly to bell hooks (2004), Dyson demonstrates how the draws of the market can be a powerful factor in encouraging young Black men, who might have otherwise not been socialized into harmful masculine performativity, might be lured in by the promise of a possible career in music.

However, in spite of the ubiquitous connections between drill music and criminality, evidence suggests that rap artists even at the harder edge of the scene view music as a route away from offending behaviours. The 'drillers' in Stuart's (2020) study spent long periods, often while enduring bouts of homelessness and destitution, scraping limited resources together to create content to build their social media followings and subsequently social networks. They would leverage these networks, playing up aspects of the popular media depiction of Chicago as the 'murder capital', to create potentially advantageous possibilities for themselves in business and their personal/romantic lives. While there were moments where local rivalries, some of which played out via social media and rap feuds, boiled over into life-altering or in specific instances life-ending episodes of hyperviolence, there was a sense that these episodes were more symptomatic of the longstanding malaise of the racialized American ghetto than being a direct result of the influences of social media and rap music.

Bakkali (2021) highlighted a similar process whereby young men from 'road' (UK urban street culture) would leverage Bourdiesian-inspired forms of 'road capitals' to make transitions into more included social positions. The cultural clout which could be accumulated via status as a rap artist was one such strategy, whereby street comportment and associations, which are typically treated punitively in mainstream institutions, could be inverted into marketable qualities, creating legitimate income streams and higher social standing. We can see evidence of young men, like Stormzy, Konan and Krept, who have gained traction via success in UK rap music, transitioning into a more included social status and becoming important social commentators, television personalities and entrepreneurs.

Schwartze and Fatsis (2023) argue that the association and mobilization of violent content in UK rap subgenres like drill and trap are used as a lure to generate interest through controversy and the appeal of culturally transgressive attitudes. To take 'fictive' accounts designed to sell music too literally runs the risk of doing 'violence to high standards of evidence' in criminal prosecution. They highlight the fact that artists commonly consciously exploit aspects of 'ghetto life' as a 'sought after commodity' ripe for online consumption. Stuart (2020) also found that while artists were from environments which were replete with interpersonal violence, they were even more deeply saturated with the monotony of contemporary urban poverty and limited possibilities.

We can see here the deeply ambivalent situation in which drill artists and others find themselves. They have the potential to achieve commercial success and representation for their communities on a national and global level, but the genre which catapults a small number of them to these heights also contributes to the deepening of racialized structures of meaning. These sedimentary assemblages are able to re-form bringing the spectres of older stereotypes into new times. In the next and penultimate section, we will see how the state seeks to work to uphold and strengthen these sets of meanings while simultaneously denouncing them and the values they say are associated with them.

Attitudes and responses in policy: resolidifying and upping the viscosity

The fallout surrounding drill music has become articulated in state responses to the 'gang problem' (Gunter, 2017). Since the 1990s, issues of serious criminality in the UK have increasingly been framed in this way, understood as a growth in US-style street gangs. However, this orientation towards gang-based framings of criminal and social issues, along with their subsequent interventions, has been beset by definitional issues (Marshall et al, 2005) and conceptual problems (Williams and Clarke, 2016). Of particular relevance are the disproportionate ways in which the gang label has been applied to BAME communities, in particular Black men (Williams and Clarke, 2016; Amnesty International, 2020), creating a set of understandings and a policy environment that contribute to the 'pathologization and essentialization of black youth as a peculiar social problem' (Joseph and Gunter, 2011: 3).

This is reflected by the disproportionality on display in the Metropolitan Police's Gang Matrix, which seeks to keep a database on all 'gang nominals' in London, while also giving them a semi-predictive risk score which informs the kind of policing response that individuals will trigger. An investigation by Amnesty International found that nearly 80 per cent of all gang nominals in the system were Black males. This is vastly disproportionate compared to both the population of Black men in London as well as Black men involved in violent crime (Amnesty, 2018). Amnesty International found that there were very inconsistent evidence thresholds in terms of how someone might end up on the database, as well as issues around the proper protection of those individuals' data once they were on there, with it being routinely shared across stakeholders without significant justification, making it illegal in relation to the Data Protection Act (2020). There were even instances of young people's data being leaked on to and shared across social media, potentially putting them at risk.

In keeping with this framing of the problem, a recent report by Falkner for the Policy Exchange (2021) claimed that at least 23 per cent of 41 'gang related homicides' were linked to drill music, which led to a robust response through the criminal justice system, but also political and cultural leadership that would pressure brands and others to denounce music that they claim promotes violence, stating: '[w]e must end the naïve societal acceptance and legitimization of gang culture and acknowledge the violence that accompanies it' (Falkner, 2021: 15). While the condemnation of violence is potentially admirable, perhaps there is a lack of understanding of the 'situatedness' (Bakkali, 2021) of those individuals who find themselves involved in musical expression and even possibly violence. The Policy Exchange's narrative is one in keeping with the state's response to the controversies arising out of drill music, which seeks to suppress and punish those involved in making it, while offering little in relation to solving the multitude of causes, including racisms, which underpin it. Indeed, the state has adapted a range of measures, designed to tackle the gang problem and to a lesser extent the threat of terror attacks, to wield against those making drill music.

The Policing and Crime Act (2009) was the first piece of legislation to try to define a gang, though in relatively vague terms, which allowed for the creation of the gang injunction – commonly referred to as the 'Gangbo' due to its similarities to the earlier anti-social behaviour order (ASBO) (Randle, 2011). This creates the possibility for individuals who are thought to be in a gang to have limits placed on their ordinary activities, even if they have not been convicted of any specific crime – though if they breach the limitations set in a gang injunction, they can face criminal conviction. Typically, these limitations prohibit individuals from being in certain locations, with particular people or wearing specific items of clothing (thought to communicate gang affiliation) (Aldridge et al, 2011). This has been further mobilized against UK rap artists, with several groups and individuals receiving orders which limit their possibilities to create music. Brixton-based artists AM x Skengdo received a gang injunction in August 2018 which prohibited them from performing or broadcasting lyrics that mention rival groups, rappers or entering into their 'perceived territories' (Hancox, 2019). The Metropolitan Police also run Operation Domain, which seeks to remove online content from sites like YouTube which are deemed to be likely to incite violence, which has also been known to target drill videos (Fatsis, 2019a).

There have been mixed responses to the use of gang injunctions and operation domain against rap artists. The Youth Violence Commission identify the crux of the issue as the tension between the responsibility of social media companies and the police to remove content deemed 'hurtful, negative or humiliating', and the protection of artists' rights to free speech (Youth Violence Commission, 2020: 31). It is also important to remember that these decisions are being made in the context of post-2010 Conservative-led policies of austerity which have led to large-scale cuts in spending on vital services upon which those in marginal communities might rely. Immediately after their election in 2010, the Conservative-led Coalition cut the Educational Maintenance Allowance, which offered up to £30 per week to support those from the poorest backgrounds to pursue further education, despite previously offering assurances that they would not (Mullholland, 2011). In addition, the Conservatives have overseen large-scale cutbacks on spending for youth services. All these cuts disproportionately affect those at the margins, further exacerbating existing problems.

Digital content made by young people involved in the drill/trap music scene has increasingly come under observation from the authorities, which treat it as a criminal intelligence database (Rawlinson, 2018). This has been evidenced in the increasing numbers of music videos and other forms of digital content used in court by prosecutors seeking to evidence criminal intent and generally to establish an unfavourable character profile for the defendant. Of course, in the context of a market that conditions young people to exaggerate their performance of street cultural and racialized tropes, it is difficult to ascertain to what extent the types of performativity deemed to indicate genuine criminality by prosecutors are actually a carefully manicured aesthetic performance on the part of a young person who recognizes the market conditions which value such performativity as transgressive.

Ilan (2020) points out that there have been instances whereby drill artists have been found guilty of offences such as drug dealing, using this as a partial explanation for the punitive response from the state. Irwin-Rogers and Pinkney (2017) also add some credence to the possibility that drill music could be connected to real-world violence. However, this is in the context of existing street cultural value systems, whereby disrespect is felt keenly. Irwin-Rodgers and Pinkney claim that social media can act as an amplifier for interpersonal/group conflicts between young people, raising the stakes by making perceived slights more public and potentially more damaging to the self-respect of the victim. This increased intensity is reflected in the work of Lane (2016), who, working in the context of Harlem, New York, observed that interactions between those involved in street culture were taking place both in physical spaces and online. However, this evidence seems to point to the fact that social media is a new platform into which old problems leak out rather than being a causal factor in some kind of new problem. The lack of action by authorities in terms of seeking to redress social issues seems to demonstrate a reluctance to genuinely tackle youth violence at its root, instead choosing to protect the status quo along with the interests of capitalism.

To characterize the state response could be regarded as punitive and repressive. They have sought to target rap artists, predominantly young Black and brown men, attempting to make them solely responsible for social problems for which the music they create could be better regarded as symptomatic. This has been done at a time where services on which people in these communities may depend have been systematically removed. This is an approach which in effect deepens the marginality of Black and brown youths as well as further entrenching the stereotypes cast over their lives. In Baumanian terms, we can see the glaciation process in action as the state responds to shifting technologies and cultural flows to reinforce racialization and the status quo. We also see increased viscosity in the lives of Black and brown people as they encounter new technologies designed to police and contain them, as well as the public fallout, strengthening stereotypes that depict them in a negative light. This process further disadvantages this generation of young people, who have to find ways to manage and resist the sets of meanings applied to them.

Conclusion

This chapter has tried to utilize tools provided by the liquid metaphor to outline some of the complexities relating to race and racism emerging from the current 'crisis' concerning certain subgenres of rap music. It is not intended to try to argue 'realities on the ground' or whether or not there are truths to state and media depictions of drill music; instead, the chapter has sought to demonstrate how the confluence of different flows of sedimentary racisms have a causal relationship to these problems. The 'drill rapper' has already been preceded by the 'mugger' and the 'bad buck' to an extent, in that these labels are symptomatic of the relationship between the centre and the margins. Instead of being able to confront the causes of these social problems, state interventions deny their realities and exacerbate them with their interventions.

Young Black and brown people carry the weight of racism in their everyday lives to differing extents, delimiting their agency and ability to meet their needs and ambitions to the same extent as others. They are also seduced by the media, which carries with it the desires that reflect the racialized dynamics of Western societies, which will materially reward Black and brown people for performing 'authentic' and 'transgressive' displays of otherness. In the digital world where attention-seeking behaviours are monetized, this type of transgressive consumption can be pushed to extreme limits, including those which decide fates – life and death.

This is a circumstance of deep ambivalence, as the success of this Black musical genre at some level increases representation, opportunity and joy for those partaking in it, while also shedding much-needed light on the realities of many lives lived at the margins. However, it also acts as a lure to some young people, who, given the promise of fame and success, may be willing to behave in ways that may harm themselves and others, legitimizing interventions from law enforcers and policy makers that further serve to disadvantage themselves and others. Indeed, little is known about how many young people fall by the wayside in relation to this area of the creative industries, what their fates are and where they go next. We know the stigma of having been involved in the harder edge of drill music would have to be carefully managed to make transitions into the main*stream*.

Intervention is needed, but without exacerbating existing inequalities and marginalities. Interventions which provide projects for personal and collective improvement would ultimately help to relieve the problematic content, as well as violence among young people. However, we can see that state interventions ignore this, mostly focusing on punitive solutions which both deny the realities of racism and how they contribute to insecurity and social problems, as well as reifying the status quo and neoliberal logics in the liquid age.

7

Conclusion: The viscosity of contemporary racism(s)

Bauman and his work on late modernity, specifically the condition of liquidity, is useful in terms of understanding how the formation of power emerges out of a liquefaction of solidified or 'modern' structures of modernity. However, the persistence of the monster of racism beyond the liquefaction of the solid formations of power, politics and bureaucracy which facilitated the horrors of the Holocaust may appear problematic for Bauman's concept of liquid modernity. This work has contributed two significant interventions relating to theories of late modernity in the main*stream* social sciences canon. The first of these interventions is to demonstrate the ways in which Bauman's concept of liquidity can be applied meaningfully and substantively to issues concerning 'race', which have been largely absent in main*stream* canonic theorizing on the conditions of late modernity, especially in the works of Bauman himself (see Rattansi, 2016, 2017). We feel this intervention is significant because it serves as a conduit for further conceptual development of Baumanian social thought to (re)position Zygmunt Bauman back into the critical tradition of social theory.

The second intervention relates to the bridging of the gap between significant bodies of Bauman's work. Drawing upon Rattansi's (2017) extensive critique on Bauman's lack of engagement with issues concerning 'race' required us to attempt to resolve this issue by demonstrating how the liquid metaphor critically informs understandings of 'race' and racism in the context of late modernity. Through this process, we have drawn connections between Bauman's older work on bureaucratization in the facilitation of the Holocaust, and his later theoretical contributions regarding liquid modernity. The organizational structures of modernity which facilitated the kind of bureaucratization that allowed the horrors of the Holocaust to unfold represent solidified structures through which top-down authorities were able to exercise control and racialized and xenophobic violence. One of the most significant points to which we draw attention in the early stages of the book are the parallels which can be drawn between the structures that facilitated the Holocaust and those which facilitated the African slave trade under the Western European colonial project. As the solid structures which facilitated both the Holocaust in the context of Nazi Germany and the African slave trade in the context of the Western European colonial project have undergone processes of liquefaction, their legacies have been sustained and maintained through the racialized flows which come to inform power dynamics in the context of liquid modernity. This brings something of a resolution to Bauman's body of work, in that we are able to both bridge the gap between his study of bureaucratization and that of liquid modernity in a way which also makes a theoretical contribution to understanding the nuances, subtleties, and uncertain and unpredictable ways in which the dynamics of racialization play out in late modernity.

There were of course challenging premises for us to engage with and resolve in the process of applying the concept of liquid modernity to the state of race relations in contemporary society. A distinction that has been perhaps most useful throughout this book is the distinction between late modernity and states of being within it. Our application of Bauman's concept of liquidity sees 'liquid modernity' as a state of being, the conditions which characterize late modernity, and while the terms have been (and in many ways can be) used interchangeably by late modern theorists, this distinction is important. We do not, for example, contend that there is no such thing as late modernity, or that late modernity and liquid modernity are different from each other. We simply contend, as Bauman (2000) did, that late modernity is characterized by *liquidity* and it is this that distinguishes it in its relationality to modernity. From this conceptual starting point, in Chapter 2 we considered the contemporary state of play in terms of the dynamics of society, as well as the history of structures in the context of modernity. This required considering the impacts of defining characteristics of modernity, which we concluded saw modernity incarnate as an anathema to the rationalized vision of the European modern project. In place of the vision of a structured, predictable and ordered world, modernity has been characterized by various risks which themselves have been the fruit of modernity's systems of rationalization (Giddens, 1999). These conditions would come to inform a calling for an alternative way of thinking about the world in the form of postmodernism. Within this new vision, the oppressive and destructive characteristics of modernity can be reimagined and reified in the social world. Postmodernity would abandon the modernist understandings of knowledge and knowledge production being rooted in foundationalist systems of understanding the social world informed by the principles of scientific enquiry. The knowledge systems of postmodernity reject the very notion of foundationalist presumptions, but conversely would contend that claims to truth are all equally valid.

As we have considered previously, efforts to establish racialized hierarchies in the context of modernity were driven by anxiety over the risks that cultural and social ambivalence(s) posed for colonial powers looking to sustain their exploitation of colonized people. The work of Knox in particular was also driven by the notion of 'moral anatomy', which he adopted from Quetelet on translating his work. His adoption of this concept was informed by the assumption that the sciences of the Enlightenment would reaffirm notions of racial hierarchy and that once this was achieved, it would represent a definitive statement on the 'ethics' of colonialism. In short, if the sciences concur with the notion of racial hierarchy, then the abominations of colonialism could in some way be justified on this basis. As we have outlined previously, it is not only the fact that Knox failed in his efforts to actually find a scientific basis for the notion of 'race', but it also is the effort to do so which is perhaps more important. While Knox was not a lone actor in this effort, he has been described as 'the real founder of British racism, and one of the key figures in the Western movement towards a dogmatic pseudo-scientific racism' (Curtin, cited in Richards, 1989: 374). What the work of Knox and others like him represents is an effort to trigger a solidification or freezing around the notion of 'race' which would actively obscure the cultural and social ambivalences that posed a threat to the established order of colonialism in the Victorian moment. Thus, the condition(s) of racism in modernity are framed through the solidification effort to remove cultural and social ambivalences which undermine notions of racial difference. The fact that we have been able to draw out examples of this legacy through the case study chapters demonstrates the extent to which modernity persists, with the liquefaction and variances in viscosities around racialized flows over time and in the contemporary moment representing the *liquidity* that characterizes *late*, rather than *post*, modernity.

In light of this, in Chapter 2 we also asked the following question: how might racism then manifest in postmodernity? Postmodernity preoccupies itself with fantasy and the imaginary as the process of self-construction and otherness. However, this proposition raises implications for our position, as well as that of Zygmunt Bauman. Our application of the concept of liquidity itself to race relations today has demonstrated the various ways in which racism continues to function in the contemporary moment. Within the understanding presented here, the implicit relativism which underpins the epistemological and ontological premises of postmodern claims to knowledge becomes undermined by the very ability to continue to critically analyse, observe and understand racism. The premises of postmodern claims to knowledge would suggest that individuals are able to construct their own realities within which they have complete autonomy in terms of how far racism does or does not exist in their understanding of the world. We have demonstrated not only that racism continues to permeate our present social world, but also the ways in which it impacts disparately for social actors. At each stage of this book, we have identified examples of racialized disparities and inequalities as our starting point for evaluating the applicability of liquidity to understand it. The case study chapters have each demonstrated how, while it is possible for white individuals to live and function without acknowledging racism, their actions will invariably contribute to racialized flows regardless of such a lack of acknowledgement. In the interests of presenting a coherent theoretical piece of work for the reader, it was necessary for us to outline the theoretical apparatus and our position on modernity in the early stages of the book. This was designed to familiarize the reader with the notion of liquidity before we got to each of the case studies so that there was clarity on the conceptual ideas under consideration. However, there has been a strategic effort in each of the case study chapters to subject these conceptual ideas to evaluation by reference to observable examples of racism in contemporary contexts. This approach was conscious – a way of contending with anticipated accusations of tautological determinism to the theoretical project. The anchoring of the concept of liquidity to examples of contemporary racisms ensures that our analysis is embedded in an observable reality which situates our work firmly in the context of late modernity. Therefore, our work cannot be accommodated within a postmodern understanding of reality, and nor can Bauman's overall analysis of the contemporary moment.

Bauman's position has been a point of contention, with there being a debate over the extent to which his own position has shifted over time, and critically what this means for continuity across his intellectual and theoretical contributions to understanding the social world. Bauman's position in his earlier work identifies that a key feature of the European modernity project has been the bureaucratization of society, a process which required the emergence and reification of institutions as regulatory organizations. In order for such institutions to exercise regulatory function, the conditions of modernity required their formulation as solidified structures, capable of exercising power directionally. What is interesting in the process of considering how Baumann's work can be applied in debates on the present state of modernity is that his own academic positioning has been presented as embodying understandings of modernity which are not easily reconcilable. For example, Bauman's work on bureaucratization actively focuses on 'race', with his deconstruction of institutionalized bureaucracy demonstrating the capacity for the legitimation of extreme racialized violence in the Holocaust and, as such, is clearly important for our purposes in terms of understanding how his work can be applied to 'race' in the context of modernity. However, the positioning of this earlier work is perhaps most usefully understood as that of a critical social theorist, and within this understanding there are implications for the character of modernity that is being theorized. Bauman's later work in the early 1990s appears to embody a postmodern turn; however, he later acknowledges this as a 'fleeting affair' with postmodernism, and something of a epistemological stop-gap in his theorizing which would be resolved in the form of his final works on liquid modernity. Nevertheless, this intellectual journey posed a problem which needed to be engaged with for our purposes as there were two important implications. The first would be the existential question of how far we are able to make sense of the extent to which we are a state of modernity or postmodernity, while the second is how far we are able to resolve Bauman's position on modernity across his epistemological journey. With regard to the first of these implications, we considered how far along the spectrum from modernity to postmodernity present reality is situated. We can see that while there have been significant shifts and changes from the characteristics of modernity, there has not been a fundamental shift which would constitute the reframing of our understanding of contemporary society in postmodern terms. The premises of exploring the concept of liquid racism is predicated upon outlining the ways in which the legacies of 'race' in the context of modernity and have persisted. As we explored, the proposed conditions of postmodernity would invariably embody the complete dissolution of racialized identification, and the annihilation of racialized dynamics in social context. As we have demonstrated, not only have racialized power relations persisted into our contemporary social world, but the ways in which they continue to function also have longstanding connections with the older more solidified forms through which racism was manifested in the context of modernity. It is the ability to continually identify the connections between existing social dynamics in the context of liquid modernity and previously established social dynamics in modernity which reaffirms that the present reality is far from postmodern. While there have been significant changes in the ways in which structure and agency function, these changes have most substantively impacted on the forms and methods through which power dynamics have come to be reified and channelled in late modernity. We also contend that, given the inevitable legacies of history, postmodernity remains elusive, unachievable and perhaps even undesirable as an aspirational social reality. As such, achieving a state of postmodernity from this perspective would require the end of history and, in particular, our understandings of the history of modernity itself. The requirement for such a cataclysmic erasure of knowledge would also carry the implications that the subjects of any such society that emerged within that context would have no way of being able to identify that they were indeed existing in a state of postmodernity. A more accurate reading of the state of the contemporary social world would need to acknowledge the legacies of the old solid structures of modernity as they have come to be reconstituted through more fluid manifestations of power flows, and the varying states of liquidity, viscosity and solidification individuals encounter as they navigate social life according to their social locatedness in the context of liquid modernity.

Liquidity is therefore key to our ability to understand both the persistence of racism and its fluidity in the present as well as the more solidified structural characteristics of modernity which underpin it. Having established at this point in the work substantively what we intend to contribute, there is a question concerning positionality, authorship and even ownership of conversations on 'race' in the social sciences. In no way do the authors here make any claims to ownership of discussions on race; rather, we simply make a contribution which we hope will bring about more critical ways of thinking about 'race' into main*stream* discussions of late modernity as well as the social thought of Zygmunt Bauman. Our intention is to demonstrate how enmeshed racism and late modernity are and to provide an analytical tool in the application of Bauman's liquid metaphor to make sense of this. Two of the authors are writing from the positionality of being white academics, and this needs to be noted and acknowledged. Thus, in the main, the contributions here are not accompanied by a backdrop of lived experiences of racism. However, all three of the authors have lived in the context of whiteness, and two of us know it intimately through the lived experiences which have brought us to writing this book. Rather than seeing racism as a niche subject, we contend that racism is white society's problem to take responsibility for and work to deconstruct. This has to be done carefully and in ways which take leadership from intellectual groups that do draw on experiences of racism. With this in mind, we take comfort in the notion that this work will be subjected to evaluation within such spaces, and we see this as part of the process of attempting to use our positionality against the interests of whiteness more generally. Our contributions to this work as white authors may assist in confronting racism in the present in a meaningful way (as, of course, we hope it does), or it may represent a problematic embodiment of white saviourism. History will no doubt let us know.

Of course, the third substantive conceptual notion that we had to contend with in developing this work was that of the postracial state. The concept of postracialism is significant, not least because the implications might suggest that racialized dynamics had been completely eroded away as part of the process of late modernity entering the postmodern realm. The notion of the postracial has also come to inform political mobilizations primarily organized around libertarian notions of the right to free speech, opposition to cancel culture, and the advocation of individual liberties and freedoms. The predication of these kinds of political stances has invariably been informed by apparent indicators of progress regarding race relations, manifested in examples such as Barack Obama's presidency. As we have demonstrated, such moments may represent some indication of progress in terms of race relations, but these moments have been met with a substantive political backlash which has had highly racialized implications. The flowing back and forth of the politics of race in liquid modernity has seen the emergence of the alt-right, the 'left behind' and the main*stream*ing of populism in Europe as examples where notions of progressiveness have been met with resistance of varying viscosities. Integral to our understanding of racism in late modernity has been the history of racism in modernity. The postracial state, characterized perhaps by the complete erosion of notions of 'race', has been far from achieved in our contemporary reality. Furthermore, we contend that, as with postmodernity itself, coming to such a state would require the erasure of history. This would on the surface indicate the end of racism, but this would also require that the character of dominant public political cultures is negotiated equitably on the way towards a postracial state. We maintain here that the liquidity of racism in late modernity would make this process difficult if not impossible, short of a moment of freezing at precisely the point where equitability is achieved. While it is possible that this frozen moment could embody a 'postracial state', this would exist as a point in time in late/liquid modernity rather than as a singularity from which the only way forward is postraciality. As we established in Chapter 3, this leaves the postracial state as a notional rather than tangible entity, and one which fails to deliver on its promise of the erosion of racialized inequities. Rather, the notional postracial state primarily serves as a moment within which false claims that racial equality has been achieved dominate the public political space, and in turn trigger counterflows containing sediments of white resentment which collectively build up to derail flows of progressive racial politics. Thus, the postracial state not only fails to deliver on its promise, but also serves to maintain the existence of the racialized flows which characterize liquid modernity. Within this understanding, the postracial state is unachievable, other than as a notional moment in time which in the very best scenario could be subjected to freezing, but which would inevitably thaw and return the politics of 'race' to the unstable, unpredictable and ever-changing manifestations of racist flows in liquid modernity.

We have sought to explore the manifestations of these racist flows through three case studies. These three case studies were used as a way of grounding the theoretical premises outlined in the book. Brexit, or the referendum on the UK leaving the EU in 2016, was the first case that was considered. Brexit represented a good example of how racism can be manifested at the macro-level in the context of liquid modernity and provides insights into how matters of 'race' were located in relation to a national political issue in an international context. Key to our analysis is the recognition that the political conditions which underpinned Brexit cannot be separated from the older solid structures of racism in modernity – most significantly, the colonial project of which Britain was at the forefront. As society transitioned into late modernity, the liquefaction of the old colonial order has seen the breakdown of formal empire, and this has resulted in its dissolution into murky and ambiguous waters where colonial histories are washed away from mainstream understandings of 'race' in the contemporary moment. While this process leads to increasing ambiguities concerning the extent to which 'race' and racism still function in liquid modernity, the sediments of colonialism remain, meandering within and between white British and racialized minority groups. This process sees sediments gradually build in ways which impact differentially based on which side of the ever-growing embankment individuals find themselves based on their relationality to whiteness. Racialized minority groups, including those with histories of colonial rule under Britain but also many economic migrant groups, find themselves exposed to varying and nuanced viscosities of resistance in navigating through their experience of civic life. The specifics of these experiences are based on the intersections of their identities and how these play out in their relationality to whiteness and national identification. For those favoured by the flows of whiteness, the sedimentary build-up comprises old and confused messages, as legacies and relics of the colonial project are no longer solidly intact, no longer clearly attributable to the unapologetic aspirations to racial domination from which they are derived. These flows convey messages which have seen their connection to racism eroded away such that matters of 'race' become reformulated and attributable to other, more palatable political issues. Anti-immigration politics is no longer a reserve for the active racist. Immigration becomes strategically reframed as simply detrimental for employment opportunities for white Britons – particularly the working classes (see Chapter 5 for our analysis of 'race' and education in liquid modernity). The process of liquefaction in this context allowed for the co-signing of anti-immigration sentiments which underpinned much of the leave campaigns without having to acknowledge the ways in which these were invariably tied up with the state of race relations more widely. Furthermore, the legacies of the colonial project which underpinned much of the anti-immigration rhetoric around Brexit are so well obscured in the murky and ambiguous waters of contemporary politics that, for the most part, they go unnoticed and unacknowledged.

There are also implications for the liquefaction of the colonial project beyond the experiences and political participation of individuals in the context of Brexit. The state of liquidity which has characterized late modernity has obscured the realities of the 'role of state violence' and 'expansion of colonialism' (Carrington et al, 2016: 3) for states in the Global North. 'Great Britain' was at the forefront of the colonial project, and while the solidified structures of colonialism have been subjected to liquefaction through the breakdown of Empire, Britain has worked to maintain its position of hegemonic dominance in the late modern global order. To paraphrase Ciocchini and Greener (2021), flows of goods, capital and services alongside the concentration of economic influence in the Global North have impacted the Global South in ways that have sustained highly racialized socioeconomic problems. The UK has been a key part of this process, and the notion of hanging on to historical notions of 'Great Britain' has invariably informed the politics around Brexit – in particular, the perception that it would lead to greater economic positioning in an increasingly liquid global order. Of course, this notion is far from new and clearly echoes Gilroy's (2004) postcolonial melancholia. However, the conditions of Brexit were specifically characterized by anxieties around not only the observable realities of immigration and economic recession, but also the increasing sense of ambivalence and instability around flows of people and resources in the post-New Labour era. Whereas Blair had championed economic migration and embraced freedom of movement within the EU, the addition of new EU Member States would trigger waves of resentment which would become heavily racialized, specifically in relation to Eastern European migrant workers. Similarly, issues of asylum would also be significant, with distorted perceptions of refugee crises representing a double-edged sword from the late 1990s to the early 2000s. The UK's obligation to process claims for asylum were met with public resistance and increasingly restrictive legislative frameworks. The processing of asylum claims in other states such as France and the Netherlands would also be a significant factor, with EU nationals who had been granted refugee status in such states gaining access to freedom of movement and exercising it to move to Britain as economic migrants. Significant proportions of the diasporic communities which emerged in the early 2000s were EU nationals living alongside those with shared cultural backgrounds who *were* seeking asylum in Britain. The intersection of these flows informed a massively distorted picture of asylum, which would in turn lead to increasing resentment towards refugees, asylum seekers and the government. It is the very conditions of liquid modernity which facilitated the intersection of these flows, as well as the ambiguities, uncertainties and inaccuracies which would culminate in an increasing sedimentary build-up in resistance to all matters pertaining to immigration. What is also important here is that this happens in the context of Britain as a nation state in the Global North working to continuously maintain its global position at the expense of the Global South. However, the liquefaction of the solidified entity of Great Britain and its Empire obscures this reality such that it results in ambiguities and anxieties about what 'British' actually means in late modernity for citizens of the state. The transition from the notion of a 'Britannia' that 'rules the waves' to a nation state interdependent on others and answerable to the EU represented the dissolving of long-understood notions of Britishness. For 'leavers', independence from the EU would represent a moment of resolidification, with Britain reclaiming sovereignty on its path to once again becoming 'Great'. Brexit represents a perfect conundrum, where this motivation for 'leavers' was gradually built up out of sediments of resentment regarding notions of lost sovereignty and the perceived impacts of immigration on individual access to resources within the nation state. 'Remainers', on the other hand, can be seen as complicit in the neocolonial project, whereby the ambiguities of liquid modernity obscure a more tacit commitment to exploiting economic migrants as a strategy to sustain a global economic position comparable to their previous, more solidified position as a colonial global power.

Considering the political context around Brexit exposes underlying tensions regarding the impacts of immigration on access to resources which were facilitated by the increasing uncertainties and obscurities of liquidity in late modernity. As we moved to consider the case study of education, we can break down some of these anxieties into more tangible manifestations, incarnate in the concerns of both affluent but also socioeconomically deprived white British groups. We are able to trace the sediments of the 2016 referendum back to New Labour's championing of economic migrants and freedom of movement in the EU. This represents a clear embodiment of *mixophilia* or attraction towards the 'other' – in this case, economic migrants. As we move through the late 1990s and into the early 2000s, the legacy of this manifesting was seen through what Vertovec (2007, 2009) describes as increasing superdiversity. These cumulative waves of economic migration, alongside the distorted perception of the scale of those seeking asylum, were absorbed into political mobilizations characterized by far-right conservative convictions – such as those manifested in UKIP and the BNP, and accompanied by informal movements such as the English Defence League (EDL). These mobilizations purposefully positioned themselves in opposition to the increasingly liberal flows of the 'loony left', who had taken matters of diversity too far at the expense of 'real Brits'. Attempts to stem both migration flows and the political rhetoric which had seemingly facilitated them were subsequently co-opted by the Conservative Party, with then Prime Minister David Cameron offering a referendum on Britain's membership of the EU as part of the 2015 general election campaign. Whereas UKIP, the BNP and even the EDL had coexisted, their political influence had in many ways remained niche, confined to concentrated pools of political resistance to main*stream* political agendas. However, the shift in Conservative strategy that saw the party entertain the possibility of Britain leaving the EU resulted in a significant increase in flows of political rhetoric on immigration and sovereignty which flooded the plains across which the pooling of UKIP, BNP and EDL political sentiment had coexisted. This process necessarily resulted in some dilution – the Conservative Party fell short of the anti-Muslim rhetoric of the EDL and the overtly nationalistic politics of the BNP. On the issue of the EU, the Conservatives also fell short of replicating UKIP's rhetoric – the party offered the *opportunity* for British voters to *have their say* on leaving the EU rather than positioning their campaign on *advocating* for leaving the EU, as UKIP did. Nevertheless, this process of flooding led to the Conservatives absorbing voters who would have previously voted UKIP or BNP, while seemingly offering a legitimate political space for advocated of the EDL to exercise anti-immigration politics. Brexit is an important example of how the ambiguities that characterize politics in liquid modernity allowed the Conservatives to secure power without having to subscribe overtly to the politics of the right-wing from which they would secure new voters. Cameron was even vocal about stepping down as Prime Minister should the outcome of the referendum result in Britain leaving the EU. While much of Brexit was characterized by the build-up of anti-immigration sentiment, the Conservative campaign arguably focused more on the economic implications, with 'Brexiters' in the party claiming a number of financial benefits for Britain on leaving the EU. However, separating matters of immigration and economics is not possible in the case of Brexit owing to cross-flows of anxieties over economic migrants, the cost of asylum seekers and refugees to the government, and increased competition for employment – particularly for white Britons living with high levels of socioeconomic deprivation.

Our focus on education as the second site for our enquiry offers important insights into how much of the political tension which underpinned Brexit came to be. It also allows us to deconstruct the ways in which sediments of white resentment built up against a perception of 'progressive' politics overlooking the interests of the white working classes in the case of the education system. The notion of the white working classes as the 'new underachievers' in education can be traced back to around 2007 and was the result of misleading news media reporting and the misrepresentation of educational attainment statistics. The educational attainment of white boys who qualify for FSM is, of course, a cause for concern for such groups as stakeholders in education. However, the way in which this has been framed as a case where white groups are experiencing disadvantage *because* they are white is a massive misrepresentation of the problem: the reality that the attainment gap between white boys who do not qualify for FSM and those who do is greater than the gap between attainment for white boys and Black African boys who quality for FSM. Consequently, the disadvantage that white boys who qualify for FSM face in education is the result of the impacts of *poverty*, not the result of their whiteness. It is also telling that the statistics must be fractured by gender to generate this gap, and that the comparison is not the wider category of Black British boys, but the highest-achieving Black British group. The most alarming aspect is the way in which the news media reported these attainment gaps. Headlines favoured the term 'working class' over 'boys who qualify for Free School Meals', culminating in the construction of the much-distorted narrative that 'the white working classes are the new underachievers in education'. We worked through this deconstruction in Chapter 5 in further detail, but in short the projection of the proportion of white boys who qualify for FSM (around 14 per cent of the population) onto the working classes (somewhere between 50 and 60 per cent of the population) is not only irresponsible, but also played a significant role in the tensions which have culminated in the 'left behind'. The proportion of white groups who qualify for FSM maps almost perfectly onto the 'precariat' in Savage et al's (2013) social class model, a group which make up around 13 per cent of the population. The legitimate viscosities in education experienced by these groups do leave them disempowered, but because of *poverty*, *not* because of any systemic racialized processes in education eroding away white interests – a reality embodied through the comparative success of their more economically affluent white peers.

These ambiguities between working-class identity, 'race' and poverty have done much to convey obscured messages on *who* is disempowered, *how* and *why* in education in the context of liquid modernity. These ambiguities have led to anxieties around how far matters of race and working-class identity have started to work against the interests of white stakeholders in education in the contemporary moment. Nevertheless, even in the face of this confusion, those white groups who are most impacted by poverty in education *do* represent one example of Bauman's 'wasted lives' – the casualties of liquid modernity. Furthermore, the tension around immigration, economic migrants, asylum seekers and refugees, and the implications of this for children of the 'precariat' represent a confluence of 'wasted lives', or casualties of liquid modernity, competing for security and resources in education and beyond. The notion of the white working classes as the new underachievers in education is one example of the ways in which the anti-immigration politics of the 'left behind' emerged as a misdirected backflow targeted at immigrant communities rather than their white affluent counterparts. Within this political narrative, immigration is the inevitable consequence of 'real' leftist politics gradually becoming diluted into liberal flows (Winlow et al, 2017: 145), meandering around the interests of the white working classes to collide with racialized backflows of resentment, within which immigrants are perceived of as the 'human waste of distant parts of the globe unloaded into "our" own backyard' (Bauman, 2003b: 56).

The backflows of resentment which have characterized white resistance to immigration flows have sat at the centre of both narratives around Brexit and the 'wasted lives' of the 'left behind' in education. Bauman's (2000) liquid metaphor has allowed us to reveal and understand the ways in which racialized marginality not only persists in late modernity, but also how vastly differing perceptions of the state of race relations have come to be. Relationality to whiteness sits at the centre of the ways in which racialized flows are experienced, with processes of filtration, sedimentary build-up and meandering all impacting on white perceptions of racialized marginality which obscures the reality of their socioeconomic domination. In considering the white precariat as 'wasted lives', we of course acknowledge that we are discussing a white group. But 'white' in this context only makes sense as an identifier for the group we are discussing. Their marginality is not a product of any racialized oppression; rather, relationality to whiteness still works to alleviate the threat of race-based inequality relative to racialized minority groups in comparable socioeconomic conditions. Thinking about 'race' and socioeconomic marginality in this way leads to thinking about the spaces and places within which marginality across both streams occurs. We typically see this in areas of high deprivation in large cities, within which the combination of these concurrent flows spirals, resulting in confusion and ambiguity regarding the realities of racialized oppression – both for those within and those spectating from more affluent streams. The intensity that has characterized these tensions exacerbates a process of *spiralling*, which inevitably erodes downwards through spaces characterized by high socioeconomic deprivation and high levels of racial diversity. Eroding downwards results in increasingly insurmountable banks surrounding flows of racialized and socioeconomic oppression, as they spiral and erode, leading to pooling. In this context, both the 'left behind' and racialized minorities are vagabonds, but their experiences are distinguished from each other as they encounter viscosities comprising differing constitutions. While racialized minority groups are faced with highly racialized flows and viscosities in their stream, the sedimentary composition of concurrent streams of white marginality filters perception for the left behind such that they see their marginality as racial. It is within these pools that we see tensions between 'race' and class also inform the negotiation of cultural flows deriving from the diversities of city spaces.

This led us to consider how the conditions of liquidity impact for young people living in inner-city spaces, but also how cross-flows of cultural production and consumption lead to the intensification of racism and structural violence. Indeed, perceptions of road culture are characterized by associations with Blackness which reproduce longstanding tropes on Black men, criminality and policing. This process is characterized by tension – both in the present and historically – as the fetishization of Black cultural consumption relies on ascribing aspects of controversiality in perceptions of Black masculinity. The flow between road culture as a lived experience and how it is perceived in the wider main*stream* opens up ambiguities which soak into pre-existing racialized flows. Historically, Black cultural flows have been subject to damming, with Black cultural production being controlled, policed and restricted in ways which have limited cultural expression. There are serious implications to both the damming Black cultural expression and the pooling of racialized flows in the context of the city. Misrepresentations of life 'on road' equate aspects of road culture with criminality; however, Bakkali (2019), among others, has demonstrated the more mundane aspects of road life. Nevertheless, many have argued that the immediate challenges of life 'on road' necessitate resistance in the form of 'toughness' in efforts to navigate the viscosities in flows of both racialization and socioeconomic marginalization in inner-city spaces. This process is complicated, and in no way do we look to establish truth in stereotypes. Rather, it is the viscosities around racialized socioeconomic marginality which set the conditions for the embodiment of 'hardened masculinities' in street cultural settings. The realities of these masculinities are also ambiguous, with their depiction implying a state of toughness as a constant feature, which may only exist temporally, momentarily or performatively – if at all. Where masculinities do become embodied in this way, their development is a product of racism, disparately affecting minoritized people.

There are complex dynamics which inform this process, as street masculinities have also been considered a response to the difficulties of life 'on road' combined with pressures regarding expectations of men in the context of patriarchy (Miller, 1958; Bourgois, 1996; bell hooks, 1999). Where hypermasculinities become embodied, they derive from hegemonic masculinities being recontextualized and actualized at the limits of marginality. The conditions of life 'on road' are such that men are positioned at a disadvantage in the labour market, with viscosities affecting access to legitimate economic activity and opportunities to negotiate social status. Our case study in education is particularly relevant here, as disproportionate educational marginalization and exclusion impact significantly on access to legitimate economies. These conditions may leave those most marginalized to be confronted with being unable to embody dominant or main*stream* masculinities, leading to hypermasculine performances of gender. Legacies of colonialism also have a role, with white powerholders in the colonial project propagating stereotypes regarding colonized people being characterized by hyperviolence, low intelligence and hypersexuality. The sedimentary effects in white majority societies with colonial histories mean that masculinities of Black/brown men cannot be separated from the history of their oppression. From this understanding, where Black/brown men do embody hypermasculinities/street masculinities, this is heavily informed by their socialization in the context of white supremacist societies (Orelus, 2010: 78–79).

The internalization of hypermasculine tropes has invariably informed approaches to policing, racial profiling and disproportionality in practices such as stop and search, arrests and custodial sentencing. These processes of criminalization are invariably bound up with the ways in which Black British cultural production has been historically policed. The restriction of access to main*stream* platforms for artists who embodied a 'street image' has been eroded away with the emergence of digital technologies facilitating cultural flows across new online and social media platforms. While these developments have opened flows of cultural production, there have been negative impacts on young people located at the fringes of street cultures. Within these contexts, social status can be highly sensitive and precarious, and slights against young men specifically can result in violent conflicts. The emergence of social media alongside this not only provides platforms for the further consumption of hypermasculine representations, but also serves as a new space within which the value systems that lead to violent conflicts can be amplified (Irwin-Rogers and Pinkney, 2017, 2018). Representations in both traditional and social media present desires which mirror racialized dynamics of white majority societies with colonial histories and, in this context, Black and brown people are materially rewarded for performing transgressive displays of otherness. These transgressive displays can be taken to the extreme in social media spaces, at times resulting in the difference between life and death. The production and consumption of street aesthetics has sat at the centre of drill music, and while this genre is not the first to embody such imagery, its allusions to violence and more provocative aspects of inner-city life have resulted in it attracting main*stream* attention and concern. The overflow between the lyrical imagery that characterizes drill as a cultural product and the ambiguities around what constitutes 'life on road' reflects longstanding racialized narratives on young people and violence which have been commodified for main*stream* consumption. This dynamic is characterized by deep ambivalence, with digital platforms opening flows of cultural production which were previously dammed, but also offering promises of fame and fortune which may lead some to transgress and cause harm. This dynamic cannot be understood without acknowledging the sedimentary legacies of the Western European colonial project.

Concluding thoughts

Our application of liquidity has helped in explaining the pervasiveness of racism in late modernity, particularly the ways that it has shifted and changed under conditions of liquefaction. The notion of racism as ongoing and pervasive has been met with resistance in public political discourse, and Bauman's (2000) liquid metaphor allows us to evidence and identify its ongoing effects in the contemporary moment. Concepts such as sedimentary legacies, meandering and confluences, damming and glaciation can be applied to understand the ever-changing yet ongoing presence of racism in late modernity. We have provided examples of this across our three case studies: Brexit, education, and road culture. Liquidity has also helped us to analyse the contemporary state we are in regarding how far we are still in late modernity versus postmodernity. The liquefaction of the old structures of the colonial project may have given the appearance of society moving away from the legacies of modernity in ways which may eventually lead the way into postmodernity. However, Bauman's liquid metaphor allows us to evidence ongoing legacies of histories which cannot and have not been washed away in the contemporary moment. Rather, the liquefaction of racist apparatus has allowed racism to operate unseen by those whose experiences of racialized flows are clouded by the filtration of colonialism's sedimentary legacies afforded by relationality to whiteness. This understanding allows us to explain not only that neither postmodernism nor a postracial state can exist; it also explains why white groups perceive the state of race relations so differentially from racialized minorities.

Bauman's (2000) concept of liquidity can be applied meaningfully to understand some of the complexities regarding race in contemporary society which are overlooked in other theories of late modernity. In the process, we have opened up Baumanian thinking to a wider vocabulary of application, allowing race to sit at the centre of canonical theorizing on late modernity. This is something of a political project, where theories of modernity can be held to account for overlooking the complexities of race relations in the contemporary moment. We are fully indebted to bodies of work on critical race theory, Black criminology and wider contributions to knowledge on 'race' and racism. This book does not intentionally make any claims of novel application other than in developing the extent to which Bauman's work can be applied to matters of 'race'. Our intention is to provide a book on main*stream* theorizing on late modernity which brings 'race' to the centre, with the intention that matters of 'race' do not become eroded from canonical bodies of work on modernity moving forwards. We also hope that this book will lead some on a path towards engaging with more critical perspectives on 'race'. While this book has focused on the application of Bauman's (2000) liquid metaphor to experiences of 'race' and racism, this is part of a larger project on Baumanian social thought. The authors aim to conceptually develop Bauman's notion of liquidity further by applying it to a range of contemporary social issues.

References

Abranches, M., Theuerkauf, U.G., Scott, C. and White, C.S. (2021) 'Cultural violence in the aftermath of the Brexit referendum: manifestations of post-racial xeno-racism'. *Ethnic and Racial Studies*, 44(15), 2876–2894.

Adorno, T.W. (1947) *Composing for the Films*. New York: A&C Black.

Adorno, T.W. (1964) *Night Music: Essays on Music 1928–1962*. New York: Seagull Books.

Adorno, T.W. (1966) *Negative Dialectics*. New York: A&C Black.

Adorno, T.W. and Horkheimer, M. (1944) *Dialectic of Enlightenment*. London: Verso.

Agamben, G. (1998) *Homo Saucer: Sovereign Power and Bare Life*. Stanford: Stanford University Press.

Ahmed, S. (2000) *Strange Encounters*. London: Routledge.

Al-Jazeera (2020) 'Know their names: Black people killed by the police in the US'. [online] Available from: https://interactive.aljazeera.com/aje/2020/know-their-names/index.html

Aldridge, D.P. and Stewart, J.B. (2005) 'Introduction. Hip hop history: past, present and future'. *Journal of African American History*, 90(3), 190–195.

Aldridge, J., Ralphs, R. and Medina, J. (2011) 'Collateral damage: territory and policing in an English gang city', in B. Goldson (ed.) *Youth in Crisis?* Abingdon: Routledge, pp 72–88.

Alkaraan, F. and Floyd, D. (2020) 'Rethinking of the UK strategic public decision: outsourcing, accountability, and governance perspectives'. *Strategic Change*, 29(6), 625–632.

Amnå, E. and Ekman, J. (2014) 'Standby citizens: diverse faces of political passivity'. *European Political Science Review*, 6(2), 261–281.

Amnesty (2018) *Trapped in the Matrix: Secrecy, Stigma and Bias in the Met's Gang Database*. London: Amnesty International UK.

Amnesty International (2020) 'What is the Gangs Matrix?' [online] Available from: https://www.amnesty.org.uk/london-trident-gangs-matrix-metropolitan-police

Anderson, B. (1983) *Imagined Communities: Reflections on the Origins and Spread of Nationalism*. London: Verso.

Anderson, E. (2000) *Code of the Street: Decency, Violence, and the Moral Life of the Inner City*. New York: WW Norton & Company.

Anderson, E. (2004) 'The cosmopolitan canopy'. *Annals of the American Academy of Political and Social Science*, 595(1), 14–31.

Andrews, K. (2016) 'The psychosis of whiteness: the celluloid hallucinations of amazing Grace and Belle'. *Journal of Black Studies*, 47(5), 435–453.

Archer, M.S. (2012) *The Reflexive Imperative In Late Modernity*. Cambridge: Cambridge University Press.

Atkinson, R. (2006) 'Padding the bunker: strategies of middle-class disaffiliation and colonisation in the city'. *Urban Studies*, 43(4), 819–832.

Atkinson, R. (2016) 'Limited exposure: social concealment, mobility and engagement with public space by the super-rich in London'. *Environment and Planning A: Economy and Space*, 48(7), 1302–1317.

Augé, M. (1992) *Non-places: Introduction to an Anthropology of Supermodernity*. London: Verso.

Back, L. (2007) *The Art of Listening*. Oxford: Berg.

Back, L., Keith, M., Khan, A., Shukra, K. and Solomos. J. (2002) 'New Labour's white heart: politics, multiculturalism and the return of assimilation'. *Political Quarterly*, 73(4), 445–454.

Baird, A., Bishop, M.L. and Kerrigan, D. (2022) ' "Breaking bad"? Gangs, masculinities and murder in Trinidad'. *International Feminist Journal of Politics*, 24(4), 632–657.

Bakkali, Y. (2018) 'Life on road: symbolic struggle and the munpain'. Unpublished PhD Thesis, University of Sussex.

Bakkali, Y. (2019) 'Dying to live: youth violence and the munpain'. *Sociological Review*, 67(6), 1317–1332.

Bakkali, Y. (2021) 'Road capitals: reconceptualising street capital, value production and exchange in the context of road life in the UK'. *Current Sociology*, 70(3), 419–435.

Bakkali, Y. (2022) 'Road capitals: reconceptualising street capital, value production and exchange in the context of road life in the UK'. *Current Sociology*, 70(3), 419–435.

Bakkali, Y. and Chigbo, E. (2023) 'Tainted love: intimate relationships and gendered violence on-road', in J. Levell, T. Young and R. Earle (eds) *Exploring Urban Youth Culture Outside of the Gang Paradigm*. Bristol: Bristol University Press, pp 39–58.

Ball, S. (2008) *The Education Debate*. Bristol: Policy Press.

Bang, H. (2005) 'Among everyday makers and expert citizens', in J. Newman (ed.) *Remaking Governance: Peoples, Politics and the Public Sphere*. Bristol: Policy Press, pp 159–178.

Banton, M. (1983) *Racial and Ethnic Competition*. Cambridge: Cambridge University Press.

Barth, F. (1969) *Ethnic Groups and Boundaries*. Boston: Little Brown.

Baudrillard, J. (1981) *Simulacra and Simulation*. Michigan: University of Michigan Press.

Bauman, Z. (1957) *Questions of Democratic Centralism in Lenin's Works*. Warsaw: Książka i Wiedza.

Bauman, Z. (1964) *An Outline of the Marxist Theory of Society*. Warsaw: Państwowe Wydawnictwo Naukowe.

Bauman, Z. (1967) 'Images of man in modern sociology (some methodological remarks)'. *Polish Sociological Bulletin*, 15, 12–21.

Bauman, Z. (1972) *Between Class and Elite: The Evolution of the British Labour Movement. A Sociological Study*. Manchester: Manchester University Press.

Bauman, Z. (1976) *Socialism: The Active Utopia*. New York: Holmes and Meier Publishers.

Bauman, Z. (1988) 'Is there a postmodern sociology?'. *Theory, Culture & Society*, 5(2), 217–237.

Bauman, Z. (1989a) *Modernity and the Holocaust*. Ithaca, NY: Cornell University Press.

Bauman, Z. (1989b) 'Sociological responses to postmodernity'. *Thesis Eleven*, 23(1), 35–63.

Bauman, Z. (1990a) 'Philosophical affinities of postmodern sociology'. *Sociological Review*, 38(3), 411–444.

Bauman, Z. (1990b) *Thinking Sociologically*. Oxford: Blackwell.

Bauman, Z. (1991a) *Modernity and Ambivalence*. Cambridge: Policy Press.

Bauman, Z. (1991b) 'A sociological theory of postmodernity'. *Thesis Eleven*, 29(1), 33–46.

Bauman, Z. (1992) *Intimations of Postmodernity*. London: Routledge.

Bauman, Z. (1993) *Postmodern Ethics*. Cambridge, MA: Blackwell.

Bauman, Z. (1995a) *Life in Fragments: Essays in Postmodern Morality*. Cambridge, MA: Blackwell.

Bauman, Z. (1995b) 'Making and unmaking of strangers'. *Thesis Eleven*, 43(1), 1–16.

Bauman, Z. (1997) *Postmodernity and Its Discontents*. New York: New York University Press.

Bauman, Z. (1998) *Globalisation: The Human Consequences*. Cambridge: Polity Press.

Bauman, Z. (2000) *Liquid Modernity*. Cambridge: Polity Press.

Bauman, Z. (2001a) 'The journey never ends: Zygmunt Bauman talks with Peter Beilharz', in P. Beilharz (ed.) *The Bauman Reader*. Oxford: Blackwell, pp 334–344.

Bauman, Z. (2001b) *Community: Seeking Safety in an Insecure World*. Cambridge: Polity Press.

Bauman, Z. (2003a) *Liquid Love*. Cambridge: Polity Press.

Bauman, Z. (2003b) *Wasted Lives: Modernity and Its Outcasts*. Cambridge: Polity Press.

Bauman, Z. (2005) *Liquid Life*. Cambridge: Polity Press.

Bauman, Z. (2006a) *Liquid Fear*. Cambridge: Polity Press.

Bauman, Z. (2006b) *Liquid Times*. Cambridge: Polity Press.

Bauman, Z. (2007) *Consuming Life*. Cambridge: Polity Press.

Bauman, Z. (2011a) *Collateral Damage: Social Inequalities in a Global Age*. Cambridge: Polity Press.

Bauman, Z. (2011b) *Culture in a Liquid Modern World*. Cambridge: Polity Press.

Bauman, Z. (2016) *Retrotopia*. London: Wiley.

Bauman, Z. (2017) *Strangers at Our Door*. Cambridge: Polity Press.

Bauman, Z. (2020) 'Modernity, racism, extermination', in L. Back and J. Solomos (eds) *Theories of Race and Racism*. Abingdon: Routledge, pp 277–293.

Bauman, Z. and Donskis, L. (2013) *Moral Blindness: The Loss of Sensitivity in Liquid Modernity*. Cambridge: Polity Press.

Bauman, Z. and Donskis, L. (2016) *Liquid Evil*. Cambridge: Polity Press.

Bauman, Z. and Lyon, D. (2012) *Liquid Surveillance: A Conversation*. Cambridge: Polity Press.

Bauman, Z. and Lyon, D. (2013) *Liquid Surveillance: A Conversion with Zygmunt Bauman*. Cambridge: Polity Press.

Bauman, Z. and Yakimova, M. (2002) 'A postmodern grid of the worldmap? Critique and humanism'. [online] Available from: https://www.eurozine.com/a-postmodern-grid-of-the-worldmap/

Bauman, Z., Bauman, I., Kociatkiewicz, J. and Kostera, M. (2016) *Management in a Liquid Modern World*. Cambridge: Polity Press.

BBC News (2011) 'Ed Miliband condemns David Starkey's race comments'. [online] Available from: https://www.bbc.co.uk/news/uk-14531077

Beck, U. (1992) *Risk Society: Towards a New Modernity*. London: Sage.

Beck, U. (1998) *World Risk Society*. Cambridge: Polity Press.

Beck, U. (1999) *What Is Globalization?* Cambridge: Polity Press.

Beck, U. (2009) *World at Risk*. Cambridge: Polity Press.

Begum, N., Mondon, A. and Winter, A. (2021) 'Between the "left behind" and "the people": racism, populism and the construction of the "white working class" in the context of Brexit', in S. Hunter and C. van der Westhuizen (eds) *Routledge Handbook of Critical Studies in Whiteness*. Abingdon: Routledge, pp 220–231.

Beilharz, P. (2001) *The Bauman Reader*. London: Wiley.

Bell, D. (1980) 'Brown and the interest-convergence dilemma', in D. Bell (ed.) *Shades of Brown: New Perspectives on School Desegregation*. New York: Teachers College Press, pp 90–106.

bell hooks (1992) *Black Looks: Race and Representation*. Boston, MA: South End Press.

bell hooks (1994) *Teaching to Transgress Education as the Practice of Freedom*. New York. Routledge.

bell hooks (1999) *Feminism Is for Everybody: Passionate Politics*. London: Pluto Press.

bell hooks (2000) *Feminist Theory: From Margin to Center*. London: Pluto Press.

bell hooks (2004) *We Real Cool: Black Men and Masculinity*. New York: Psychology Press.

Ben-Shahar, O. (2016) 'The non-voters who decided the election: Trump won because of lower democratic turnout'. [online] Available from: https://www.law.uchicago.edu/news/omri-ben-shahar-false-account-how-trump-won

Benjamin, W. (1929) *One-Way Street and Other Writings*. London: Verso.

Benson, M. and Lewis, C. (2019) 'Brexit, British people of colour in the EU-27 and everyday racism in Britain and Europe'. *Ethnic and Racial Studies*, 42(13), 2211–2228.

Berman, M. (1982) *All That Is Solid Melts into Air: The Experience of Modernity*. London: Verso.

Best, S. (1998) 'Zygmunt Bauman: personal reflections within the mainstream of modernity'. *British Journal of Sociology*, 49(2), 311–320.

Bhambra, G.K. (2017) 'Brexit, Trump, and "methodological whiteness": on the misrecognition of race and class'. *British Journal of Sociology*, 68, 214–232.

Bhambra, G.K. and Holmwood, J. (2021) *Colonialism and Modern Social Theory*. Hoboken, NJ: John Wiley & Sons.

Bhattacharyya, G. (1999) 'Teaching race in cultural studies: a ten-step programme of personal development', in M. Bulmer and J. Solomos (eds) *Ethnic and Racial Studies Today*. Abingdon: Routledge, pp 73–85.

Bhopal, K. (2004) 'Gypsy travellers and education: changing needs and changing perceptions'. *British Journal of Educational Studies*, 52(1), 47–64.

Bhopal, K. (2011) ' "This is a school, it's not a site": teachers' attitudes towards Gypsy and traveller pupils in schools in England, UK'. *British Educational Research Journal*, 37(3), 465–483.

Biddiss, M.D. (1976) 'The politics of anatomy: Dr Robert Knox and Victorian racism'. *History and Medicine*, 69, 245–250.

Billig, M., Condor, S., Edwards, D., Gane, M., Middleton, D. and Radley, A. (1988) *Ideological Dilemmas: A Social Psychology of Everyday Thinking*. London: Sage.

Blackshaw, T. (2005) *Zygmunt Bauman*. London: Routledge.

Blair, T. (1999) 'Prime Minister's speech to the Labour Party conference, September 26th 1999', Bournemouth, UK.

Boakye, J. (2017) 'Boys to mandem: grime and the masculinity barrier', in J. Boakye (ed.) *Hold Tight: Black Masculinity, Millennials and the Meaning of Grime*. London: Influx Press, pp 355–361.

Bogle, D. (1973) *Toms, Coons, Mulattoes, Mammies and Bucks: An Interpretive History of Blacks in American Films*. London: Bloomsbury.

Bonilla-Silva, E. (2013) *Racism without Racists: Color-Blind Racism and the Persistence of Racial Inequality in the United States*. New York: Rowman & Littlefield.

Bonnett, A. and Alexander, C. (2013) 'Mobile nostalgias: connecting visions of the urban past, present and future amongst ex-residents'. *Transactions of the Institute of British Geographers*, 38, 391–402.

Bottero, W. (2009) 'Relationality and social interaction'. *British Journal of Sociology*, 60(2), 399–420.

Bourgois, P. (1996) 'In search of masculinity: violence, respect and sexuality among Puerto Rican crack dealers in East Harlem'. *British Journal of Criminology*, 36(3), 412–427.

Boym, S. (2001) *The Future of Nostalgia*. New York: Basic Books.

BPI (2023) 'The new music democracy'. [online] Available from: https://www.bpi.co.uk/media/3742/bpi-streaming-report-2023.pdf

Breen, D. (2018) *British Muslim Communities, 'Faith' Schooling and Critical Race Theory. Muslim Schools, Communities and Critical Race Theory: Faith Schooling in an Islamophobic Britain?* London: Palgrave Macmillan.

Breen, D. (2023) 'From securing whiteness to securing publics? Marginalized communities and differential stakeholdership in domestic security in the UK'. *Journal of Global Faultlines*, 10(1), 58–70.

Breen, D. and Meer, N. (2019) 'Securing whiteness? Critical race theory (CRT) and the securitization of Muslims in education'. *Identities*, 5, 595–613.

Bryant, A. (2007) 'Liquid modernity, complexity and turbulence'. *Theory, Culture & Society*, 24(1), 127–135.

Bryant, A. (2013) 'Bauman's challenge: metaphors and metamorphoses', in M. Davies (ed.) *Liquid Sociology: Metaphor in Zygmunt Bauman's Analysis of Modernity*. Abingdon: Routledge, pp 39–56.

Bulman, M. (2017) 'Government faces High Court challenge for collecting data on school pupils' nationality and country of birth'. [online] Available from: https://www.independent.co.uk/news/uk/home-news/school-pupils-nationality-country-birth-data-information-high-court-challenge-government-education-a8094996.html

Burnett, J. (2012) 'After Lawrence: racial violence and policing in the UK'. *Race & Class*, 54(1), 91–98.

Burnett, J. (2017) 'Racial violence and the Brexit state'. *Race & Class*, 58(4), 85–97.

Busby, E. (2019) 'Black students more likely to engage in studies – but still attain lower degrees, study finds'. [online] Available from: https://www.independent.co.uk/news/education/education-news/black-students-degrees-universities-advance-he-study-a9179226.html

Butler, J. (1997) *Excitable Speech: A Politics of the Performative*. Abingdon: Routledge.

Butler, J. (2004) *Precarious Life: The Powers of Mourning and Violence*. London: Verso.

Bygnes, S. (2013) 'Ambivalent multiculturalism'. *Sociology*, 47(1), 126–141.

Bygnes, S. and Erdal, M.B. (2017) 'Liquid migration, grounded lives: considerations about future mobility and settlement among Polish and Spanish migrants in Norway'. *Journal of Ethnic and Migration Studies*, 43(1), 102–118.

Byrne, B., Alexander, C., Khan, O., Nazroo, J. and Shankley, W. (eds) (2020) *Ethnicity, Race and Inequality in the UK: State of the Nation*. London: Palgrave Macmillan.

Campbell-Stevens, R. (2020) 'Global majority: we need to talk about labels such as "BAME"'. [online] Available from: https://www.linkedin.com/pulse/global-majority-we-need-talk-labels-bame-campbell-stephens-mbe

Camus, A. (1951) *The Rebel*. London: Penguin.

Carrington, K., Hogg, R. and Sozzo, M. (2016) 'Southern criminology'. *British Journal of Criminology*, 56, 1–20.

Castells, M. (1991) *The Network Society*. Oxford: Blackwell.

Charles, M. (2018) 'Grime Labour'. *Soundings*, 68, 40–52.

Children's Society (2021) 'What is drill?' [online] Available from: https://www.childrenssociety.org.uk/what-we-do/blogs/culture-of-drill-music

Choak, C. (2021) 'Hegemonic masculinity and "badness": how young women bargain with patriarchy "on road"'. *Boyhood Studies*, 14(1), 63–74.

Choi, K.J. (2011) 'Should race matter? A constructive ethical assessment of the post racial ideal'. *Journal of the Society of Christian Ethics*, 31(1), 79–101.

Christian, M. (2005) 'The politics of black presence in Britain and black male exclusion in the British education system'. *Journal of Black Studies*, 35(3), 327–346.

Ciocchini, P. and Greener, J. (2021) 'Mapping the pains of neo-colonialism: a critical elaboration of southern criminology'. *British Journal of Criminology*, 61(6), 1612–1629.

Clegg, J. Stackhouse, K.F. Murphy, C. and Nicholls, S. (2009) 'Language abilities of secondary age pupils at risk of school exclusion: a preliminary report'. *Child Language Teaching and Therapy*, 25(1), 123–140.

Coard, B. (1971) *How the West Indian Child Is Made Educationally Subnormal in the British School System: The Scandal of the Black Child in Schools in Britain*. London: Self-published.

Coates, T. (2015) *Between the World and Me*. Melbourne: Text Publishing.

Connell, R. (1995) *Masculinities*. Abingdon: Routledge.

Connell, R. (2007) 'The northern theory of globalization'. *Sociological Theory*, 25(4), 368–385.

Cubitt, G. (2007) *History and Memory*. Manchester: Manchester University Press.

Curtice, J. (2019) 'Three years on: still divided'. *NatCen Social Research*. [online] Available from: https://whatukthinks.org/eu/three-years-on-still-divided/

Cutler, C. (2007) 'Hip-hop language in sociolinguistics and beyond'. *Language and Linguistics Compass*, 1(5), 519–538.

Crenshaw, K. (2017) 'Race to the bottom: how the post-racial revolution became a whitewash'. [online] Available from: https://thebaffler.com/salvos/race-to-bottom-crenshaw

Crouch, C. (2017) 'Globalization, nationalism and the changing axes of political identity', in W. Outhwaite (ed.) *Brexit: Sociological Responses*. London: Anthem Press, pp 101–109.

Cressey, P. (1999) 'New labour and employment, training and employee relations', in M. Powell (ed.) *New Labour, New Welfare State?* Bristol: Bristol University Press, pp 171–190.

Cruz, J.M. and Sodeke, C.U. (2021) 'Debunking Eurocentrism in organizational communication theory: marginality and liquidities in postcolonial contexts'. *Communication Theory*, 31(3), 528–548.

Davis, M. (ed.) (2013) *Liquid Sociology: Metaphor in Zygmunt Bauman's Analysis of Modernity*. Abingdon: Routledge.

Day, J. (2006) 'Radio 1 glorifies knife crime, says Tory leader'. [online] Available from: https://www.theguardian.com/media/2006/jun/07/radio.conservativeparty

De Lima, P. and Carvajal, L. (2020) 'International migration: sustaining rural communities', in M. Vittuari, J. Devlin, M. Pagani and T. Johnson (eds) *The Routledge Handbook of Comparative Rural Policy*. Abingdon: Routledge, pp 147–161.

De Saussure, F. (1993) *Course in General Linguistics*. London: Duckworth.

Debord, G. (1967) *Society of the Spectacle*. Baltimore, MD: Black & Red.

Deleuze, G. and Guattari, F. (1977) *Anti-Oedipus*. London: Bloomsbury.

Deleuze, G. and Guattari, F. (1988) *A Thousand Plateaus: Capitalism and Schizophrenia*. Minneapolis: University of Minnesota Press.

Dempsey, N. and Johnston, N. (2018) 'Political disengagement in the UK: who is disengaged?' Briefing Paper no. CBP-7501. House of Commons Library.

Dennis, A. (2007) 'Poetic (in)justice-rap music lyrics as art, life, and criminal evidence'. *Columbus Journal of Law & Arts*, 31, 1–41.

DfE (Department for Education) (2010) *The Importance of Teaching: The Schools White Paper*. London: HMSO.

DfE (2016) *School Census 2016 to 2017: Guide for Schools and LAs – A Guide to Help Schools and Local Authorities (LAs) Complete and Submit Their Autumn 2016 to Summer 2017 School Census Data*. London: HMSO.

DfE (2017) *Permanent and Fixed Period Exclusions in England: 2015 to 2016*. London: HMSO.

DfE (2020) *Free School Meals – Autumn Term 2020–21*. London: HMSO.

Department for Education & Employment (1997) *Excellence in Schools*. London: HMSO.

Department for Education & Skills (2006) *Department for Education and Skills Departmental Report 2006*. London: HMSO.

Department for Transport (2015) *British Social Attitudes Survey Statistical Release*. London: HMSO.

Derrida, J. (1981) *The Ear of the Other: Otobiography, Transference, Translation*. Lincoln, NE: University of Nebraska Press.

Derrida, J. (1993) *Specters of Marx: The State of the Debt, the Work of Mourning and the New International*. Abingdon: Routledge.

Dixon, T.L. and Linz, D.G. (1997) 'Obscenity law and sexually explicit rap music: understanding the effects of sex, attitudes, and beliefs'. *Journal of Applied Communication Research*, 25(3), 217–241.

Dorling, D. and Thomlinson, S. (2019) *Rule Britannia: Brexit and the End of Empire*. London: Biteback.

Du Bois, W.E.B. (1897) 'Strivings of the negro people'. *The Atlantic*, 194–198.

Du Bois, W.E.B. (1903) *The Souls of Black Folk*. Oxford: Oxford University Press.

Duinker, B. and Martin, D. (2017) 'In search of the golden age hip-hop sound 1986–1996'. *Empirical Musicology Review*, 12(1–2), 80–100.

Dunleavy, P. (1994) 'The globalization of public services production: can government be "best in world"?'. *Public Policy and Administration*, 9(2), 36–64.

Dyson, M.E. (2008) 'Gangsta rap and American culture', in T. Strode and T. Wood (eds) *The Hip Hop Reader*. New York: Pearson, pp 140–184.

Eatwell, R. and Goodwin, M. (2018) *National Populism: The Revolt against Liberal Democracy*. London: Penguin.

Electoral Commission (2021) 'Results and turnout at the 2015 UK general election and 2016 EU referendum'. [online] Available from: https://www.electoralcommission.org.uk/who-we-are-and-what-we-do/elections-and-referendums/past-elections-and-referendums/uk-general-elections/results-and-turnout-2015-uk-general-election

El-Enany, N. (2020) *Bordering Britain: Law, Race and Empire*. Manchester: Manchester University Press.

Elias, N. (1939) *The Civilising Process*. London: Wiley.

Elgot, J. (2016) 'May wanted to "deprioritise" school places for children of people illegally in UK'. [online] Available from: https://www.theguardian.com/uk-news/2016/dec/01/may-wanted-to-deprioritise-school-places-for-children-of-people-illegally-in-uk

Elliott, A. (2004) *Subject to Ourselves: Social Theory, Psychoanalysis and Postmodernity*. London: Routledge.

Elliott, A. (ed.) (2013) *The Contemporary Bauman*. Abingdon: Routledge.

Emery, E.E. and Trist, E.L. (1973) *A Social Ecology: Contextual Appreciation of the Future in the Present*. New York: Springer.

Engbersen, G. (2013) 'Labour migration from Central and Eastern Europe and the implications for integration policy', in J.W. Holtslag, M. Kremers and E. Schrijvers (eds) *Making Migration Work: The Future of Labour Migration in the European Union*. Amsterdam: Amsterdam University Press, pp 104–121.

Engbersen, G. and Snel, E. (2013) 'Liquid migration: dynamic and fluid patterns of post-accession migration flows', in B. Glorius, I. Grabowska-Lusińska and A. Rindoks (eds) *Mobility in Transition: Migration Patterns after EU Enlargement*. Amsterdam: Amsterdam University Press, pp 21–40.

Engels, F. and Marx, K. (1848) *The Communist Manifesto*. London: Vintage Press.

Falkner, S. (2021) *Knife Crime in the Capital: How Gangs Are Drawing Another Generation into a Life of Violent Crime*. London: Policy Exchange.

Fanon, F. (2008 [1952]) *Black Skin, White Masks*. London: Pluto Press.

Fatsis, L. (2019a) 'Policing the beats: the criminalisation of UK drill and grime music by the London Metropolitan Police'. *Sociological Review*, 67(6), 1300–1316.

Fatsis, L. (2019b) 'Grime: criminal subculture or public counterculture? A critical investigation into the criminalization of Black musical subcultures in the UK'. *Crime, Media, Culture*, 15(3), 447–461.

Featherstone, M., Robertson, R. and Lash, S.M. (1995) *Global Modernities*. London: Sage.

Fenton, S. (1999) *Ethnicity, Racism, Class and Culture*. Basingstoke: Palgrave Macmillan.

Findlay, A.M. (2006) 'Challenges arising from the UK's policy on attracting global talent', in C. Kuptsch and P. Eng Fong (eds) *Competing for Global Talent*. Geneva: International Institute for Labour Studies, pp 65–86.

Foucault, M. (1969) *The Archaeology of Knowledge*. New York: Harper Row.

Foucault, M. (1986) 'Of other spaces'. *Diacritics*, 16(1), 22–27.

Foucault, M. (1988) *Technologies of Self*. Amherst: University of Massachusetts Press.

Fukuyama, F. (1989) 'The end of history?' *The National Interest*, 16, 3–18.

Franco, S.H. (2019) 'Favelas and townships: place making, everyday racialization, and the postracial'. *International Journal of Sociology and Social Policy*, 39(11/12), 962–974.

Frankenberg, R. (1993) *White Women, Race Matters: The Social Construction of Whiteness*. Minneapolis: University of Minnesota Press.

Frankenberg, R. (2001) 'The mirage of an unmarked whiteness', in B. Ramussen, E. Klinenberg, I. Nexica and M. Ray (eds) *The Making and Unmaking of Whiteness*. Durham, NC: Duke University Press, pp 72–91.

Fryer, P. (1986) 'Musicians as heroes: Black singers in the United States and Jamaica'. *New Community*, 13(2), 208–213.

Gallagher, C.A. (2003) 'Color-blind privilege: the social and political functions of erasing the color line in post-race America'. *Race, Gender & Class*, 10(4), 22–37.

Gane, N. (2001) 'Zygmunt Bauman: liquid modernity and beyond'. *Acta Sociologica*, 44(3), 267–275.

Garreau, J. (1991) *Edge City: Life on the New Frontier*. New York: Doubleday.

Garrett, P.M. (2012) 'From "solid modernity" to "liquid modernity"? Zygmunt Bauman and social work'. *British Journal of Social Work*, 42(4), 634–651.

Garland, D. (2018) *Punishment and Welfare: A History of Penal Strategies*. Louisiana: Quid Pro Books.

Garcia, D.F. (2017) *Listening for Africa: Freedom, Modernity, and the Logic of Black Music's African Origins*. Durham, NC: Duke University Press.

Geertz, C. (1973) *The Interpretation of Cultures*. New York: Basic Books.

Gentleman, A. (2019) *The Windrush Betrayal: Exposing the Hostile Environment*. London: Faber & Faber.

Glynn, M. (2014) *Black Men, Invisibility and Crime: Towards a Critical Race Theory of Desistance*. Abingdon: Routledge.

Giddens, A. (1990) *The Consequences of Modernity*. Cambridge: Polity Press.

Giddens, A. (1991) *Modernity and Self-Identity: Self and Society in the Late Modern Age*. Cambridge: Polity Press.

Giddens, A. (1994) *Beyond Left and Right: The Future of Radical Politics*. Stanford: Stanford University Press.

Giddens, A. (1999) *Runaway World: How Globalization Is Reshaping Our Lives*. London: Profile.

Giddens, A. (2003) 'The globalizing of modernity', in D. Held and A. McGrew (eds) *The Global Transformations Reader: An Introduction to the Globalization Debate*. Cambridge: Polity Press, pp 60–66.

Gillborn, D. (2005) 'Education policy as an act of white supremacy: whiteness, critical race theory and education reform'. *Journal of Education Policy*, 20(4), 485–505.

Gillborn, D. (2008) *Racism and Education: Coincidence or Conspiracy?* London: Taylor & Francis.

Gillborn, D. (2009) 'Who's afraid of critical race theory in education? A reply to Mike Cole's "the color-line and the class struggle"'. *Power and Education*, 1(1), 125–131.

Gillborn, D., Demack, S., Rollock, N. and Warmington, P. (2017) 'Moving the goalposts: education policy and 25 years of the Black/white achievement gap'. *British Educational Research Journal*, 43(5), 848–874.

Gilroy, P. (1987) *There Ain't No Black in the Union Jack*. Abingdon: Routledge.

Gilroy, P. (1993) *The Black Atlantic: Modernity and Double Consciousness*. Cambridge, MA: Harvard University Press.

Gilroy, P. (2004) *After Empire: Melancholia or Convivial Culture*. London: Taylor & Francis.

Gilroy, P. (2007) *Black Britain: A Photographic History*. London: Saqi.

Giroux, H.A. (2013) 'Neoliberalism's war against teachers in dark times'. *Cultural Studies: Critical Methodologies*, 13(6), 458–468.

Goldberg, D.T. (2015) *Are We All Postracial Yet?* London: John Wiley & Sons.

Goodhart, D. (2017) *The Road to Somewhere: The Populist Revolt and the Future of Politics*. London: Penguin.

Goodwin, M. and Heath, O. (2016) 'The 2016 referendum, Brexit and the left behind: an aggregate-level analysis of the result'. *Political Quarterly*, 87(3), 323–332.

Greene, K.J. (1998) 'Copyright, culture & (and) black music: a legacy of unequal protection'. *Hastings Communications and Entertainment Law Journal*, 21, 339–360.

Gunter, A. (2008) 'Growing up bad: Black youth "road" culture and badness in an East London neighbourhood'. *Crime, Media, Culture*, 4(3), 349–366.

Gunter, A. (2010) *Growing up Bad? Black Youth, 'Road' Culture and Badness in an East London Neighbourhood*. London: Tufnell Press.

Gunter, A. (2017) *Race, Gangs and Youth Violence: Policy, Prevention and Policing*. Bristol: Policy Press.

Habermas, J. (1981) *Theory of Communicative Action*. London: Polity Press.

Habermas, J. (1985) *The Philosophical Discourse of Modernity*. Cambridge, MA: MIT Press.

Habermas, J. (2016) 'Core Europe to the rescue: a conversation with Jürgen Habermas about Brexit and the EU crisis'. *Social Europe*. [online] Available from: https://www.socialeurope.eu/2016/07/core-europe-to-the-rescue/

Habermas, J., Derrida, J. and Borradori, G. (2003) *Philosophy in a Time of Terror: Dialogues with Jurgen Habermas and Jacques Derrida*. Chicago: University of Chicago Press.

Hall, S. (1989) 'Ethnicity: identity and difference'. *Radical America*, 23(4), 9–20.

Hall, S. (1997) (ed.) *Representation: Cultural Representations and Signifying Practices*. London: Sage.

Hall, S. (2015) 'Cultural identity and diaspora', in L. Chrisman and P. Williams (eds) *Colonial Discourse and Post-colonial Theory*. Abingdon: Routledge, pp 392–403.

Hall, S. and du Gay, P. (eds) (1996) *Questions of Cultural Identity*. London: Sage.

Hall, S., Critcher, C., Jefferson, T., Clarke, J. and Roberts, B. (1978) *Policing the Crisis: Mugging, the State and Law and Order*. London: Bloomsbury.

Hamilton, D.G. (2018) 'Too hot to handle: African Caribbean pupils and students as toxic consumers and commodities in the educational market'. *Race Ethnicity and Education*, 21(5), 573–592.

Harvey, D. (1989) *The Condition of Postmodernity*. London: Wiley.

Harvey, D. (2006) *Spaces of Global Capitalism*. London: Verso.

Harvey, D. (2007a) *A Brief History of Neoliberalism*. New York: Oxford University Press.

Harvey, D. (2007b) 'Neoliberalism and the city'. *Studies in Social Justice*, 1(1), 2–13.

Hallsworth, S. and Silverstone, D. (2009) '"That's life innit": a British perspective on guns, crime and social order'. *Criminology & Criminal Justice*, 9(3), 359–377.

Hancox, D. (2009) 'The triumph of grime'. [online] Available from: https://www.theguardian.com/commentisfree/2009/feb/14/music-grime-dan-hancox

Hancox, D. (2019) 'Skengdo and AM: the drill rappers sentenced for playing their song'. [online] Available from: https://www.theguardian.com/music/2019/jan/31/skengdo-and-am-the-drill-rappers-sentenced-for-playing-their-song

Harding, S. (2014) *The Street Casino*. Bristol: Policy Press.

Harrison, A.K. (2008) 'Racial authenticity in rap music and hip hop'. *Sociology Compass*, 2(6), 1783–1800.

Hayward, K.J. (2012) 'Five spaces of cultural criminology'. *British Journal of Criminology*, 52(3), 441–462.

Hawley, G. (2017) *Making Sense of the Alt-Right*. New York: Columbia University Press.

Helm, T., Taylor, M. and Davis, R. (2011) 'David Cameron sparks fury from critics who say attack on multiculturalism has boosted English Defence League'. [online] Available from: http://www.guardian.co.uk/politics/2011/feb/05/david-cameron-speech-criticised-edl

Hickel, J. (2017) *The Divide: A Brief Guide to Global Inequality and Its Solutions*. Washington DC: Random House.

Holdaway, S. (1999) 'Understanding the police investigation of the murder of Stephen Lawrence: a "mundane sociological analysis"'. *Sociological Research Online*, 4(1), 107–114.

Hooghe, M. and Dejaeghere, Y. (2007) 'Does the "Monitorial Citizen" exist? An empirical investigation into the occurrence of postmodern forms of citizenship in the Nordic countries'. *Scandinavian Political Studies*, 30, 249–271.

Howe, D. (2011) 'New Cross: the blaze we cannot forget'. [online] Available from: https://www.theguardian.com/commentisfree/2011/jan/17/new-cross-fire-we-cant-forget

Ilan, J. (2012) '"The industry's the new road": crime, commodification and street cultural tropes in UK urban music'. *Crime, Media, Culture*, 8(1), 39–55.

Ilan, J. (2015) *Understanding Street Culture: Poverty, Crime, Youth and Cool*. London: Palgrave Macmillan.

Ilan, J. (2017) *Understanding Street Culture: Poverty, Crime, Youth and Cool*. London: Bloomsbury.

Ilan, J. (2020) 'Digital street culture decoded: why criminalizing drill music is street illiterate and counterproductive'. *British Journal of Criminology*, 60(4), 994–1013.

Independent, The (2011) 'Cameron: my war on multiculturalism'. [online] Available from: https://www.independent.co.uk/news/uk/politics/cameron-my-war-on-multiculturalism-2205074.html

IRR (Institute of Race Relations) (2020) 'Racial violence statistics'. [online] Available from: https://irr.org.uk/research/statistics/racial-violence/

Irwin-Rogers, K. and Pinkney, C. (2017) 'Social media as a catalyst and trigger for youth violence'. [online] Available from: https://www.catch-22.org.uk/resources/social-media-as-a-catalyst-and-trigger-for-youth-violence/

Irwin-Rogers, K., Densley, J. and Pinkney, C. (2018) 'Gang violence and social media', in J.L. Ireland, C.A. Ireland and P. Birch (eds) *Routledge International Handbook on Human Aggression*. Abingdon: Routledge, pp 400–410.

Jacobsen, M.H. (2013) 'Solid modernity, liquid utopia–liquid modernity, solid utopia: ubiquitous utopianism as a trademark of the work of Zygmunt Bauman', in A. Elliott (ed.) *The Contemporary Bauman*. Abingdon: Routledge, pp 217–241.

Jacobsen, M.H. (ed.) (2016) *Beyond Bauman: Critical Engagements and Creative Excursions*. Abingdon: Routledge.

Jacobsen, M.H. and Poder, P. (eds) (2016) *The Sociology of Zygmunt Bauman: Challenges and Critique*. Abingdon: Routledge.

Jameson, F. (1991) *Postmodernism, or, the Cultural Logic of Late Capitalism*. Durham, NC: Duke University Press.

Jenkins, R. (1997) *Rethinking Nationhood: Arguments and Explorations*. London: Sage.

Johnson, D. (2019) *Hateland: A Long, Hard Look at America's Extremist Heart*. New York: Prometheus Books.

Jones, K., Visser, D. and Simic, A. (2019) 'Fishing for export: calo, recruiters, informality and debt in international supply chains'. *Journal of the British Academy*, 7, 107–130.

Jordan, E. (2001) 'Exclusion of travellers in state schools'. *Educational Research*, 43(2), 117–132.

Joseph, I. and Gunter, A. (2011) *What's a Gang and What's Race Got to Do with It? Politics and Policy into Practice*. Milton Keynes: Runnymede.

Kajikawa, L. (2021) 'Leaders of the new school? Music departments, hip-hop and the challenge of significant difference'. *Twentieth-Century Music*, 18(1), 45–64.

Kalkan, H. (2022) 'The American ghetto, gangster, and respect on the streets of Copenhagen: media(tion)s between structure and street culture'. *Journal of Contemporary Ethnography*, 51(3), 407–434.

Kar, D. and Spanjers, J. (2015) 'Illicit financial flows from developing countries: 2004–2013'. *Global Financial Integrity*, 1–10.

Kerrigan, N. (2018) *A Threatened Rural Idyll? Informal Social Control, Exclusion and the Resistance to Change in the English Countryside*. Wilmington: Vernon Press.

Khan, U. (2022) 'A guilty pleasure: the legal, social scientific and feminist verdict against rap'. *Theoretical Criminology*, 26(2), 245–263.

Kierkegaard, S. (1846) *Samlede værker*. Copenhagen: Gyldendal.

King, B. and Swain, J. (2023) 'The characteristics of street codes and competing performances of masculinity on an inner-city housing estate'. *Journal of Youth Studies*, 26(8), 1046–1063.

Klein, N. (2003) 'The rise of the fortress continent'. *Nation*, 276(4), 10–12.

Knox, R. (1850) *The Races of Men: A Fragment*. London: H. Renshaw.

Komaromi, P. (2016) 'Post-referendum racism and xenophobia: the role of social media activism in challenging the normalisation of xeno-racist narratives'. [online] Available from: http://www.irr.org.uk/news/post-referendum-racism-and-the-importance-of-social-activism/

Kristeva, J. (1982) *Powers of Horror*. Princeton: Princeton University Press.

Kubrin, C.E. (2005) 'Gangstas, thugs and hustlas: identity and the code of the street in rap music'. *Social Problems*, 52(3), 360–378.

Kulz, C. (2019) 'Mapping folk devils old and new through permanent exclusion from London schools'. *Race Ethnicity and Education*, 22(1), 93–109.

Kundnani, A. (2007) *The End of Tolerance: Racism in 21st Century Britain*. London: Pluto Press.

Lacan, J. (1973) *The Four Fundamental Concepts of Psychoanalysis*. New York: Vintage Publishing.

Lacan, J. (1977) *Écrits: A Selection*. New York: W.W. Norton & Company.

Ladson-Billings, G. (1998) 'Just what is critical race theory and what's it doing in a nice field like education?' *International Journal of Qualitative Studies in Education*, 11(1), 7–24.

Lammy, D. (2017) *The Lammy Review: An Independent Review into the Treatment of, and Outcomes for, Black, Asian and Minority Ethnic Individuals in the Criminal Justice System*. London: Her Majesty's Government.

Lane, J. (2016) 'The digital street: an ethnographic study of networked street life in Harlem'. *American Behavioural Scientist*, 60(1), 43–58.

Lasch, C. (1979) *The Culture of Narcissism: American Life in an Age of Diminishing Expectations*. New York: W.W. Norton & Company.

Lash, S. (1999) *Another Modernity: A Different Rationality*. Oxford: Blackwell.

Lash, S. and Friedman, J. (1992) *Modernity and Identity*. Oxford: Blackwell.

Lash, S., Beck, U. and Giddens, A. (1994) *Reflexive Modernization*. Cambridge: Polity Press.

Lash, S., Szerszynski, B. and Wynne, B. (1996) *Risk, Environment and Modernity*. London: Sage.

Lentin, A. (2016) 'Racism in public or public racism: doing anti-racism in "post-racial" times'. *Ethnic and Racial Studies*, 39(1), 33–48.

Levi-Strauss, C. (1955) 'The structural study of myth'. *Journal of American Folklore*, 68(270), 428–444.

Lyotard, J. (1979) *The Postmodern Condition: A Report on Knowledge*. Minnesota: University of Minnesota Press.

Mac an Ghail, M. (1986) *Young, Gifted and Black*. Milton Keynes: Open University Press.

Macpherson, W. (1999) *The Stephen Lawrence Inquiry: Report of an Inquiry by Sir William Macpherson*. London: The Stationery Office.

Majors, R and Billson. J. (1992) *Cool Pose: The Dilemmas of Black Manhood in America*. New York: Lexington.

Marcuse, H. (1941) 'Some social implications of modern technology'. *Zeitschrift für Sozialforschung*, 9(3), 414–439.

Marcuse, H. (1955) *Eros and Civilization*. Boston, MA: Beacon.

Marcuse, H. (1964) *One-Dimensional Man: Studies in the Ideology of Advanced Industrial Society*. Abingdon: Routledge.

Marshall, B., Webb, B. and Tilley, N. (2005) *Rationalisation of Current Research on Guns, Gangs and Other Weapons: Phase One*. London: UCL Press.

Massey, D. (1994) *Space, Place, and Gender*. Minneapolis: University of Minnesota Press.

McGregor-Smith, R. (2017) *Race in the Workplace*. London: Her Majesty's Government.

McIntyre, N. Parveen, N. and Thomas, T. (2021) 'Exclusion rates five times higher for Black Caribbean pupils in parts of England'. [online] Available from: https://www.theguardian.com/education/2021/mar/24/exclusion-rates-black-caribbean-pupils-england

McLaughlin, J. and Weiler, A.M. (2017) 'Migrant agricultural workers in local and global contexts: toward a better life?' *Journal of Agrarian Change*, 17(3), 630–638.

McLuhan, H. (1962) *The Gutenberg Galaxy: The Making of Typographic Man*. Toronto: University of Toronto Press.

Meer, N. (2012) 'Racialization and religion: race, culture and difference in the study of antisemitism and Islamophobia'. *Ethnic and Racial Studies*, 36(3), 1–14.

Meer, N. (ed.) (2016) *Multiculturalism and Interculturalism: Debating the Dividing Lines*. Edinburgh: Edinburgh University Press.

Mestrovic, S.G. (2010) 'Bauman and the drama of Abu Ghraib', in K. Tester (ed.) *Bauman's Challenge: Sociological Issues for the 21st Century*. Basingstoke: Palgrave Macmillan, pp 37–61.

Mignolo, W. (2011) *The Darker Side of Western Modernity: Global Futures, Decolonial Options*. Durham, NC: Duke University Press.

Miller, K. (2012) *Playing Along: Digital Games, YouTube and Virtual Performance*. Oxford: Oxford University Press.

Miller, W.B. (1958) 'Lower Class culture as a generational milieu of gang delinquency'. *Journal of Social Issues*. https://doi.org/10.1111/j.1540-4560.1958.tb01413.x

Mills, C.W. (1959) *The Sociological Imagination*. Oxford: Oxford University Press.

Mintchev, N. (2021) 'The cultural politics of racism in the Brexit conjuncture'. *International Journal of Cultural Studies*, 24(1), 123–140.

Mitchell, S.A. (1993) *Hope and Dread in Psychoanalysis*. New York: Basic Books.

Modood, T. (1994) 'Political Blackness and British Asians'. *Sociology*, 28(4), 859–876.

Modood, T. (2017) 'Must interculturalists misrepresent multiculturalism?' *Comparative Migration Studies*, 5(1), 1–17.

Mondon, A. and Winter, A. (2020) 'Whiteness, populism and the racialisation of the working class in the United Kingdom and the United States', in Meer, N (ed.) *Whiteness and Nationalism*. London: Routledge, pp 10–28.

Mouzakitis, A. (2017) 'Modernity and the idea of progress'. *Frontiers in Sociology*, 2. https://doi.org/10.3389/fsoc.2017.00003

Mulholland, H. (2011) 'Decision to scrap EMA "stacks the odds" against poor, says Burnham'. [online] Available from: https://www.theguardian.com/education/2011/jan/19/day-action-labour-urges-rethink-scrap-ema

National Audit Office (2018) *Managing PFI Assets and Services as Contracts End*. [online] Available from: https://www.nao.org.uk/press-releases/managing-pfi-assets-and-services-as-contracts-end/

Neal, S. and Cochrane, A. (2022) 'Superdiversity through the lens of Brexit', in F. Meissner, N. Sigona and S. Vertovec (eds) *Oxford Handbook of Superdiversity*. Oxford: Oxford University Press, pp 389–400.

O'Connor, T. (2020) 'The shockingly high numbers of black children being excluded from Croydon's schools'. [online] Available from: https://www.mylondon.news/news/south-london-news/-17693580

Office for National Statistics (2020) *Child Poverty and Education Outcomes by Ethnicity: An Exploration of How Child Poverty and Educational Outcomes Vary For Different Ethnic Groups, Including A Look at Whether There Is a Relationship between These Variables That Is Consistent across Ethnic Groups*. London: HMSO.

Oliveira, dos Santos, N. (1996) 'Favelas and ghettos: race and class in Rio de Janeiro and New York City'. *Latin American Perspectives*, 23(4), 71–89.

Oliveira, P.J. (2019) 'Weaponizing quietness: sound bombs and the racialization of noise'. *Design and Culture*, 11(2), 193–211.

Orelus, P.W. (2010) *The Agony of Masculinity: Race, Gender and Education in the Age of 'New' Racism and Patriarchy*. New York: Peter Lang.

Outhwaite, W. (ed.) (2017) *Brexit: Sociological Responses*. London: Anthem Press.

Palmer, J. (2023) *Zygmunt Bauman and the West: A Sociology of Intellectual Exile*. Montreal: McGill Queens University Press.

Parekh, B. (2000) *The Parekh Report: The Future of Multi-ethnic Britain*. London: Runnymede Trust.

Persaud, E.J. (2011) 'The signature of hip hop: a sociological perspective'. *International Journal of Criminology and Criminological Theory*, 4(1), 1–22.

Pham, V.N. (2015) 'Our foreign president Barack Obama: the racial logics of birther discourses'. *Journal of International and Intercultural Communication*, 8(2), 86–107.

Phoenix, A. (2013) 'De-colonising practices: negotiating narratives from racialised and gendered experiences of education', in H. Mirza and C. Joseph (eds) *Black and Postcolonial Feminisms in New Times*. Abingdon: Routledge, pp 101–114.

Pitcher, B. (2019) 'Racism and Brexit: notes towards an antiracist populism'. *Ethnic and Racial Studies*, 42(14), 2490–2509.

Poynting, S., Noble, G. and Tabar, P. (1998) ' "Intersections" of masculinity and ethnicity: a study of male Lebanese immigrant youth in western Sydney'. *Race Ethnicity and Education*, 2(1), 59–78.

Preston, J. and Chadderton, C. (2012) 'Rediscovering "race traitor": towards a critical race theory informed public pedagogy'. *Race Ethnicity and Education*, 15(1), 85–100.

Rampton, A. (1981) *Interim Report of the Committee of Inquiry into the Education of Children from Ethnic Minority Groups – West Indian Children in Our Schools*. London: HMSO.

Randle, D. (2011) 'New "gangbo" gang injunctions aim to cut violence'. [online] Available from: https://www.bbc.co.uk/news/newsbeat-12307647

Rattansi, A. (2007) *Racism: A Very Short Introduction*. Oxford: Oxford University Press.

Rattansi, A. (2016) 'Race, imperialism and gender in Zygmunt Bauman's sociology', in M.H. Jacobsen (ed.) *Beyond Bauman: Critical Engagements and Creative Excursions*. Abingdon: Routledge, pp 65–86.

Rattansi, A. (2017) *Bauman and Contemporary Sociology: A Critical Analysis*. Manchester: Manchester University Press.

Rawlinson, K. (2018) 'Police may prosecute those who post videos glorifying violence'. [online] Available from: https://www.theguardian.com/uk-news/2018/may/30/police-prosecute-videos-glorifying-violence

Ray, L. (2013) 'Postmodernity to liquid modernity', in A. Elliott (ed.) *The Contemporary Bauman*. Abingdon: Routledge, pp 63–81.

Reid, E. and Ilan, J. (2023) 'Deen and Dunya: Islam, street spirituality, crime and redemption in English road culture'. *Theoretical Criminology* https://doi.org/10.1177/13624806231184172

Rex, J. and Mason, S. (eds) (1986) *Theories of Race and Ethnic Relations*. Cambridge: Cambridge University Press.

Richards, E. (1989) 'The "moral anatomy" of Robert Knox: the interplay between biological and social thought in Victorian scientific naturalism'. *Journal of the History of Biology*, 22(3), 373–436.

Riley, H.B. (2020) *Safe and Sound: 21st Century Country Music and Changing Perceptions of Violence*. Gainesville: Florida State University Press.

Roberts, J. (2021) '"Woke" culture: the societal and political implications of Black Lives Matter digital activism', in R. Luttrell, L. Xiao and J. Glass (eds) *Democracy in the Disinformation Age*. New York: Routledge, pp 37–57.

Rose, T. (1994) *Black Noise: Rap Music and Black Culture in Contemporary America*. Middletown, CT: Wesleyan University Press.

Rzepnikowska, A. (2019) 'Racism and xenophobia experienced by Polish migrants in the UK before and after Brexit vote'. *Journal of Ethnic and Migration Studies*, 45(1), 61–77.

Said, E. (1978) *Orientalism*. New York: Pantheon.

Said, E. (2000) 'Invention, memory, and place'. *Critical Inquiry*, 26, 175–192.

Salem, T. and Larkins, E.R. (2021) 'Violent masculinities: gendered dynamics of policing in Rio de Janeiro'. *American Ethnologist*, 48(1), 65–79.

Samanani, F. (2022) 'The long road: hope, violence and ethical register in London street culture'. *American Ethnologist*, 49(1), 64–76.

Sandberg, S. and Pedersen, W. (2009) *Street Capital: Black Cannabis Dealers in a White Welfare State*. Bristol: Policy Press.

Savage, M., Devine, F., Cunningham, N., Taylor, M., Li, Y., Hjellbrekke, J., Le Roux, B., Friedman, S. and Miles, A. (2013) 'A new model of social class? Findings from the BBC's Great British Class Survey experiment'. *Sociology*, 47(2), 219–250.

Schudson, M. (1996) 'What if civic life didn't die?' *American Prospect*, 25, 17–20.

Schudson, M. (1998) *The Good Citizen: A History of American Public Life*. New York: Free Press.

Schumacher, T.G. (1995) '"This is a sampling sport": 1 digital sampling, rap music and the law in cultural production'. *Media, Culture & Society*, 17(2), 253–273.

Schwarze, T. and Fatsis, L. (2023) 'Copping the blame: the role of YouTube videos in the criminalisation of UK drill music'. *Popular Music*, 41(4), 463–480.

Scott, C.D. (2020) 'Policing Black sound: performing UK grime and rap music under routinised surveillance'. *Soundings*, 75(75), 55–65.

Sernhede, O. (2000) 'Exoticism and death as a modern taboo: gangsta rap and the search for intensity', in P. Gilroy, L. Grossberg and A. McRobbie (eds) *Without Guarantees: in Honour of Stuart Hall*. London: Verso, pp 302–317.

Sernhede, O. (2011) 'School, youth culture and territorial stigmatization in Swedish metropolitan districts'. *Young*, 19(2), 159–180.

Seidler, V. (2018) *Making Sense of Brexit: Democracy, Europe and Uncertain Futures*. Bristol: Policy Press.

Seshadri-Crooks, K. (2002) *Desiring Whiteness*. Abingdon: Routledge.

Sibley, D. (2002) *Geographies of Exclusion: Society and Difference in the West*. Abingdon: Routledge.

Simmel, G. (1903) *The Metropolis and Mental Life*. Chicago: University of Chicago Press.

Skeggs, B. (2017) 'You are being tracked, evaluated and sold: an analysis of digital inequalities'. [online] Available from: https://www.lse.ac.uk/Events/Events-Assets/PDF/2017/2017-MT03/20170926-Bev-Skeggs-PPT.pdf

SMC (Social Mobility Commission) (2016) *State of the Nation 2016: Social Mobility in Great Britain*. London: Social Mobility Commission.

Source, The (2023) 'Today in hip hop history'. [online] Available from: https://thesource.com/2018/08/11/today-in-hip-hop-history-kool-hercs-party-at-1520-sedgewick-avenue-45-years-ago-marks-the-foundation-of-the-culture-known-as-hip-hop/

Speed, S. (2020) 'The persistence of white supremacy: Indigenous women migrants and the structures of settler capitalism'. *American Anthropologist*, 122(1), 76–85.

Standing, G. (2011) *The Precariat: The New Dangerous Class*. London: Bloomsbury Academic.

Steele, C.M. (1997) 'A threat in the air: how stereotypes shape intellectual identity and performance'. *American Psychologist*, 52(6), 613–629.

Stuart, F. (2020) *Ballad of the Bullet: Gangs, Drill Music and the Power of Online Infamy*. Princeton: Princeton University Press.

Sullivan, D. and Hickel, J. (2023) 'Capitalism and extreme poverty: a global analysis of real wages, human height, and mortality since the long 16th century'. *World Development*, 16(1), 106–126.

Sutcliffe-Braithwaite, F. (2018) *Class, Politics and the Decline of Deference in England, 1968–2000*. Oxford: Oxford University Press.

Swann Report (1985) *Education for All. The Report of the Committee of Inquiry into the Education of Children from Ethnic Minority Groups*. London: HMSO.

Swidler, A. (1986) 'Culture in action: symbols and strategies'. *American Sociological Review*, 51, 273–286.

Taggart, P. (2000) *Populism*. Buckingham: Open University Press.

Taylor, G. (2017) 'Two tribes? The winners and losers of european integration', in *Understanding Brexit: Why Britain Voted to Leave the European Union*. London: Emerald, pp 45–72.

Tester, K. (2004) *The Social Thought of Zygmunt Bauman*. New York: Palgrave Macmillan.

Tester, K. and Jacobsen, M.H. (2005) *Bauman before Postmodernity*. Aalborg: Aalborg University Press.

Thapar, C. (2021) *Cut Short: Why We're Failing Our Youth – and How to Fix It*. London: Penguin.

Timpson, E. (2019) *Timpson Review of School Exclusion*. London: Her Majesty's Stationery Office.

Titley, G. (2016) 'On "Are we all postracial yet?"' *Ethnic and Racial Studies*, 39(13), 2269–2277.

Touraine, A. (1995) *Critique of Modernity*. Oxford: Blackwell.

Tsakona, V., Karachaliou, R. and Archakis, A. (2020) 'Liquid racism in the Greek anti-racist campaign #StopMindBorders'. *Journal of Language Aggression and Conflict*, 8(2), 232–261.

UK Government (2018) 'UK population by ethnicity – regional ethnic diversity'. [online] Available from: https://www.ethnicity-facts-figures.service.gov.uk/uk-population-by-ethnicity/national-and-regional-populations/regional-ethnic-diversity/latest#ethnic-groups-by-area

UK Government (2019) 'Black Caribbean ethnic group – facts and figures'. [online] Available from: https://www.ethnicity-facts-figures.service.gov.uk/summaries/black-caribbean-ethnic-group#population

UK Government (2020) *Permanent and Fixed Period Exclusions in England: 2018–19*. London: HMSO. Available from: https://explore-education-statistics.service.gov.uk/find-statistics/suspensions-and-permanent-exclusions-in-england/2018–19

UK Government (2021a) 'Permanent exclusions and suspensions in England'. [online] Available from: https://explore-education-statistics.service.gov.uk/find-statistics/permanent-and-fixed-period-exclusions-in-england

UK Government (2021b) 'Schools, pupils and their characteristics: academic year 2020–21'. [online] Available from: https://explore-education-statistics.service.gov.uk/find-statistics/school-pupils-and-their-characteristics

UK Government (2022a) 'Ethnicity facts and figures – GCSE English and Maths results'. [online] Available from: https://www.ethnicity-facts-figures.service.gov.uk/education-skills-and-training/11-to-16-years-old/a-to-c-in-english-and-maths-gcse-attainment-for-children-aged-14-to-16-key-stage-4/latest#by-ethnicity

UK Government (2022b) 'Ethnicity facts and figures – GCSE results (Attainment 8)'. [online] Available from: https://www.ethnicity-facts-figures.service.gov.uk/education-skills-and-training/11-to-16-years-old/gcse-results-attainment-8-for-children-aged-14-to-16-key-stage-4/latest

UK Government (2023) *Stop and Search Statistics*. London: His Majesty's Government.

Valluvan, S. (2016) 'What is "post-race" and what does it reveal about contemporary racisms?' *Ethnic and Racial Studies*, 39(13), 2241–2251.

Van Hellemont, E. (2012) 'Gangland online: performing the real imaginary world of gangstas and ghettos in Brussels'. *European Journal of Crime, Criminal Law, and Criminal Justice*, 20(2), 165–180.

VCU.edu (2023) 'Magazine for alumni and friends', Virginia Commonwealth University. [online] Available from: https://magazine.vcu.edu/2023-fall/

Vertovec, S. (2007) 'Super-diversity and its implications'. *Ethnic and Racial Studies*, 30(6), 1024–1054.

Vertovec, S. (2009) *Transnationalism*. Abingdon: Routledge.

Virdee, S. (2014) *Racism, Class and the Racialized Outsider*. London: Bloomsbury Publishing.

Virdee, S. and McGeever, B. (2017) 'Racism, crisis, Brexit'. *Ethnic and Racial Studies*, 41(10), 1802–1819.

Wacquant, L. (1999) 'How penal common sense comes to Europeans: notes on the transatlantic diffusion of the neoliberal doxa'. *European Societies*, 1(3), 319–352.

Wacquant, L. (2008) *Urban Outcasts: A Comparative Sociology of Advanced Marginality*. London: Polity Press.

Wacquant, L. (2009) *Punishing the Poor: The Neoliberal Government of Social Insecurity*. Durham, NC: Duke University Press.

Warren, N. (2016) 'W.E.B. du Bois looks at the future from beyond the grave'. *African American Review*, 49(1), 53–57.

Waterson, J. (2018) 'YouTube deletes 30 music videos after Met link with gang violence'. [online] Available from: https://www.theguardian.com/uk-news/2018/may/29/youtube-deletes-30-music-videos-after-met-link-with-gang-violence

Weaver, S. (2010) 'Liquid racism and the Danish Prophet Muhammad cartoons'. *Current Sociology*, 58(5), 675–692.

Weaver, S. (2011) 'Liquid racism and the ambiguity of Ali G'. *European Journal of Cultural Studies*, 14(3), 249–264.

Weber, M. (2013 [1922]) *Economy and Society*. Berkeley: University of California Press.

Wendling, M. (2018) *Alt-Right: From 4chan to the White House*. London: Pluto Press.

Wheeler, R. (2017) 'Local history as productive nostalgia? Change, continuity and sense of place in rural England'. *Social & Cultural Geography*, 18(4), 466–486.

White, J. (2014) '(In) visible entrepreneurs: creative enterprise in the urban music economy'. Unpublished PhD thesis, University of Greenwich.

White, J. (2015) '"Just type my name in Google and see what comes up": creating an online persona in the urban music industry'. [online] Available from: https://papers.ssrn.com/sol3/papers.cfm?abstract_id=2569347

White, J. (2017) 'Controlling the flow: how urban music videos allow creative scope and permit social restriction'. *Young*, 25(4), 407–425.

White, J. (2021) 'Growing up under the influence: a sonic genealogy of grime', in W. Henry and M. Worley (eds) *Narratives from Beyond the UK Reggae Bassline: The System is Sound*. London: Palgrave Macmillan, pp 249–268.

Whittaker, F. (2018) 'DfE: schools "must no longer request" pupil nationality data', *School's Week*, 28 June 2018. [online] Available from: https://schoolsweek.co.uk/dfe-schools-must-no-longer-request-pupil-nationality-data/

Wiggan, J. (2012) 'Telling stories of 21st century welfare: the UK Coalition government and the neo-liberal discourse of worklessness and dependency'. *Critical Social Policy*, 32(3), 383–405.

Williams, M.L., Sutherland, A., Roy-Chowdhury, V., Loke, T., Cullen, A., Sloan, L., Burnap, P. and Giannasi, P. (2022) 'The effect of the Brexit vote on the variation in race and religious hate crimes in England, Wales, Scotland and Northern Ireland'. *British Journal of Criminology*. Available from: https://orca.cardiff.ac.uk/id/eprint/153093

Williams, P. and Clarke, B. (2016) 'Dangerous associations: joint enterprise, gangs and racism'. [online] Available from: https://www.crimeandjustice.org.uk/sites/crimeandjustice.org.uk/files/Dangerous%20assocations%20Joint%20Enterprise%20gangs%20and%20racism.pdf

Willis, P. (1977) *Learning to Labour: How Working-Class Kids Get Working Class Jobs*. Abingdon: Routledge.

Wilson, H.F. (2016) 'Brexit: on the rise of "(in) tolerance"'. *Environment and Planning D: Society and Space*. [online] Available from: http://societyandspace.org/2016/11/21/brexit-on-the-rise-of-intolerance/

Winlow, S., Hall, S. and Treadwell, J. (2017) *The Rise of the Right: English Nationalism and the Transformation of Working-Class Politics*. Bristol: Policy Press.

Winter, A. (2016) 'Island retreat: "on hate, violence and the murder of Jo Cox"'. [online] Available from: https://www.opendemocracy.net/en/opendemocracyuk/island-retreat-on-hate-violence-and-murder-of-jo-cox/island-retreat-on-hate-violence-and-murder-of-jo-cox

Wolfson, S. (2013) 'Giggs: prison, police harassment, cancelled tours – when will It stop'. [online] Available from: https://www.theguardian.com/music/2013/oct/05/giggs-when-will-it-stop

Xifra, J. and McKie, D. (2011) 'Desolidifying culture: Bauman, liquid theory, and race concerns in public relations'. *Journal of Public Relations Research*, 23(4), 397–411.

Young, T. and Trickett, L. (2017) 'Gang girls: agency, sexual identity, and victimisation "on road"', in K. Gildart, A. Gough-Yates, S. Lincoln and B. Osgerby (eds) *Youth Culture and Social Change: Making a Difference by Making a Noise*. London: Palgrave Macmillan, pp 231–259.

Youth Violence Commission (2020) *Youth Violence Commission Final Report*. London: HMSO.

Zappettini, F. (2019) 'The Brexit referendum: how trade and immigration in the discourses of the official campaigns have legitimised a toxic (inter) national logic'. *Critical Discourse Studies*, 16(4), 403–419.

Index

J

K

L

M

R

U

V

W

Y

www.ingramcontent.com/pod-product-compliance
Lightning Source LLC
Chambersburg PA
CBHW070929030426
42336CB00014BA/2592

9781529218480